THOSE FATAL GENERALS

GEORGE WASHINGTON

Those
Fatal Generals

by E. V. Westrate

★

KENNIKAT PRESS, INC.
PORT WASHINGTON, N. Y.

THOSE FATAL GENERALS

Copyright 1936 by Knight Publications Inc.
Reissued in 1968 by Kennikat Press
Library of Congress Catalog Card No: 68-16300
Manufactured in the United States of America

ESSAY AND GENERAL LITERATURE INDEX REPRINT SERIES

"*Those fatal generals with whom America has been cursed in every war which she has ever waged.*"

—Sir George Otto Trevelyan, Bart.
The American Revolution

Contents

Illustrations

Foreword

THIS is a story which has been unfolding for one hundred and sixty years and the end has not yet been reached—a story which always has been kept in the shadows by specious eloquence and fulsome hypocrisy. It may lack something of sweetness and light with the smokescreen swept aside, but it does have the virtue of being true.

In all its history, the United States never has lost a war. It is a matchless record. But, as a nation, we have been blinded ingeniously to all except the fact of ultimate victory which invariably has crowned our arms. We justly honor our heroic dead. We ring the welkin with their praise. We place little flags and wreaths of flowers upon their graves. But we are not permitted to stop and think how vastly too many graves there are. While the pæans of triumph are sounding, we must forget that those whose lives actually helped pave the road to victory are a pitiful minority—that all the rest were wasted wantonly.

The pacifist will find small comfort in these pages. This story has nothing to do with the horrors and evils of war as such. Its basic premise is that if there must be wars, they should be fought more efficiently. It has to do with the vicious toll which victory has not demanded but which we always have paid, the needless slaughter of those whose bitter sacrifice contributed nothing toward the victory but rather served only to prolong the desolating agony of the wars in which they were murdered.

From their countless graves, these do not shout to high heaven the magnificence of the United States' record in war. They know that record is ghastly, a hideous travesty of ever-repeated useless butchery under the incompetent commanders with which they have been cursed, a *danse macabre* whose ceaseless encores nothing ever has been done to prevent. . . . It began even before the Declaration of Independence was signed to create the nation and it has gone on, unchecked, ever since.

It may be that this is so because the darker phase of our history has been hidden so carefully. The dishonesty of half-truths and deliberate omissions on the part of our annalists has reared a gilded screen which conceals the rattling skeletons.

That is why this book has been written. It is a parade of skeletons which everyone has the right to see.

I.

Sorel

LATE in May, 1776.

The dismal camp at Sorel lay festering in the sun. It was a dreary sight. A few straggling tents housed the higher ranking officers. From these ran rows of ragged shelters, built of leaf-covered branches, brushwood, a tattered yard or two of dirty cloth—anything the men could find. Mud-hole lanes wound past the wretched quarters, out to the hastily thrown up breastworks which faced east toward distant Quebec and north on that widened expanse of the St. Lawrence known as Lake St. Peter. On the west, the camp was flanked by the swift-flowing Richelieu, tumbling into St. Peter from Lake Champlain. Southward, dank wilderness bound the riverside trail to St. John's, refuge of the daily increasing mob of stragglers who no longer could endure Sorel and still had strength enough to beat their way through sixty miles of forest.

There were twenty-five hundred men within the camp and over half of them were rotting with smallpox. The rest were gaunt, pasty-faced creatures with lack-luster eyes, who moved about with painful weariness. All of them were sick —from endless privation, exposure, bad water, bad food. For days, the only rations had been flour, which made a semi-edible paste when mixed with water, and salt pork, so near to putrefaction, it could be eaten only if the consumer held his nose tightly during the process. None of the men had uniforms. None of them had clothes enough of any kind, nothing but a few rags of homespun, as nondescript as their battered hats and the soleless shoes on their feet.

This was the main army of the fighting colonists' invading force in Canada! It was not all of the northern army. At least six hundred stragglers were scattered about St. John's, nearly half of them down with the smallpox. At Chambly, ten miles nearer the camp, were another two or three hundred. At Chambly, too, lay the commander of the army, Major General John Thomas, slowly dying of the smallpox which had stricken so many of his men. Montreal had the rest, a garrison of four hundred, under the flouted Benedict Arnold, whose untiring efforts kept them a little healthier and more disciplined than the others.

All were under the shadow of increasing peril. Across the St. Lawrence, twenty-five miles northeast of Sorel, was Three Rivers, which more than 10,000 well-armed, well-trained, well-fed British and Hessians were approaching, an ever-darkening menace to the tragic Continentals.

Yet, these same Continentals had held Quebec in siege only twenty days ago, and less than five months before some of these shambling men had charged through a driving blizzard to all but capture that citadel and with it all of Canada. Now they were an army without morale, starving, shattered by disease and left to rot through the brutal neglect and criminal bungling of those who controlled their destinies, the gentlemen of the Continental Congress, in Philadelphia assembled.

On December 31, 1775, the Americans had held Canada from Montreal to the walls of Quebec. The superhuman efforts of Brigadier General Richard Montgomery, Colonel Benedict Arnold and their valiant twelve hundred had accomplished that. A few hours later, at two o'clock in the morning of January 1, 1776, they had made their epic snow-swept attack on Quebec itself, to miss spectacular success by a hairline. With the city in their grasp, Montgomery was killed, Arnold seriously wounded and the troops, thrown into confusion by the loss of their leaders, were forced to fall back.

Congress now turned its back on the men it had sent north but Arnold refused to give up. "With a leg disabled worth more than the average general who had every limb whole,"* he gathered the remnants of his force and held Quebec in siege for three months. Given any reasonable support, he almost certainly could have captured it. Congress sent him his new commission as a brigadier general but—during January and February—not a man for reinforcement, no ammunition, not a pound of food nor a yard of cloth to cover the soldiers freezing in their rags. Smallpox struck Arnold's camp and he had no medicines. At one time, he had only two hundred and eighty-six men fit for duty—and still he held Quebec in his grasp!

Back in Albany, too ill for field duty, Major General Philip Schuyler, commander of the northern department,

* Trevelyan: *American Revolution*, Vol. II.

moved heaven and earth to support Arnold and, finally, in March, Congress let him have some raw militia from Vermont, New Hampshire and Massachusetts, signed under the idiotic three- and six-months enlistment policy which Congress favored so strongly. When these men slowly drifted to Quebec, they were half equipped and almost worse than useless. At the end of March, Arnold reported 786 men sick out of 2,505 on hand, more than half the total without military training or experience and the enlistments of 1500 due to expire in fifteen days.*

Arnold's chances were lessening now. While the opportunity to take Quebec was ripe, Congress failed to send him a single man through a few hundred miles of friendly territory. England, however, took the trouble to send 12,000 men under General John Burgoyne, in a fleet of eighty-two vessels, all the way across the Atlantic to help Sir Guy Carleton, its beleaguered commander in Canada.

Arnold was still hopeful of launching a new attack before they could arrive when Congress slapped him in the face—for the first of many times—by removing him from command. In his place, to the coldest and most trying battlefield of the war, was sent the oldest man in the Continental army, Brigadier General David Wooster, a giddy incompetent, aged 66!

Wooster arrived on April 1. Next day, he celebrated his advent by wasting ammunition in a silly bombardment with six-pounders whose shot bounced harmlessly off the Quebec walls while the British soldiers gathered on the embattlements and howled their derision. It was not without result, however. Arnold's horse, startled by the firing,

* Arnold's Report to Washington, March 30, 1776.

stumbled and fell, throwing its rider heavily on his wounded leg. In disgust, he asked for leave of absence which Wooster granted hastily, glad to be rid of him. Arnold acted characteristically. Instead of seeking a comfortable place to recover, he hurried to Montreal and spent his "leave" working day and night to infuse the campaign with new life for the defense of the conquered area still held.

Wooster spent a month capering about Quebec, wasting more ammunition and gaining nothing. By the end of April, he was practically out of powder and had food enough for only six days. But Congress had moved again. On May 2, Major General John Thomas arrived, bringing with him two more regiments and the authority to take over the command. He also brought two tons of powder and five hundred new muskets, sent not by Congress but by the despairing Schuyler, who had purchased them with money from his own pocket.

Winter was not yet gone from Quebec. It snowed on the night of April 30. But the ice in the St. Lawrence was cracking up and the British transports were coming through the floes, so near now that Thomas could see their masts. This meant the last chance for attack was gone and on May 5, Thomas wisely decided to abandon the siege. His wisdom stopped there. He kept no watch on the British fleet and, in his confused mismanagement of the preparations for retreat, five of the transports were permitted to crash through the ice, and a thousand men slipped into Quebec under his very nose. Worse, he took no precautionary measures. Noting this, the wily Carleton made a swift sally with his strengthened force, despite Thomas's superior numbers. The encounter was not a battle. It was a rout. Taken completely by surprise in the midst of breaking up camp, the Americans were driven off in disorderly flight, leaving to the British more than two hundred of their sick comrades* and nearly all their equipment, including the two tons of sadly needed powder and the five hundred new muskets.

In the pell-mell retreat, Thomas hesitated at Deschambault, but did not stop until he reached Sorel, a hundred miles from Quebec. When the denuded forces finally halted there to pitch some sort of camp, they were utterly demoralized, half-starved and exhausted, easy prey for the smallpox, flux and other diseases which swept the damply unhealthy location like wildfire. General Thomas himself was infected a few days after his arrival.

A check-up revealed that the battered army was short one ton of lead and fifty quires of paper for wadding, to bring the ammunition up to even twenty-four rounds per man. Thomas wrote Congress, telling of his illness and begging for munitions. Congress responded magnificently. It sent to Sorel one entire hogshead of paper which, when opened, proved to be too heavy for use in musket cartridges and too light for Sorel's five cannon!**

It went further. To help the ailing Thomas, it sent Baron Siegfried de Woedtke, late—by his own accented affirmation—of the advisory staff of Frederick the Great, no less. Broken-down European fortune hunters already were flock-

---

* Carleton's treatment of the prisoners was extraordinarily humane. He gave them the best medical care at his disposal, kept them until they were well and then paroled them home. His less admirable conduct toward Americans developed after the Revolution.

** Trevelyan: *American Revolution,* Vol. II.

ing to America to offer the fighting colonists their swords—
in return for high posts of command. De Woedtke was one
of these. Without investigating either his credentials or his
personal habits, Congress clasped him to its grateful bosom,
made him a brigadier general and sent him to Sorel. The
baron celebrated his appointment by getting gloriously
drunk and then simply stayed that way on the entire journey north. When he reached St. John's, he was not impressed with what the stragglers there told him about Sorel,
so he halted for some really serious drinking while he
thought it over. Then he stopped thinking and just devoted
himself exclusively to the drinking.

Meanwhile, Congress had made another gesture. It had
seemed unable to bear the thought of sending reinforcements or supplies to Arnold but, as early as February 15, it
had voted to send a commission to inspect the northern
front. For some reason—probably because it was cold up
there and nobody wanted to go—no commission was
formed for nearly six weeks. Then the 70-year-old Benjamin Franklin and Samuel Chase, two of the truly great
men in the Congress, volunteered and took with them
Charles Carroll of Maryland and his brother, the Rev. John
Carroll, the latter to attempt a religious conciliation with
the French-Canadians. Neither of the Carrolls was a mem-
ber of Congress at the time, although Charles became one
on July 4. The significant date of his entry was not mere
coincidence. He was sent for frantically, to supplant another
Maryland delegate and guarantee a majority from that
colony for the Declaration of Independence. He arrived just
in time to cast his vote and served with real distinction
thereafter—one of the painfully few who did.

The commissioners finally left Albany on April 2, doing a leisurely but thorough job. They did not reach Montreal until April 29* and then they remained there for some time. The elderly Franklin, whose health was seriously impaired on the chilly journey, and the ministerial Carroll, finding his mission hopeless, turned back on May 11. By that time, it was unnecessary for Chase and Charles Carroll to go to Quebec to see the main force of the northern army. The main force was coming in their direction as fast as weary, shoeless feet could carry them.

But now Congress was all adither about the Canadian campaign, months after it was too late. During May, at a time when Washington could least afford to spare them, four regiments were detached from his army and assigned to the forces in Canada. At the same time, Brigadier General John Sullivan was appointed to lead them. This was tantamount to giving him supreme command of the northern army in the field, as he was the senior brigadier and Thomas already was too ill to continue in active command himself. St. John's was designated as the point where the new reinforcements should gather for the advance to Sorel.

They were slow in coming, however, and, on May 21, General Thomas, no longer able to leave his cot, turned over the command of Sorel to Brigadier General William Thompson. He himself was taken to Chambly by boat with the despairing hope that he might recover away from the pest-hole camp.

His successor was a lean, hard-bitten man with a fiery

* "Journal of Charles Carroll of Carrollton During His Visit To Canada." Published by Maryland Historical Society, May, 1876.

fervor in his deep-set eyes. He was bitter against Congress, despised the drunken De Woedtke who still lingered over his rum jugs at St. John's and burned with fury over the incompetence and neglect which had brought the army to its existing condition. Without material resources, he tried desperately to bring some sort of order out of the dismal chaos of the camp but, on May 24, we find him writing to Schuyler in a not-too-hopeful vein:

"The army is in an evil state with little to do that may improve its condition. What may be done I shall endeavor to do until General Sullivan shall come. General Thomas continues exceeding sick and I am moved to say I fear he will never rise from his bed again. We anxiously await word of the new troops but from them nothing as yet. Of the enemy, we hear but little and that uncertain. Some would have us believe they are not in pursuit but this I mistrust. That they move slowly would seem true but that they are moving I have no particle of doubt. Should they reach Three Rivers in force ere our reinforcement comes, our position would be perilous indeed. I have word from General Arnold at Montreal that the Honourable Commissioners of the Congress will be here on the morrow. From that which has gone before, I hope but faintly that their visit will bring to us the relief of which we have such sore need."

In spite of his skepticism, General Thompson was graciousness itself to Commissioners Chase and Carroll when they reached Sorel, though he took a grim satisfaction in permitting the horrors of the camp to reveal themselves to the visitors with a bomb-like effect. He was astonished, however, when neither of the grave-faced commissioners attempted to excuse a solitary phase of the army's condition on behalf of the Congress they represented.

"This is frightful, sir," the earnest Chase exclaimed; "more, it is beyond pardon."

And Carroll, his smoldering eyes sweeping over the camp, declared, "It would seem the Congress has been somewhat remiss—and that I say with rare restraint. I have never seen a condition so appalling." He turned to Thompson. "You may rest assured, sir, that we shall do our utmost—our very utmost—nor will our words to Congress be ameliorated with lack of force."

Nor were they. On May 27, the wholly sincere commissioners sent from Montreal one of the most scathing indictments ever to be received by any Congress, particularly when the customary stately reserve of eighteenth-century diction is considered.

"We found all things in confusion; there is little or no discipline among your troops nor can any be kept up while the practice of enlisting for a twelvemonth continues; the general officers are all of this opinion. Your army is badly paid; and so exhausted is your credit that even a cart cannot be procured without ready money or *force*. . . . The army is in a distressed condition and is in want of the most necessary articles—meat, bread, tents, shoes, stockings, shirts, &c. . . . Your army here does not number four thousand men. . . . (Referring to the prospect of reinforcements already on their way.) We cannot conceal our concern that six thousand men should be ordered to Canada, without taking care to have magazines formed for their subsistence and cash to pay them. . . .

"We can not find words strong enough to describe our

miserable situation. You will have a faint idea of it if you figure to yourself an army broken and disheartened, half of it under inoculation or under other diseases; soldiers without pay, without discipline and altogether reduced to live from hand to mouth, depending on the scanty cattle and trifling quantities of flour which have hitherto been picked up in different parts of the country. Your soldiers grumble for their pay—if they receive it they will not be benefited as it will not procure them the necessaries they stand in need of. You have in your war chest eleven thousand dollars paper. You owe your soldiers here treble that sum and the inhabitants of the country fifteen thousand dollars more.

> "Samuel Chase,
> "Charles Carroll."*

No clearer picture could be drawn of the quality of the Continental Congress as a whole than the response which was elicited by this message which would have moved a stone image. The reply was immediate. Congress forwarded to Sorel the one thing the commissioners had said would be of the least use—money—and the total of that was less than one fourth the amount due the troops in back pay. And, as a substitute for "the most necessary articles"— food, clothing and medicine—Congress sent "a spirited Resolve in favour of national independence!"**

After General Thomas's illness became known in Philadelphia, the inspired congressmen began sending their commissioners in the north repeated suggestions that the ridicu-

* American Archives, Vol. VI, pp. 589, 590.
** General Sullivan to George Washington, June 6, 1775.

lous Wooster be restored to command. The indignant Chase and Carroll exploded. Just before they left Montreal at the end of May for the journey back, they took time to write Congress another letter which fairly sizzled.

"When the interests of our country and the safety of your army are at stake, we think it improper to conceal our sentiments, either with regard to persons or things. General Wooster is, in our opinion, unfit—totally unfit—to command your army and conduct the war."*

A little indignant on his own account when he heard about this, Wooster resigned his commission. He was even more indignant when the resignation was accepted.**

After the commissioners had gone and Sorel continued to wallow in misery, General Thompson renewed his own efforts to improve matters and, at the same time, keep an eye out for the British. The reports he received were distinctly conflicting but, on June 1, a scout brought him word that his suspicions of a definite British advance were correct. The enemy had reached Three Rivers but with only 800 men, the rest of Burgoyne's army following at a dawdling, leisurely pace. June 2 brought another message that the British force at Three Rivers was only three hundred strong. At the same time came news from the south

* The Commissioners to Congress, May 27, 1776. American Archives.

** Wooster refused to believe he was not a military genius and upon his return home, despite his age, was made major general of the Connecticut militia. The following year—April 27, 1777—he was killed in the first skirmish of the battle of Ridgefield, during Tryon's raid. With poetic fitness, it was Benedict Arnold, on leave to visit his children, who then took command and routed the British.

that Sullivan had finally arrived at St. John's the afternoon before. Impatiently unwilling to delay any longer in
a situation he felt to be crucial, Thompson sent for Colonel
Arthur St. Clair.

He liked the sharp-featured colonel. A former officer in
the King's army, St. Clair was one of the few regimental
commanders at Sorel who made sincere efforts to restore
discipline to their ranks. He had not yet had the opportunity to display those weaknesses which were to make him
one of America's "fatal generals" throughout his disastrous
military career.

"I'm troubled about Three Rivers," Thompson began
abruptly when the colonel reached his headquarters. "I
want you to take six hundred of our best men and go over
to Nicolet tonight. Scout Three Rivers from there. If the
enemy force there is as small as has been reported, take the
town and begin fortifying it immediately. With three thousand men on their way here with Sullivan, they can be
rushed to your support as soon as they arrive. Behind
strong breastworks, they may be able to stop Burgoyne's
advance until we are further reinforced. If we delay, the
chance may be gone. But remember, making the attack
depends entirely upon the town's being lightly held. And
keep me informed of everything."

Finding six hundred men at Sorel in condition to fight
was no easy task, but St. Clair finally accomplished it,
equipped his force as best he could and set out on the
twenty-five-mile march to Nicolet.

All of June 3, Thompson awaited new assurance of
Sullivan's approach but the only messenger who came that
day brought tragic word from Chambly. General Thomas

had died the day before, exactly one month after he took command of the northern army. In the tensity of the situation, however, this expected news seemed almost unimportant. Thompson received it stolidly and resumed his restless vigil.

Early in the afternoon of June 4, he heard a sudden shout sweep over the camp, repeated again and again, "Sullivan's coming!" He hurried out of his tent to the bank of the Richelieu, where one glance to the south banished all doubt. Far upstream, a veritable swarm of boats was approaching.

The news served to bring out every man at the camp who was still on his feet; they gathered in a ragged mob along the river's edge, a muttering mob, feverishly hopeful, yet scarcely daring to guess what the advent of the new force and a new commander might mean. A curious silence fell over them as the vast flotilla drew nearer. Then a hoarse cry, something like a cheer, burst from their throats as the boats in the van came opposite them, then swung sharply toward shore.

It was a strange sight to those who had seen nothing but rags and destitution for months. Bateau after bateau filled with stalwart, healthy men, clean of face, hair neatly clubbed, each wearing a bright new uniform, each with a new rifle and gleaming bayonet at his side, each with a knapsack which seemed promisingly well filled.

The leading bateau grated against the bank. As its occupants arose, they waited respectfully for their leader to be the first to step ashore. He was a tall, impressive figure as he strode up the bank, a large man, with a red face and a tuft of hair thrust out from each side of his head which gave him a curiously lynx-like appearance, an effect heightened by his narrowed eyes, sharp nose and stubborn mouth. As he stepped forward and greeted General Thompson, a distinct touch of hauteur marked his bearing.

General Sullivan had arrived.

2.

For the Sullivan "Honor"

JOHN SULLIVAN was a major general because he was
a lawyer—which is less of a non-sequitur than appears
at first glance. After several years of office study, he began practising law at Durham, N. H. Here his conde-
scending but determined efforts to be popular were highly
successful. His business increased rapidly and he gained a
public prominence almost sufficient to gratify even his
inordinate vanity. His imposing gift of words and his natural ability to look and act impressive won him the cap-
taincy of Durham's militia company. He saw no active
service but, in due course, the awed respect he demanded
elevated him to the rank of major.* By the time the Revolution began, his practice had made him wealthy—at 34—
and he had succeeded in identifying himself with the
patriot cause so well that he was chosen one of New Hampshire's two delegates to the Continental Congress.

After Lexington and Concord, that august body awoke

* Sparks, Jared: *Life of Major General John Sullivan.*

to the necessity of an army, if a war was to be fought. In all the fearful and wonderful methods it employed in military affairs, nothing quite equalled its first move in that field. An unorganized mob of thousands of "minute men" was flocking toward Boston at the time. Without consulting them, the gentlemen in Philadelphia adopted this force en masse and declared it the Continental Army. Then Congress started at the top to fill in the gaps it thought it saw and provided for countless future gaps which might develop by creating major generals, brigadier generals, colonels and majors, in wholesale bargain lots.

It was all engagingly simple. The army needed officers. Plenty of personal friends and *their* personal friends wanted to be officers. A few strokes of the congressional pen made officers. Presto! It was as easy as printing money —another favorite and resultful pastime of the Continental Congress. Outside a comic opera, no force ever equalled the Continental Army for quantity of generals per enlisted man, to say nothing of colonels and lower-ranked officers. But then, the redundant list of commissions made a lot of nice men happy. The happiness of the men who had to serve under them was overlooked somehow.

By some accidental miracle, George Washington, the one man who did not want the job, was made commander-in-chief. In the rest of its appointments, Congress did not score a very high average. But, with a live major in its own midst, in the form of John Sullivan, only one procedure was possible. With considerable éclat, Fellow-Congressman Sullivan was commissioned a brigadier general* and sent on his way rejoicing, to take command of the

* June 22, 1775.

New Hampshire troops. It made no difference that this powerful contingent of Washington's army had been raised almost entirely by the untiring efforts of the doughty John Stark. The Durham lawyer, who was one of the "boys," was given the call over the man who had done the work.

During the months of watchful waiting at the siege of Boston, Sullivan was chiefly a drill-master, at a time when the Continental Army needed drill-masters more than it needed guns—which is saying a great deal. He must have been rather good at it. There seems to be no other possible explanation for the high favor he won with the commander-in-chief.

Washington made extremely few mistakes in his judgment of men. Sullivan was one—and well-nigh fatal. The transmuted lawyer had the first of many chances to prove his generalship when he was sent to the northern army in May, 1776. In less than four months, he all but wrecked the patriot cause by nearly destroying both its armies. In fact, nothing but miraculous luck prevented that calamitous result.

When he went north, Congress bestowed lavish blessings upon him. His new troops comprised the four best-equipped, best-drilled regiments in the Continental Army. One of them was commanded by Colonel Anthony Wayne, who was worth a regiment in himself. But Sullivan accepted these favors with great calm, as nothing more than his just due.

Such a man could neither tolerate nor remotely understand the conditions he faced in Canada. He listened only to what he wished to hear and, once an idea became fixed in his mind, nothing could change it, not even the wholesale slaughter of the men he sacrificed to his mulish convictions.

With unbounded faith in his own intellectual powers, he leaped to conclusions without investigation of the facts. His first contact with the northern front came on June 1, at St. John's, where he found the inebriated De Woedtke and a mob of disgruntled stragglers. This was all he needed. Within a few hours he passed a sweeping judgment on the entire situation. This he transmitted in a long letter—not to Schuyler, his immediate superior, nor to Washington, his commander-in-chief, but to the president of Congress, John Hancock—who hated Washington and was probably the only man in the country who surpassed Sullivan himself in vanity.

He began with an irritated condemnation of everything. "I can, in a word, inform you that no one thing is right." He was hearing things, too. Some of those he found at St. John's, "beset by Fear," reported the British advancing in force but "persons who have come from 80 miles below Quebeck declare that there is no Appearance of men or Ships on this Side of that city and for my own part *I am fully convinced that the latter report is true.*" He did not say why. Then he went into a vitriolic denunciation of the "Infamous Retreat from Quebeck" and grandly projected the immediate correction of the "dreadful errors" made by all his predecessors.*

Arrived at Sorel, he was much less disturbed by the horrible condition of the troops he found there than the incomplete state of the camp's defenses. He immediately set everyone at work building breastworks and intrenchments

* Sullivan to Hancock, June 1, 1776.

and kept them at it all of June 5. Then, with a contented sigh, he wrote to Washington.

"I arrived here at a very critical moment," he stated modestly. "I can reduce this army to order and put a new face upon affairs here." At considerable length he also described the touching happiness of everyone over his coming.*

Incidentally, he brought De Woedtke with him from St. John's. He mentioned the baron several times in his dispatches but seems to have had a great deal of trouble with his name. It is spelled differently each time—and never correctly—ranging from "Woodkle" to "Woteke." This may have been because of the befuddled gurgle with which its owner pronounced the name in his prevailing condition.

Sullivan had nothing but disdain for the officers he found at Sorel and he impatiently refused to listen to any useful information they had to offer. Instead, he moulded everything he saw and heard to fit his own preconceived notions. This led him to a momentous conclusion and he called a council of war. Or, rather, he assembled an audience.

"The situation here is unspeakable," he declared to his officers. "I can scarcely comprehend how such incredible mistakes have been made. But," he drew himself up arrogantly, "they will be rectified. It is well I have come." He paused only long enough to draw his breath and, frowning impressively, continued. "A vast area captured last year has been lost in a most disgraceful manner. That ground will

* Sullivan to Washington, June 5, 1776.

be recovered—at once. Henceforth, our watchword will be 'advance.' 'Retreat' is a word my men do not know."

He fixed his cat-like eyes on General Thompson. "A somewhat abortive expedition has gone to Nicolet," he went on. "That gesture will be transformed into decisive action. Tomorrow, General Thompson, you will assemble the regiments of Colonels Wayne, Maxwell and Irvine, join St. Clair and attack Three Rivers without delay."

"But, sir," protested the startled Thompson, "we have received no word from Colonel St. Clair. Surely, it would be advisable to await his report."

"And waste more valuable time?" Sullivan stared at him coldly. "No, General Thompson. That is what has been wrong here. My honor demands that I strike now to begin the redemption of this army. It is my decision that the attack be made forthwith. I am convinced the British force is small. Opportunity awaits us."

Thompson's deep-set eyes flashed but his voice was even as he replied, "Your orders will be obeyed of course, sir, but the failure to hear from Colonel St. Clair would seem to indicate he has encountered difficulties of which we should know."

Sullivan smiled. "If I may be permitted to say so," he retorted, with heavy sarcasm, "I fear Colonel St. Clair's hesitation is prompted by the spirit which I found prevalent here." Thompson flushed angrily, but Sullivan went on in a lofty tone. "My own information convinces me Three Rivers is occupied by a very small force. You will move to Nicolet tomorrow. With the addition of the three fresh, *fighting* regiments you will have 2,200 men. If you move on Three Rivers during the night and attack before dawn, your victory should be easy and overwhelming. That is what I am expecting." He turned to the other officers. "That is all, gentlemen."

So, within two days after his arrival in a region of which he was totally ignorant, General Sullivan directed that his new and valuable troops be hurled against an enemy of whose position he was uncertain and whose strength he did not know or even trouble to learn. In his final, written instructions, he gave Thompson a certain amount of lee-way but declared he expected him to "open the Way for our Recovering that Ground which former troops have so shamefully lost."* Sullivan's complete ignorance of the country is sharply revealed in his report to Schuyler in which he constantly referred to Three Rivers as "forty-five miles distant." The actual distance was scarcely more than half that.

When Thompson reached Nicolet he found an apologetic St. Clair. The colonel had learned practically nothing in his four days' absence from Sorel. The terrain on the north side of the St. Lawrence had proved treacherous. The extensive swamps along the shore made approach toward Three Rivers difficult for scouting. A few ships had been sighted but, on the whole, his meager information led him to believe the British garrison was small. His chief prize was a French-Canadian guide he had engaged, who professed to know every inch of the country and who now offered to lead the army to Three Rivers by the shortest route for ten dollars, hard money, paid in advance.

Thompson was dissatisfied but, under his instructions, he felt he had no recourse but to launch an immediate attack.

* Sullivan to Thompson, June 6, 1776.

Since the easiest method of approach to Three Rivers was by boat, the army embarked shortly after dark. But the flotilla was badly piloted, the night was cloudy and when the boats finally touched shore again, it was nearly midnight and the troops had to land in pitch darkness. After a brief survey, the guide declared he had oriented himself and that they were nine miles from their destination.

Lined up on shore, the troops marched off briskly with Thompson and the guide in the van. But the vigorous pace did not continue long. Within fifteen minutes, they were floundering in grass-tangled mud which deepened as they advanced.

"Are you sure this is the way?" Thompson demanded of the guide.

"Oh, yes, monsieur," was the quick reply. "We must cross this to reach the short path. Only ten, fifteen minutes more."

The "ten, fifteen" minutes lengthened into an hour and the swamp grew worse. Cursing roundly, the men struggled on, through muck which first rose above their ankles, then their knees, and finally they were beating through mud and water up to their thighs while the tangled roots in the morass tore their fine new uniforms to shreds. Wallowing profanely in the van, Thompson became more exasperated by the moment. "I think you've lost your own way," he exclaimed, angrily. "This can't be right."

There was no answer and the general stopped, trying to peer through the blackness. "Guide!" he called, sharply, "guide, where are you?" He turned toward the splashing men behind him and shouted, "Silence, there—halt!" When the force paused in semi-quiet, he once more called for the guide but there was no response.

"We've been tricked!" Thompson roared. "Turn back. Turn back until we find solid ground."

For two miles, the soldiers fought their way through the slimy ooze before they had freed themselves.* But there was no breathing spell. They had spent three hours in the marsh and time was pressing. Thompson swung back toward Three Rivers, following the shore as closely as possible and had not gone half a mile before he stumbled into another swamp.** This time there was no recourse but to go on and they did, in raging desperation.

Two more hours they slogged through the quagmire and now dawn was almost upon them. Already the first streaks of light were beginning to appear, revealing a world of tangled morass, wrapped in heavy mist, almost as impenetrable as the night.

"Hurry, hurry," Thompson urged unceasingly but hurry was beyond these bedraggled and weary men. Panting, wet, shivering and utterly spent, they began to emerge at last, all of them in a sorry state. Many of them had lost their guns. Others had found their powder soaked. All were so exhausted they could scarcely stand.

Daylight was full upon them now and with it came the sun thinning the mist and driving the shroud from the river. A sudden, confused cry of alarm ran along the line of men struggling to solid ground. Anthony Wayne, striding beside Thompson, gripped the general's arm, while the

* Sullivan's Report to Washington, June 12, 1776.
** Unsigned Letter of June 12, 1776: American Archives. Also, Carrington: *Battles of the American Revolution*.

leader of the Continentals looked up and a volley of curses burst from his lips. St. Clair had said "a *few* boats." The vanishing mists uncovered a veritable fleet, a line of British war vessels riding at anchor before them, beside them, far back of them, all along the shore, so near, the Americans could have thrown stones aboard them. And, on the land side, directly above, frowned the intrenchments of Three Rivers.

"We're trapped," Thompson exclaimed, bitterly. "This is what comes of planning attacks without information. I warned him, but no, he knew there were only ——"

He was cut short by a flash and a roar from one of the gunboats, then another and another. As the Americans had seen, so they had been seen and, in half a dozen minutes, the guns of the entire fleet were roaring, blasting ghastly holes through the huddling groups still floundering from the swamp. Men were dropping in bloody heaps. Simultaneously, the intrenchments above them awakened. A musket fired, then another and then there was a blaze of flame along the whole line of breastworks.

"There's nothing for it but to fight," Thompson shouted. "It's murder to stay here and we cannot retreat past those boats. Our only hope is attack. A determined rush may save the army."

"Let me take the van to the left," Wayne cried, eagerly. "I believe we have a chance to flank the works."

"It's yours," Thompson said. "Place your men in position." He hurried along the lines, where the officers were attempting to organize their troops in furious haste, giving swift orders. He placed Irvine's regiment on the right, with Maxwell in support and sent St. Clair behind Wayne. The hail of shot still tore ragged holes in the lines but the men were deploying feverishly, weary as they were, grateful for any action in preference to standing helpless under the leaden storm.

Thompson hurried to the advance wave. "I trust this will satisfy the demands of General Sullivan's honor," he exclaimed, savagely, as he passed Wayne. Then he swung about abruptly. "Let every man see that his rifle is loaded," he shouted. "Fix bayonets!" His sword flashed from its scabbard and he waved it above him. "Forward!"

Something in the sharp command, something in the sense of battle sent an electric impulse along the lines. With their last gasp of energy, the men sprang forward, the dynamic Wayne leading them all. With each step of advance, men were pitching forward on their faces, dead and dying, as again and again the intrenchments whipped out their blazing lash of lead. The forward line faltered under the hail of death. The second line caught up with its remnants, plunged doggedly on only to be met by a new storm of raking fire which crumpled its ranks but Wayne leaped before them, eyes ablaze.

"No falling back!" he roared. "Come on! Come on! Forward!"

Inspired by his reckless example, the wavering line steadied, moved on once more. The men paused to fire at glimpsed redcoat targets behind the breastworks, reloaded quickly and stumbled on, while the British lines flamed with an unbroken hurricane of fire. Dead and dying men fell in droves but still the decimated ranks went grimly ahead. And suddenly, over the deafening roar of the volleys, sounded a wild, ringing yell as the remnants of the assaulting array leaped upon the breastworks, clung there for an agonizing moment and then were sent hurtling back—those who were not spitted on redcoat blades to gasp out their lives on the crest.

As the shattered ranks reeled back down the slope, they stumbled over the broken, bleeding forms of more than seven hundred of their comrades who lay there as fruit of the attack for General Sullivan's honor. And now after them came the British, a giant wave of red, whose members numbered several times the 800 Sullivan had fondly chosen to believe as the garrison's maximum, a horde of fresh, unwearied men who leaped over the intrenchments and rushed in pursuit. Caught, front and rear, the Continentals, already tried beyond human endurance, broke wildly. On the right, where General Thompson was roaring imprecations as he made desperate attempts to rally his lines, the British caught up with Irvine's force, swarmed over it. There was a wild confusion of savage melee and then the Americans, cut off, were engulfed by the redcoat mass.

The remaining Continentals fled down the river bank, trying to run the gauntlet of the gunboats. Wayne rushed to protect their rear with a bare handful of men he hastily gathered together. With these he beat back one charge and though he was shot in the leg, ignored his wound as he fought on grimly in his rearguard defense. The broken troops staggered down the bank and into the swamps but nowhere was there safety from the booming fire of the fleet which swept them with fearful havoc, littering the bank with mangled bodies while the wounded within the swamps were sucked out of sight into the mire.

Wayne refused to leave the north shore of the St. Lawrence at once. For three days, he moved about tirelessly, picking up stragglers one by one until he was certain no more of the shattered Continentals could be recovered. During those three days, other fragments of the American force filtered into Sorel, but even when Wayne had brought back the last, few more than half of the twenty-two hundred had returned. The slaughter before the intrenchments had been a second Bunker Hill with the opponents reversed in position.* The gunboats had taken a fearful toll and General Thompson, Colonel Irvine and two hundred men had been captured.

General Sullivan had not won an "overwhelming victory." But he had created an immortal precedent. He had established the great American tradition of useless butchery in the name of war.

* Letter of an American chaplain who was present at Three Rivers: American Archives.

3.

Retreat à la Sullivan

ON THE day of the battle, General Sullivan wrote a fantastic letter to Washington. Inspired by the sound of the firing which could be "clearly heard, although forty-five miles distant," he enthusiastically described the certain victory his troops were winning—as he visioned it.* Four days later, he was writing Washington again, a very different sort of letter, one which fairly exuded tears and heartbreak. It contained not a word of regret over the criminal waste of so many good men, of which the colonies never had enough, nor of the suffering and death to which he had subjected them. He only bemoaned their failure to do the impossible and wailed over the stunning surprise of discovering that Burgoyne had stationed more than 5,000 men at Three Rivers without telling him about it. Although he admitted he did not yet know what had happened to Wayne and his men, he brazenly offered the estimate of his losses at "about 150"! But he slipped concerning his real

* Sullivan to Washington, June 8, 1776.

41

knowledge of the disaster when he went off into a mood of high tragedy and wrote, grandly, "I now think only of a glorious death or a victory against superior numbers."*

His rebound was quick, however. He had about 2,600 men in camp of whom 1,000 were in fairly good condition. Twenty-five miles away, Burgoyne was rapidly assembling an army of more than 10,000—almost 100-per-cent healthy and ready to fight. This made no difference to Sullivan. With his customary opera-bouffe grandiloquence, he proclaimed his intention of standing his ground and facing the foe to the bitter end. "I am determined," he wrote, "to hold the most important post, so long as one stone is left upon another."**

His subordinates were aghast. They had no illusions as to the menace which hung over them and they protested violently, insisting upon an immediate retreat to a spot less exposed to annihilation. Sullivan was furious.

"You cringe in fear of an enemy you have not even seen," he shouted angrily.*** "Well, I am not afraid. We will proceed at once to the complete fortification of the camp."

"With due apologies, sir," Colonel Thomas Maxwell replied, "some of us have seen the enemy. His force is so superior that nothing but catastrophe can result from an attempt to hold this camp."

"Your words are intolerable," Sullivan exclaimed, his mouth tightly stubborn. "Let the enemy come. It will grant

* Sullivan to Schuyler, June 12, 1776.
** Sullivan to Washington, June 12, 1776.
*** Sullivan to Schuyler, June 19, 1776.

us opportunity to redeem ourselves. We will prepare for defense to the last extremity."

The retort of the officers stunned him. *More than forty of them immediately turned in their resignations to him.** But he refused to be moved from his stand. He also refused to accept any of the resignations and compelled the troops to strengthen the hopeless camp's defenses. For six days after the Three Rivers tragedy, he maintained his mulish attitude, six days during which an orderly and safe retirement could have been made with a minimum of hardship for the disheartened and physically weakened troops, six days of anxious peering to the northeast by officers and men alike. Then, on the morning of June 14, the word swept through the camp that a vast British fleet was in sight.

With the first alarm, Wayne and St. Clair were on the northern breastworks where they shortly were joined by the sullen-faced commander. Through their glasses, they made out no less than fifty vessels, most of them transports, the rest gunboats and other fighting ships.

Wayne turned to Sullivan. "Surely, sir, we can wait no longer," he said, earnestly. "If that force attacks us, we will be wiped out. As it is, we barely have time to escape."

"Escape?" Sullivan thundered. "We are not seeking escape. We will stand our ground." Again he looked through his glass at the fleet which was moving steadily westward along the north shore of Lake St. Peter. And, slowly, his face brightened. He lowered his glass and swung toward the two colonels in smug triumph. "I have it," he cried. "They are going to give us unsurpassed opportunity. They do not plan to attack here. Their objective is Montreal, of

* Sullivan to Schuyler, June 19, 1776.

course. Let them go to Montreal. Once they have passed this point, our road is open. We can cross the lake unhampered and sweep on to take Quebec."

Wayne stared at him in blank incredulity. "And what, sir," he demanded, "if, after they have passed us, instead of going on they suddenly land and cut off *our* rear. There would be nothing left but surrender."

Sullivan gave him a startled glance then reddened with anger. "We will never surrender," he exclaimed. "We will die honorably, if need be, but surrender—never!"

Wayne's long-held temper suddenly flamed. "Sir," he retorted, "it would seem more in keeping with the advancement of our cause to retreat honorably and save our soldiers to fight again."

"Your tone smacks of disrespect, Colonel Wayne," Sullivan flared, drawing himself up. "This is my last word on the matter. We will wait until the purpose of the enemy is manifest."

So he waited, all through the long June day, waited while the British ships drew nearer and nearer, waited until, late in the afternoon, the fleet suddenly veered from its westerly course and made directly for Sorel, waited until the sloops in the van were less than two hours' sail from the camp. Then, his florid face a shade paler, Sullivan leaped down from his perch on the breastworks and gave the command to abandon camp.

He was days too late to make the retreat by land. He was hours too late to retire safely by the Richelieu. Now there was only one glimmer of hope—compel the half-starved sickly men to take to the boats and row for their very lives. In sheer criminal stubbornness, General Sul-

JOHN SULLIVAN

livan had wantonly risked the complete destruction of the northern army.

In some amazing manner it escaped. With the enemy only an hour and a half distant, the haggard, emaciated troops went to work with feverish frenzy, razed the camp, carried more than a thousand sick men and placed them in the bateaux, loaded all their cannon, their muskets and rifles, their powder and shot, their food and personal effects—all meager enough—aboard the boats and pulled away, rowing as lustily as their enfeebled condition would permit. And when the last bateau was gone, the British van was less than an hour away.*

The Americans had sixty miles to go to reach the hoped-for security of St. John's. They had to row upstream against a strong current, fifty miles, to reach Chambly and then disembark again. The twelve miles of the Richelieu from Chambly to St. John's are filled with dangerous rapids through which the loaded boats could not be taken safely.

Somehow, the army did it. The oarsmen rowed desperately, all night and all the following day. They rowed until they had to wrap their hands in rags, and continued to row until the rags were bloody and their bodies were numb and their arms seemed ready to pull from their sockets. But they did it. It was nightfall of June 15 when they reached Chambly and now again they did the impossible. The boats were unloaded of all equipment which the men could take on their backs, the sick were carried bodily and then the boats were towed, poled and partially rowed along the shore through the rapids. Evening of the 17th found them at St. John's at last, but still they were

* Sullivan to Schuyler, June 19, 1776.

not safe. Then Sullivan had had another brilliant inspiration. He had decided upon a new place to make a stand. So the boats were loaded once more, the men climbed aboard and the oarsmen rowed out to a small flat island below St. John's, the Isle aux Noix. Here the French had fortified themselves against the British fifteen years before. Here Sullivan believed he could stop Burgoyne and here, completely exhausted, the harassed army collapsed, unable for hours even to pitch camp.

Sullivan believed he had made a masterly retreat to achieve a brilliant escape, and he so informed Schuyler. Actually, the miracle of Burgoyne's decision to postpone his pursuit and push on to Montreal was all that saved him. Had the British commander grasped the opportunity Sullivan's reckless stupidity had given him, the American force could have been captured at once and the way would have been open for a British sweep from the north which would have shattered the Revolution.

But Sullivan was far from through. For two days after he abandoned Sorel, he sent no warning to Arnold. In the face of the certainty that the British would strike for Montreal, the commanding general of the American force completely failed to notify his subordinate of the danger which threatened him.

Arnold escaped by one of the most ironic miracles of the war. Six weeks before, when General Sullivan and the four new regiments were assigned to northern service, another man was detached from Washington's army and sent alone to join the northern force, a very young man, aged nineteen, rather stocky as to figure, with cold eyes and thin lips set in a face rather too broad. His name was

James Wilkinson, a captain, personally commissioned by
no less than General Washington himself. Since he will
be met frequently in this record, he merits a somewhat
more complete introduction.

He was born in Tidewater, Md., not far from the
Virginia estates of the Washingtons, in 1757. When he was
fifteen, he went to Philadelphia to study medicine. While
there he became acquainted with several officers of the
British regiment garrisoned at Philadelphia, an association which "inspired in me that love of things military
ever after the guiding star of my life."*

By the time he was seventeen, he had acquired all the
knowledge of anatomy, drugs and elementary surgery then
available, and went back to Maryland; but in the summer
of 1775, he made his way to Cambridge and became a
private in a rifle company. A gentleman of extremely
ingratiating manners, good education and—more important—an earnestly acquired mastery of the manual of arms,
Wilkinson stood out like a sore thumb in the ragged array.
Moreover, he had the gift of meeting the "right people."
Always willing to work unstintingly if he saw a chance
for personal benefit, he performed his duties so ener-
getically and efficiently that he was brought to the attention
of the commander-in-chief. Happy to hear that his youthful neighbor from back home was so excellent a soldier,
Washington gave him a captain's commission in March,
1776.

Sent north, he reached St. John's almost a month ahead
of Sullivan. He found "the post without garrison or command but infested with stragglers from the army. . . .

* Wilkinson: *Memoirs of My Own Times.*

Being myself without orders, written or verbal, I yielded to the natural impulse of my breast and determined to reinforce the weakest point. Accordingly, having taken under my command every man who acknowledged himself a soldier, I marched, upward of a hundred strong,"* to Lachine where Arnold was, about twelve miles from Montreal.

Perhaps because of this admirable act, perhaps because he had a crisp military air, but more likely because he had breeding and education, Arnold made Wilkinson his personal aide—and the gods probably laughed out loud. In less than a month, Wilkinson already had begun the undermining tactics which led, in no small measure, to the final wrecking of Arnold.

On June 15, however, he was the heroic rescuer of the leader he was attempting to undo. Entirely ignorant that Sorel had been abandoned, Arnold sent Wilkinson on his way there that day, with a message for Sullivan. He did not go far. A few miles from Montreal, the young captain suddenly ran into the vanguard of Burgoyne's army, newly landed and marching rapidly toward the city. Wilkinson barely escaped capture but managed to turn and gallop at top speed to warn his chief, with British bullets flying all about him. Arnold immediately sounded the alarm, assembled his garrison of three hundred and fifty, loaded them into boats and was just starting across the St. Lawrence to La Prairie when the advancing British appeared behind him.**

But for Wilkinson's accidental encounter, the Montreal

* Ibid.
** Arnold to Sullivan, from La Prairie, June 16, 1775.

force undoubtedly would have been captured. Arnold would have been a prisoner and by another of Sullivan's blunders, the British would have had the chance to defeat the Americans and end the Revolution almost before the ink was dry on the Declaration of Independence. For it was Arnold and Arnold alone who, later in that year of 1776, stopped the British in the north and forced the postponement of Burgoyne's invasion for one year, and then it was to be Arnold who would stop them again.

From La Prairie, Arnold hurried his force cross-country to St. John's and then joined the rest of the American army at Isle aux Noix where Sullivan now had assembled all the northern troops then north of Crown Point, a total of nearly 6,000. The menace of British pursuit was more present than ever and Isle aux Noix was anything but a health resort, so Arnold immediately urged Sullivan to take the army to assured safety at Crown Point. But Sullivan bluntly refused to retreat farther and so the army was subjected, for eight days, to the unspeakable horrors of the island camp.

Sorel, with all its hideousness, was a paradise compared with Isle aux Noix. The land was low and swampy, the oppressive midsummer atmosphere above it, muggy and miasmatic. The water which surrounded it was covered with scum.* The entire place was a breeding ground for insects which almost drove the sickly soldiers to madness as they swept upon them in huge swarms. There was no reasonable place to camp. Nowhere could a shelter be raised which could be protected against the soggy dampness of the soil or the myriad flying pests overhead.

* Trevelyan: *American Revolution*, Vol. II.

Here there was no escape from the ravages of smallpox, dysentery and a dozen other diseases which felled the men like wheat before a scythe. In eight days the number of smallpox cases alone increased from 2,000 to more than 4,000. Roll calls became a mockery, with only a handful of men able to answer to their names. Even the immovable Sullivan's reports sounded a note of despair.

"One fortnight longer in this place will not leave us well enough to Carry off the Sick. The Raging of the Smallpox deprives us of whole Regiments in the Course of a few days and we have nothing to give them but rotting* Salt Pork, Flour & the Poisonous water of this Lake. This Wretched Army is now perhaps the most pitiful one that ever was formed."**

On that report, there was no return whatever from the entire battalion of Colonel John Patterson. On April 21, he had marched north with his New York force of six hundred men, not one of them on the sick list. Now he had only five men able to stand—exactly two months later!

At least thirty men died every day—died and were buried like dogs, their only grave the huge death trench dug at one end of the island. Every morning the festering shelters

---

* The "rotting" pork can not be charged against Congress. The teamsters who hauled the army supplies were responsible for that. They found the vats of salt pork rather heavy so, to lighten the burden on their teams, they simply drained off the preserving pickle water before they started on their journeys through the hot midsummer sun. "Not a pound could possibly be in a good state on arriving," Schuyler wrote to Congress, in an indignant report when he discovered the practice.

** Sullivan to Washington, June 24, 1776.

of the troops were combed for those who had stopped breathing during the night. Then the cadavers were simply dragged out and thrown into the trenches without ceremony.

Day by day, the foul stench which hung over the island grew worse as more men died and more men became sick. Day by day, the conditions became more frightful and still Sullivan refused to leave the pest hole. "I will not retreat farther," he fretfully told a meeting of his officers on June 24. "This is the last bit of Canada which we hold and I propose to keep it. I do not credit the prevailing belief of an early British invasion. Moreover, we are safe here. The British can not reach us."

"Not unless they've no objection to wet feet," Arnold said, drily, "and that's all they'd risk through the shallow water which separates us from shore. Sir," he added, earnestly, "our only security lies behind the works at Crown Point. We can go there easily at this time when the British are not yet upon us. We may not be so fortunate a week or two hence."

"I tell you we have nothing to fear," exclaimed Sullivan and once more his lips set obstinately. "I can not, in honor, retreat another foot at this time."

Arnold stared at him with flint in his eyes. "General Sullivan," he said, shortly, "do you stand willing to sacrifice 6,000 soldiers for your honor?"

Sullivan turned on him in fury. "My honor, sir—" he began with a roar but Arnold made an apologetic wave of his hand.

"No offense, sir, I assure you," he said, with a frigidity which was worse than invective. As he spoke, young Captain Wilkinson approached him, bowed to General Sullivan and then spoke hastily in his own chief's ear. Arnold looked at him, startled, then swung toward Sullivan with a grim smile. "This may alter your convictions somewhat," he said. "Captain Wilkinson informs me of the arrival of one of my scouts with the report that General Burgoyne is at Chambly."

Sullivan looked at him in consternation. "Chambly!" he ejaculated. "Then he is only twenty miles distant." He stood staring for a minute, then, with a gesture of exasperation, said, "Very well. Order the men to abandon camp. We will go to Isle la Motte. That at least is healthier than Aux Noix."

"Why not to Crown Point at once, general?" Arnold demanded.

"Isle la Motte," Sullivan exclaimed in an angry voice. "I will not retire to Crown Point except by specific orders from General Schuyler."

Arnold looked at him quizzically but merely said, "Very well, sir," and went out.

So once more the weakened, pestilence-ridden army was forced to rush to escape under pressure. It was harder work this time, for the men were in worse condition than at Sorel and there were more of them. But the panting force finally had everything aboard the bateaux and pushed for the twenty-five-mile row up Lake Champlain to Isle la Motte. All except Arnold. He waited over at St. John's until every Continental had started south except the two oarsmen waiting in his own boat. Then he rode northward, rode for five miles until he was in sight of Burgoyne's advancing troops, coming inexorably to wipe out the last vestige of the Canadian conquest he himself had conceived and had begun so brilliantly nine months before. At last he turned and galloped back to St. John's, where he boarded the waiting boat. He was the last American to leave Canadian soil.

He did not stop at Isle la Motte. Mindful of Sullivan's words, he went on to Crown Point, procured a horse there and went galloping to Albany and Schuyler. On July 1, Sullivan received Schuyler's command to fall back to Crown Point and, in deep chagrin, he ordered the retirement. Again he was tragically late. The troops were transferred safely enough but now were so permeated with disease that Crown Point was a charnel house that summer. In less than two months, the northern army lost five thousand men!

The Continentals' tragic retreat from Canada is one of the most completely suppressed episodes of the Revolutionary War. Even John Fiske, whose *American Revolution* has been the most widely accepted authority on the war for the past fifty years, dismisses the entire Canadian campaign of 1776 with the following: "In the spring, the enterprise was taken up by Wooster and Sullivan with fresh forces. But, by this time, the Hessians had come over and Carleton, reinforced until his army numbered 13,000, was enabled to recapture Montreal and push back the Americans until, in June, after a hazardous retreat, *well-conducted by Sullivan,* the remnant of the invading army found shelter at Crown Point." In a historian of Fiske's caliber, this is an almost incredible evasion and perversion of the facts.

So much importance was accorded the campaign by both Congress and Washington that, in numbers, the "remnant of the invading army" (nearly six thousand), combined with the garrisons at Crown Point and Ticonderoga, gave the northern army a strength only 1,000 less than the "grand army" which Washington took to New York at the same time Sullivan was retreating.

More troops actually fought in the disastrous attack on Three Rivers than met at Bunker Hill, Trenton, Princeton, Camden, King's Mountain, Cowpens and a dozen other well-publicized pitched battles of the Revolution. For sheer horror, during its brief occupation, Isle aux Noix surpassed Valley Forge.

4.

The Death Trap on Long Island

CHANGES now came to the north—though not necessarily for the better. The lynx merely gave way to the hyena. A few days after the staggering army poured into Crown Point, a sly-faced, gray-haired man by the name of Horatio Gates appeared there with the Congressional ukase to relieve Sullivan of command. The Durham lawyer was not the only person to be stunned by the change. It came as an equally disagreeable shock to Washington and Schuyler and the manner of its development inscribed some ominous handwriting on the wall.

In May, 1776, Washington had sent Gates—then his adjutant general with the rank of brigadier—to Philadelphia on army business. Despite his aging bones, Gates fairly sprinted all the way and then remained for so long that Washington began to wonder what had become of him. The commander-in-chief eventually found out. Late in June, he was informed officially that the Continental Congress had signalized its recognition of Gates' military genius. It had made him a major general and, on June 17, had appointed him to command the "army in Canada."

Washington was enraged. He had been cognizant, at least, of the previous moves in the north and Sullivan had been sent there at his recommendation, but nothing had been said to him about the elevation of Gates until the matter was concluded. General Schuyler, commander of the Northern Department, was treated even more shabbily. Not only was he not consulted; he was not even informed of the change which so vitally affected the region under his jurisdiction. He knew nothing about it until Gates appeared at Albany on his way to Crown Point to take command.

Both Washington and Schuyler protested to Congress vigorously but Gates had done his personal lobbying well, so well that it stands out as the one thorough accomplishment of his life, a ringing testimonial to his ability in underhanded conniving. Stealthy, venal and soft-spoken, a natural sycophant, he was the very type to which most of the members of Congress were susceptible. In an incredibly short time, he had developed an extraordinary bloc in that noble body, dedicated to the proposition that he was Heaven's gift to the colonists' hopes. Before he left for the north, many of the congressmen were wondering if it had not been a serious mistake to make Washington the commanding general when so sterling a warrior as Gates was available. It was a thought which influenced them for a long time to come. That Gates was able to supplant one of Congress's own previous pets was not surprising. The Continental Congress was like that. A more flighty, inconsistent, ungrateful and short-memoried aggregation never existed. At the moment, Sullivan was down and Gates was up. That was all there was to it. Gates kept the job.

Sullivan caustically wrote both Washington and Congress, declining to serve under Gates, and went to Philadelphia to resign his commission. From the standpoint of the Revolutionary cause, the psychological situation was unfortunate, as Washington's own indignation placed him on Sullivan's side. He persuaded the disgruntled brigadier to remain in the service and welcomed him back to his own army in New York City.

It must be remembered that Washington was not as yet in a position to know the truth concerning Sullivan's debacle in the north, owing to the uncertainty and slothfulness of communications. As for Congress, it had not even heard of Three Rivers at the time of Gates' appointment. Sullivan was not removed because of his failure but simply because Gates asked Congress for the post, after convincing its dominant New England contingent that his inspired talents had little opportunity for expression under the tyrannical Virginian who unfortunately had been made commander-in-chief. More strength was added to Sullivan's claims of unjust treatment when Congress, probably a little shamefaced over its action, tried to make partial amends. August 9, 1776, was another commissioning day at Philadelphia and Sullivan drew a major generalship from the grab bag. Incidentally, among the others honored that same day was Colonel Arthur St. Clair, who was made brigadier general for no conceivable reason other than that Congress probably thought it was his turn to get something.

Sullivan's promotion soothed his wounded vanity* and restored his self-esteem, just in time to permit him to throw Washington's army on the altar of sacrifice, just as he had offered Burgoyne the rejected opportunity to destroy the northern army in June.

Sir William Howe, commander of the British army, was on Staten Island with 30,000 men, preparing to make a drive for the capture of New York City. His brother, Admiral Richard, Lord Howe, was in the harbor with the British fleet. In order to hold New York, Washington had to keep Brooklyn Heights, which commanded New York just as Bunker Hill and Dorchester Heights commanded Boston. He had about 18,000 men at the time, 10,000 of them raw militia of less than a month's service and he had to scatter half this force to garrison widely separated points, as far apart as King's Bridge at the north end of Manhattan Island, Paulus Hook on the New Jersey shore and Governor's Island, just below the city proper. He devoted most of the militia to this purpose as the surest means of keeping them out of his way. With ample justification, Washington never had any faith in the short-term militia Congress always thrust upon him.

The rest of the army, nearly 8,000 Continentals and 1,000 militia, he put behind the newly built breastworks of

* Washington was not altogether blind to Sullivan's defects. In a letter to Hancock, written in a rather amused vein after receiving one of Sullivan's glowing prospectuses from Sorel, he freely said that Sullivan obviously was aiming for undisputed command in the north and added: "He has his wants and his foibles. The latter are manifested in his little tincture of vanity and in an overdesire of being popular, which sometimes leads him into embarrassments." Truthful, but a little on the conservative side, that comment.

Brooklyn Heights under the command of Sullivan who, after one of his customary ten-minute surveys of the situation, immediately wrote Washington he was prepared to withstand the entire British army. It was Sullivan's misfortune that, every time he indulged in this sort of bombast, something dull and heavy struck him. In this case, the day after he issued his flourishing dispatch, Washington sent over the irascible Major General Putnam to relieve him and Sullivan, his feelings injured again, was relegated to the command of a division.

With a British attack certain, Washington's plan was extremely simple. He could not expect to defeat the overwhelming enemy force in a pitched battle. His one hope was to inflict heavy losses when the encounter came and present such an impregnable front to Howe that his tenuous grip on New York could be retained long enough to bolster the morale of the newly declared independent states. To accomplish this, he directed Putnam to establish strong outposts below Brooklyn Heights. When the British attacked, they were to put up a strong resistance as long as it was reasonably safe to do so, then retire in good order behind the breastworks. He was justifiably confident that Howe would hesitate to risk another Bunker Hill slaughter on the slopes of Brooklyn Heights.

Putnam sent out 5,000 men, all he could afford. The right division was placed under the command of Lord Stirling (Brigadier General William Alexander of New Jersey), the left under Sullivan, who was the ranking officer on the field. These troops were deployed on a series of hills, those occupied by Sullivan being heavily wooded and particularly easy to defend by open-country fighters such as he had under his command—provided they were well directed.

On August 22, Howe landed 20,000 men at Gravesend Bay, well to the left of the American position. It became obvious at once that Sullivan held an exposed position which demanded the utmost in precautionary measures to protect it. Alive to this, Washington sent him explicit instructions to watch his left and keep close observation on the British movements, to avoid being flanked. Putnam supplemented these with additional warnings and, having no other troops to spare, stationed a militia patrol at Jamaica. With Sullivan on the alert, he was confident this patrol would suffice to spread the alarm of any major flanking movement by Howe.

Sullivan was not on the alert, however. Before he went into action, Howe cautiously reconnoitered for four days, during which Sullivan simply ignored the warnings of his superiors. He sent out no mounted scouts and from noon of August 26 made no effort whatever to keep himself accurately informed concerning Howe's activities.

The British commander was not so comatose. During the night of August 26, he set his entire force in motion. Nine thousand men were sent due west to make a frontal attack on Stirling and Sullivan. At the same time, under Howe's personal supervision, 11,000 troops, commanded by Sir Henry Clinton and Lords Cornwallis and Percy, made a long night march to Sullivan's rear. These divisions met not a solitary American soldier until they reached Jamaica, where they gobbled up the militia patrol, almost without stopping, just before dawn.

Shortly after sunrise of August 27, General Grant and

his Scottish Highlanders, probably the stoutest enemy troops on the field, attacked Stirling while General von Heister's Hessian regiments moved on Sullivan. Stirling put up such a terrific defense and inflicted such heavy casualties that he was justly beginning to hope the "retirement in good order" would be unnecessary. He reckoned without Sullivan.

On the American left, an almost indescribable scene was unfolding. Not only had Sullivan failed completely to protect his doomed division from Howe's circling movement, he had stationed his men so poorly that they were unable properly to defend their position even from frontal attack! The first rush of the Hessians told the story. The confusion caused by the weak arrangement of the Continentals made it impossible for them to hold against the charge of the superior enemy force, although Stirling's well-placed troops were wholly successful against the same odds.

Sullivan's line yielded at fatal points. The Hessians gained the crests and the whole left division of the Americans was forced back. They gave ground stubbornly but their efforts were not well coördinated and every minute made the situation worse. Sullivan was in the midst of mad and futile dashes, trying to untangle the snarls which never should have been possible, when a wild yell from his unguarded flank and rear caused him to make the demoralizing discovery that a huge force of British was directly behind him.

He had one meager chance, an immediate dash to the right; but he stubbornly refused to take it. Confused and bewildered by the disastrous turn of events, but still mindful of his honor which forbade retreat, he tried to fight his way through a force of British and Hessians which outnumbered his command six to one and had him trapped on three sides. Suffering tremendous losses, his men were driven back and forth through the woods between two raking fires and the whole tragic mess was over in an hour. A few of the Continentals slashed their way out of the closing circle, but the rest were hopelessly trapped and more than one thousand were forced to surrender. In a last despairing effort to escape, Sullivan attempted to hide in a cornfield* but the British routed him out and he was hauled back to Cornwallis, a prisoner.

On the right, Stirling still fought desperately, ignorant of the fate of the left wing. With his Maryland brigade immortalizing itself, he held his ground for four hours, refusing to yield an inch until he was dumfounded to see a wave of redcoats appear on his left and rear, fresh from the rout of Sullivan. Unlike that general, Stirling's only thought was to save his division and he started back to Brooklyn Heights. With scarcely two thousand men left to him, he surged back, fighting off a force ten times as strong, through two bitter hours. At the cost of his own freedom, he won. With his Marylanders battling shoulder to shoulder, furiously beating back the British and Hessian rush, he succeeded in extricating his division, though its final dash into Brooklyn Heights was a disorderly flight and in the savage rear-guard fighting, Stirling himself was taken, though only a handful of his men were captured.

The Continentals' demoralized rush into the breastworks

* Shaver: *History of Long Island.*

threw the entire force at Brooklyn Heights into a confusion from which it did not recover for hours. Had Howe pressed his advantage at once, there is little doubt that he could have overwhelmed Putnam's force and wiped out practically all of Washington's army. As it was, the unaccountable British delay again saved the country from suffering the full fruits of Sullivan's vainglorious stupidity. It gave Washington the chance to make his famous escape from Brooklyn Heights without the loss of a man or a piece of equipment, though he was forced into precipitate retreat.

The Battle of Long Island was one of the greatest disasters suffered by the Americans during the Revolutionary War. Of the five thousand Continentals engaged, nearly three thousand were killed, wounded or captured. It forced the immediate abandonment of New York City and led directly to the long chain of disasters which continued to mount for months to come—each a new stone in the bloodstained monument Sullivan was erecting to himself.

★ ★ ★ ★ ★ ★ ★ ★ ★

5.

Disaster Marches On

1776! MAGIC date of American history. Mere mention of it is sufficient to make patriotic breasts swell and loyal hearts throb with pride—all because of its one miracle day, July 4.

As a matter of fact, 1776 was one of the sorriest years in the annals of the country, a year marked by unending catastrophe from early spring to its final week, the year when the United States came nearest to losing all chance for the independence it had so newly proclaimed, the year when more good lives were sacrificed to jealous, self-seeking, vicious blundering and unvarnished treachery than any other period in the Revolutionary War, the year which caused Thomas Paine to cry out, "These are the times that try men's souls."

Today, July 4, 1776, and its significance overshadow everything else of that period. The people of 1776 had no such sentiments. The historians have painted the events of July 4, that year, and its immediate consequences, in the most fantastic of colors. We are told of a nation swept with a wave of untrammelled enthusiasm which coursed from Maine to Georgia as soon as the word went forth. We are told that all of Philadelphia went wild with the first peal of the Liberty Bell to announce the signing of the Declaration of Independence.

This has made interesting reading to warm the patriotic cockles, but nothing could be farther from the truth. There was no enthusiastic wave of rejoicing. The only persons who were excited were the members of Congress who signed the Declaration. The people of the colonies accepted it entirely as a routine matter, not as a world-shaking event. To them, the actual signing of a document merely meant that a group of men in Philadelphia who, more or less, represented them had reduced to writing something accomplished in fact more than a year before. The "embattled farmers" who took up arms against the British at Lexington and Concord in April, 1775, issued the real declaration of independence and it had been accepted as such from that time, to a very large degree.

The long-pictured riotous joy of Philadelphia on the historic day was absolutely non-existent. The city was far from being enthusiastic about the Revolution. It and New York City were preponderantly Tory in sentiment and remained so throughout the war. The historic truth is that the signing of the Declaration caused so little stir in Philadelphia that the *Pennsylvania Gazette*, on July 4, dismissed the entire matter with *two lines of type*! "The Continental Congress has this day declared the colonies to be free and independent states." A few days later, on July 10, when it had acquired a copy of the Declaration, the *Gazette* referred to the matter again, to wit:

"On July 4, the Congress declared the colonies to be free and independent states for the following reasons," and the "following reasons" comprised the first published draft of the Declaration.

As to the document itself, it is extremely doubtful whether Thomas Jefferson even remotely imagined the glory which time would attach to the words he penned in his room on the second floor of his boarding house in Philadelphia. Without question, it was simply another "declaration" to him, "a history of repeated injuries and usurpations" by the king as the colonists had frequently expressed them in their resolutions. It was about as original as a copy-book essay. "Many parts of it can be found, word for word, elsewhere."* Jefferson was not aiming at originality. He assembled the most emphatic phrases he could find and added some excellent ones of his own. To him and to the rest of Congress, the Declaration itself was not half so important as Richard Henry Lee's motion for independence which had been argued for weeks and was passed July 2.

At the time, the general attitude toward the Congressional action was distinctly one of indifference. Moreover, the succession of military disasters was beginning to stir the painful apprehension that the Declaration would prove to be nothing more than a "scrap of paper" which shortly might serve the king as a taper to light his pipe.

By the first of April, 1776, just after the end of the siege of Boston, Washington's army had dwindled from 16,000

* E. E. Sparks: *Thomas Jefferson.*

to less than 10,000. The other 6,000 simply had decided to go home. In May came Thomas's blundering at Quebec and the tragic retreat to Sorel. In June, Sullivan provided the slaughter at Three Rivers and his disastrous flight from Canada to deposit a broken and crushed mob of demoralized men at Crown Point after a narrow escape from destruction. In August, scarcely two months later, the same commander staged his debacle on Long Island and taxed Washington to the limit of his genius to save his battered force. As it was, the commander-in-chief had to retreat due north more than twenty-five miles from New York City before he could stop safely at North Castle, above White Plains. Then came the worst disaster of all, once more through the blundersome meddling of Congress.

In the hope of controlling the Hudson River and preventing the British fleet from sailing north, two forts had been established on the banks, Fort Washington near the north end of Manhattan Island and Fort Lee directly opposite on the New Jersey Palisades. But the river is wide at this point and it soon became evident that the British vessels could not be stopped. Further, with his army now well north of the forts, Washington recognized that they were distinct liabilities, dangerously exposed to capture with their strong garrisons and supplies.

Under these circumstances, particularly as the posts were keeping in useless idleness troops he needed for the field, Washington ordered General Nathaniel Greene, who had charge of the forts, to evacuate Fort Washington immediately and prepare to abandon Fort Lee. He issued this order just as he went to New Jersey with 5,000 men to thwart Howe's threatening feint in that direction, leaving

Major General Charles Lee, his second in command, at the head of the 7,000 men left at North Castle. Greene was allowed only sufficient discretionary powers to meet some unexpected military development which suddenly might make the evacuation unnecessary.

Greene was preparing to obey when a dispatch rider reached him from Philadelphia, a messenger who had galloped all the way, bearing a special order from Congress forbidding abandonment of Fort Washington except in "direst extremity." Torn between his conflicting instructions and himself convinced the fort could be held, Greene made the worst possible move. He reinforced the garrison from the troops at North Castle and waited in his quarters at Fort Lee for the return of Washington. When the commander-in-chief arrived, he was completely dismayed to learn nothing had been done and he prepared to execute the instant abandonment of the Manhattan fort but it was too late.

A force of 15,000 British and Hessians stormed Fort Washington on November 16 and Washington had the agony of watching the assault from the ramparts of Fort Lee. The Americans fought with desperate courage but they were outnumbered five to one and, though they inflicted casualties at the same ratio, they were forced to surrender—3,000 men and an immense quantity of sorely needed artillery and ammunition. Worse, after the surrender, some of the Hessians, infuriated by the stubborn resistance they had met, began bayoneting the prisoners in cold blood until Howe stopped them. Across the river, Washington witnessed the surrender with his usual iron immobility, but when he saw his men being mercilessly butchered, his long-tried composure gave way and he sobbed like a child, the tears streaming down his cheeks.

The capture of Fort Washington was the most crushing blow ever sustained by Washington himself. Its consequences were almost fatal. Greene did not have the luck of Sullivan in having the possibilities created by his blunders partially erased by British delay. Howe reaped the full benefit of the disaster. The splendid defensive campaign Washington was conducting was thrown into disorder immediately as Howe plunged across the Hudson in force. Greene was scarcely able to extricate his force from Fort Lee and had to abandon a considerable quantity of equipment to the enemy. Be it said for Greene that there was some excuse for his mistake in view of the Congressional order and that the Fort Washington disaster was practically his only blunder during the war. Rather, he moved forward with increasing brilliance and thereafter was Washington's right arm. In the end, he ranked second only to Washington as a consistently capable strategist and general.

Washington's immediate woes were greatly aggravated by the conduct of two other subordinate commanders whose actions can scarcely be described by so generous a term as "blunder." With the Fort Lee garrison added to his force, the commander-in-chief had only 6,000 men and, on November 17, he sent positive orders to Lee to cross the Hudson and join him at once. Lee simply disobeyed.

Charles Lee was less of a bad general than simply an out-and-out traitor. Another of the European fortune hunters who came to America seeking personal aggrandizement, the pompous, harsh-voiced insolence of this lank, sullen-faced swashbuckler so impressed Congress that he was made second ranking major general when the Continental Army was created by adoption. He accepted, although he was enraged at not being given the chief command. When old age forced Artemas Ward, the senior major general, to resign shortly after the war began, Lee automatically stepped up next to Washington. Thereafter, he exerted his best efforts to supplant his superior and, those failing, he did his best to betray the Americans altogether. Eventually, he was cashiered out of the army in disgrace.

At the time of the Fort Washington disaster, he fully recognized Washington's perilous position and, since disaster to the commander-in-chief would mean his own advancement to the chief's post, he left no stone unturned to bring it about. He refused to leave North Castle until December 1. By that time, Washington's retreat across New Jersey had developed almost into flight, although he lost none of his supplies or equipment. He did lose half his soldiers, however. Enlistments in his harassed force were running out and it was difficult to induce the men to sign again. To cap the climax, the New Englanders were smitten with homesickness—homesickness!—and pattered for their firesides as rapidly as their terms of service ended.* By the time Washington reached the Delaware, he had less than 3,000 men left. Then his only safety lay in placing the broad river between himself and the enemy, so he crossed into Pennsylvania on December 8, preventing pursuit by destroying every boat for many miles in either direction, except those he himself used.

Meanwhile, Lee, having run out of excuses, had finally

* Fiske: *American Revolution*, Vol. I.

crossed the Hudson and proceeded by exasperatingly slow marches as far as Morristown, where he stopped, fifty miles from the Delaware. Other reinforcements presumably were on their way to Washington, seven regiments from the northern army at Ticonderoga, but these were under the direction of another ambitious major general, Horatio Gates. This officer employed the same dilatory tactics as his treacherous confrere, for the same reason, and marched very slowly through northern New Jersey. As a minor additional catastrophe to the American cause, General Sullivan was exchanged and returned to the army, this partially offset by the simultaneous exchange of Lord Stirling.

Meanwhile Washington's situation on the west bank of the Delaware became more desperate daily. December, 1776, was his low tide of the war. But he was most dangerous when he was most desperate and, in his extremity, with his own army reduced to a remnant, his reinforcements withheld by treacherous subordinates, he turned and struck savagely at the enemy.

Under competent commanders American soldiers have always been more than merely good. They have been brilliant. In all the tragic record of their wholesale slaughter through the succeeding generations, there runs the bright relief of smashing victories, often won against tremendous odds, with their own losses so small as to be insignificant when they were well led. So, just as Sullivan at Three Rivers established the tradition of useless butchery, now Washington set the standard of brilliant victory almost without loss, in the first genuine battle triumph ever scored in the name of the United States.

On Christmas night, 1776, with almost incredible daring

but with a perfection of plan which had foreseen every contingency, he threw his army back across the Delaware for his immortal blow at Trenton. He struck at dawn and, in less than an hour, had captured the entire garrison of 1,000 Hessians. With the same lightning speed, he then shot back to the safety of his camp in Pennsylvania and when the complete check-up had been made, his casualties totalled exactly four—two men frozen to death on the night march and two killed in action!

In the succeeding week, the aroused Lord Cornwallis, commanding the British on the Delaware, swung into an enveloping movement with his entire force. On the night of January 1, he was so near success that he went to bed, telling his subordinates he was sure to "bag the old fox" and his entire army in the morning. But Washington staged another spectacular coup, pulled out of the trap, made a swift circling dash and, on January 2, struck Cornwallis's rear at Princeton. The sharp engagement which ensued lasted only twenty minutes. In that time, Washington cut the superior British force in two, disabled 300 of them and captured 400 prisoners, while his own casualties numbered 94.

The two cracks of the American commander's whip in such swift succession hit the British with such force that Cornwallis went tumbling back to New York with his army. In those two blows, Washington definitely turned the tide of the war, with a total loss of less than 100!

Thus glory crowned the year of misery. The Americans sustained four major field disasters during the Revolution, each worse than its predecessor, each steeped more deeply in the blood and agony of dying men, needlessly slain and three of these occurred in 1776—Three Rivers, Long Island and Fort Washington.

And with each step down the ladder, Congress bungled military matters more disastrously, but the most shameful blot of all the many on the record was placed there in 1777. At one of the most crucial moments of that year, swamped by the demands of their satellites for good government jobs, the congressmen seized upon the commissariat, took its control entirely out of the hands of the army and filled it with a host of political friends, chosen without the slightest reference to their fitness. Washington protested bitterly but as usual was overruled. Within a month, the department fell into such hopeless confusion that the armies were crippled throughout the winter season. On December 22, 1777, Washington actually was prevented from launching an action against the British which promised exceptional results because two brigades had mutinied over lack of food. For three days they had received no bread and for two days no meat. This, in the face of the fact that the bursting bins of army supplies stood within a few miles of Washington's camp, tightly locked under Congressional commissariat control.

For the next three years, the tide of war fluctuated through victory and defeat with the Continentals gradually gaining the upper hand. But no year was complete without its failure at the hands of Major General John Sullivan.

One of the mysteries of the Revolution is the strange manner in which this commander has been neglected by the historians. The convenience of ignoring unpleasant truths does not alter the fact that, for years, he played one of the bloodiest and most prominent rôles in the war.

Throughout his career he held high posts in the army and was given repeated opportunities to distinguish himself in situations of tremendous responsibility and importance. But not once did he achieve a noteworthy success, while his record of blood-drenched failure went on without relief.

On August 21, 1777, he led a strong expedition against a comparatively small enemy force on Staten Island, a project which seemed so one-sided that success was a matter of course. Sullivan bungled even this so badly that he not only failed of his object but actually was defeated when the British once more caught him in the rear to chalk up more wasted lives against his record. During the two-day foray, he marched his troops for 43 successive hours without food and with never more than a few minutes' rest.*

Twenty-two days later, on September 11, Washington, attempting to halt Howe's much larger army in its advance on Philadelphia, threw his scanty force across the British front at Brandywine Creek and almost scored a brilliant victory. But Sullivan was commanding the right wing and, as usual, was flanked with disastrous results. By desperate efforts, Washington prevented the defeat from becoming a rout, but Philadelphia had to be abandoned to the British.

In July, 1778, Sullivan commanded the land forces in the Franco-American drive to capture Newport, the last New England post held by the British. In this affair, he was more sinned against than sinning, since the French and most of his own militia walked out on the campaign. But

* Major John Taylor to Col. Moses Hazen, August 24, 1777. Taylor's many charges against Sullivan concerning the conduct of the expedition led to a Congressional investigation which gave Sullivan a very doubtful bill of health.

Newport was not taken and Sullivan had to retreat with another failure added to his list.

Months passed before he staged his denouement. It was his crowning effort and, for a time, had a curiously illusory semblance of field success. Its actual results were more ghastly than anything else he ever had done.

The Indian ravages on the New York and Pennsylvania frontiers which were climaxed with the Cherry and Wyoming valley massacres in 1778, led Washington to move for stern reprisals and a determined effort to halt the raids at their very source. This was Fort Niagara, the place where Sir John Johnson, the unprincipled British Commissioner for Indian Affairs, had his headquarters. From this poisonous fountain head, Johnson, Colonel John Butler and his son Walter—three of the blackest names in American history—led the Tories and the hostile Iroquois on their savage forays against the frontier settlements.

In the spring of 1779, Washington assembled a force of 5,000 to march through the Mohawk Valley and capture Fort Niagara, as a Continental garrison there would insure the safety of the northern frontier from further Indian attack. The army was instructed to guarantee the elimination of the Iroquois menace by completely devastating the tribal lands on the way. Against the known inferior strength of the Tories and redskins—the success of the expedition seemed so certain—Washington did not hesitate to give the command to Sullivan, the general he could most easily spare from his own army.

The drive began well and Sullivan actually scored a battle victory. At Newtown (now Elmira), N. Y., he defeated a considerable force with great slaughter, while the American loss was less than fifty. Then he moved through the home country of the Iroquois nations and the region was laid waste with extreme thoroughness. All the grain fields were destroyed, the stock seized and the villages burned, leaving the Long House in irreparable ruin.

But Sullivan's leadership developed its typical ineptitude. The army moved at an inexcusably slow pace. The food supplies ran out and many of the men became sick. By the time the force reached the Genesee River, still more than sixty miles from its objective, Sullivan decided it was too late in the year to move on Fort Niagara, so he turned around and came back and the Tory-Indian headquarters remained undisturbed.

Ironically enough, when he returned, his expedition was hailed as a success. And, in a sense, it was. It succeeded in arousing the devastated Indians to an unsurpassed vengeful fury. Sullivan had scarcely emerged from the Mohawk Valley when Johnson, the Butlers and Thayendanegea, the famous chieftain, loosed their forces in a storm of unexampled savagery.

With bloody ferocity, they swirled out of the northwest in a scourging torrent, wielding tomahawk and firebrand without restraint, burning, massacring, scalping men, women and children, to cause a reign of terror such as the frontier had never known. Two thirds of the population of Tryon County alone were wiped out in crimson horrors and the remaining third included a tragic host of more than 300 widows and 2,000 orphaned children. Twice, the raiding savages—red and white—swarmed to within a few miles of Albany and once a band of Tories from Niagara broke into the city itself in an attempt to assassinate General Schuyler—and nearly succeeded. For three years the vast area from the Hudson River to the Niagara and from the St. Lawrence to the Susquehanna was a ravaged, smoking ruin—desolate tribute to Sullivan's wretched fiasco.

It was his last. Sullivan himself was well content with his triumph over the Iroquois cornfields and decided to rest on his laurels. He resigned his commission when he returned from his half-finished task and the next year, 1780, he was back in Congress, among more congenial souls than were to be found on Washington's steadily improving staff.

He holds the unenviable distinction of being the first United States commander whose name is a blight on the nation's history and his everlasting memorial is built of the nameless graves of the thousands needlessly slaughtered, and of mouldering homestead ruins where women screamed and died beneath the tomahawk and children's brains were beaten out against the cabin walls.

As he left the service, the swaying fortunes of war were changing again. The fighting in the north had sagged to sporadic, attritional raids by the enemy. For their new major offensive the British turned to the south, ravaged the coast towns, scoured the interior, seized Charleston and from there spewed out merciless marauders who claimed the name of soldiers. Misfortune after misfortune dogged the Americans—and the stage was set for the last, the greatest and most unpardonable of the murderous disasters which blotched the Revolutionary pages.

6.

How an Army Is Murdered

IN SPITE of his evil career, Sullivan was not the worst blot on the Revolutionary record. That doubtful honor belongs to Horatio Gates, the "Hero of Saratoga" and the real evil genius of the American cause. In the needless butchery he caused, this darling of the Continental Congress rivalled Sullivan. Beyond that, he did more to prolong the war than any other individual, in or out of the army, stirred up more costly dissension and engaged in more treacherous intrigue. Sullivan was stupidly incompetent but, at least, he was honest. As much cannot be said for Gates.

He was all that is despicable—a coward to the core, a jealous ingrate, a narrow-minded, unresourceful incompetent, an inveterate liar, contemptibly underhanded, boorish, vain, petty, unfair, unjust, inconsiderate—"a man who turned instinctively against talent, genius and impetuous bravery."* Through all his campaigning he was under fire only once and then just long enough to flee from the field

* Roberts: *Rabble In Arms.*

HORATIO GATES

in abject terror. Yet, for much of the war he was a popular idol—The Hero—with whom Washington was compared most unfavorably.

He fooled his public completely. More surprising, he also fooled the historians. He has no apologists among them, but they confine their condemnation almost exclusively to the mere window-dressing of his character—his successful intrigue to supplant Schuyler as commander of the Northern Department; his infamous conduct toward Arnold and his plot against Washington in the Conway Cabal. Actually, these were the least harmful acts of Gates' career.

He displaced Schuyler too late to undo that general's brilliant work in trapping Burgoyne. He insulted Arnold, robbed him of his laurels and stripped him of his command, but he did not succeed in preventing Arnold from winning both battles of Saratoga and sealing Burgoyne's doom. His cabal against Washington was merely a matter of words and had no effect upon the war except to strengthen the position of the commander-in-chief and smudge Gates himself.

In any event, it is grossly slighting to James Wilkinson to give "Granny" Gates all the discredit for these moves. Gates had been calling this young officer an affectionate "Wilkie" as early as the siege of Boston days. When he went north, he drafted him from Arnold as his own aide and "Wilkie" was by his side in all that followed through the Conway Cabal, when their beautiful friendship came to an abrupt end. In the light of Wilkinson's own subsequent record, it is most doubtful whether Gates would have done so well without the able assistance of "Wilkie" in his malodorous intrigues.

Of much greater importance in their effect upon the war, however, were those acts of Gates which have been ignored almost completely and which won him his real place in the forerank of murderous commanders. Probably the reason for passing them by was the negative character of all but one of them, but the results were as costly as if each had been overt.

In December, 1776, his intentional dallying robbed Washington of reinforcements when the commander-in-chief needed them most. Trenton and Princeton were won without them, but how much more might Washington have accomplished had he had the troops to which he was entitled!

In the nine months he commanded at Ticonderoga, Gates consistently refused to take any steps to fortify Sugar Loaf Mountain which dominated the fort, declaring it humanly impossible to drag cannon up its precipitous slope. On July 5, 1777, Burgoyne's troops proved it could be done. The American garrison was forced into disorderly flight from the strongest post in the country and suffered bloody defeat at Hubbardton when the pursuing British and Hessians caught up with the Continental rearguard and cut it to pieces.

Gates' third delinquency was much more dastardly and probably prolonged the war more than any other single military factor. In the fall of 1777, the British occupied Philadelphia but Washington still held the Delaware forts and his continued possession of them would have made it impossible for Howe to remain in the city. To keep the forts which the British were certain to attack with a superior force, Washington needed reinforcements and needed them badly. After Burgoyne's surrender at Saratoga, the entire northern army under Gates was available, and Washington ordered that it be sent to the Delaware. The northern army combined with his own would have given Washington a force equal to Howe's. He could have held the forts and compelled Howe to abandon Philadelphia under pressure. Washington would have held the whip hand. Another Saratoga easily might have been the outcome with the Revolution ending in the winter of 1777-78 instead of five weary years later.

Gates absolutely refused to send his army. Savagely ambitious to supplant Washington as he had supplanted Schuyler, he traitorously sacrificed the country in the hope of causing a complete Washington disaster. He partially succeeded. By the time he was compelled to send part of the northern force to Washington's aid, the Delaware forts already had been stormed, the British retained Philadelphia, the war went on and Washington's army was condemned to the horrors of Valley Forge.

Valley Forge is a name to thrill every loyal American—with horror because of the terrible privations and sufferings of the army in winter quarters there; with pride because of the matchless fortitude with which Washington's loyal soldiers endured their trials. On December 23 Washington reported to Congress that he had in camp 2,898 men "unfit for duty because they are barefoot and otherwise naked." Because they had no blankets, many sat up "all night by fires instead of taking comfortable rest in a natural and common way." This takes no account of the hundreds of men who died of exposure and disease.

The tragic picture has been offered as a portrayal of the

acme of heroism—which it was—caused by the poverty of the country—which it was not. The country was anything but poverty-stricken. The summer of 1777 had been unusually fruitful in the fields and the looms of the patriotic women had never been more busy to meet the army's needs.

Not one moment of the suffering endured at Valley Forge was necessary.

As the denuded soldiers marched to their winter quarters on December 17, their route was traced easily in the snow by the blood which oozed from their bare frost-bitten feet. Yet, at that hour, hundreds of hogsheads of shoes, stockings and other clothing, blankets, food and complete winter equipment were lying along the roads and in the woods waiting only for the transportation and clearance which the Congress-controlled commissariat failed to provide. Washington begged for relief, the relief that was almost within his grasp, but Congress did not lift its hand—and men died of exposure and disease, and frozen hands and feet were lopped off to cripple hundreds of others for life.

Even the tolerant Fiske could not refrain from saying: "The events of that winter left a stain upon the reputation of the Continental Congress from which it never fully recovered. . . . At the end of 1777, it began visibly to lose its place in public esteem and sink, step by step, into the utter degradation and impotence which was to overwhelm it before another ten years should have expired."*

Then came the exposure of the Conway Cabal and Gates squirmed, squealed and lied until his balloon was punctured and he was shelved to garrison duty on the Hudson.

* Fiske: *American Revolution*, Vol. II.

Soon afterward he left the service in a huff and retired to his Virginia plantation. Unfortunately, he did not remain there. He had one more string to his bow.

As affairs in the south became increasingly serious, Washington recommended to Congress that General Nathaniel Greene be appointed to command the Southern Department. But the glamour which enveloped the "Hero of Saratoga" had not been dispelled entirely, and many people began calling for Gates. Congress rose to the occasion in its best manner. Washington's wishes were disregarded as usual, and on June 13, 1780, Gates was duly appointed— and eagerly accepted.

He emerged from retirement with considerable fanfare. Richard Peters, secretary of the Board of War and one of the giddier members of Congress—although it is difficult to discriminate—wrote him effusively: "Our affairs to the southward look blue; so they did when you took command before the Burgoynade. I can only now say, 'Go and do likewise'—God bless you."

Gates' old crony, Charles Lee, who had been kicked out of the army bodily the previous year and was living in disgrace on his Virginia estate, also wrote him but in a far less congratulatory vein. "Take care," he warned, "that your northern *laurels* do not change to southern *willows.*"

With a flip of his fingers at this, Gates moved triumphantly to Hillsborough, N. C., from which he was to launch his campaign. This was a simple project. The key point of the British activities in the interior was Camden, S. C., at the moment held by a force of less than 800 under Lord Rawdon. This made conditions propitious for an attack, and if Gates would capture it, the British would be forced to retire from all inland positions and be thrown upon the defensive at Charleston.

Gates was eager—overeager—to start immediately toward his objective, but he found conditions at Hillsborough deplorable. The troops concentrated there were greatly deficient in both arms and ammunition. They had no tents, no food, no medicines and no money—a strangely familiar condition in the Continental forces. The only seasoned soldiers on hand were some 1,400 regulars from Maryland and Delaware under the able leadership of the giant Baron de Kalb. In addition to these there were some recently recruited militia, numbering about 1,000.

No one in the entire American army was less capable of straightening out the wretched situation than Gates, but he solved it very easily. He simply ignored it.

"I am not satisfied with conditions here," he told De Kalb authoritatively, "but time is pressing. We must attack Rawdon before he can be reinforced. We will prepare to march at once."

De Kalb demurred emphatically, insisting it would be disastrous to move before the half-sick troops were better equipped, but Gates refused to listen.

"I said we would march," he snapped. "You will prepare for departure at once."

Two roads to Camden were open to Gates. One was 210 miles long, a circuitous route through fertile country, inhabited by Scotch-Irish farmers, friendly to the American cause. It was immune to sudden attack, it guaranteed plenty of wholesome food and, if the army suffered a setback, it was ideal for safe retreat. The eastern road was fifty miles shorter but it ran through a desolate region of

pine barrens. Farm houses and cultivated fields were few
and far between and these were the property of inimical
Tories. The road was exposed to flank attacks, it offered
no possibility of food and it was a death-trap for an en-
forced retreat. De Kalb and other officers urgently advised
following the westerly road, but Gates, impatient and immune as always to sensible advice, chose the other.

"We are in a hurry, gentlemen," he exclaimed irritably.
"Do you understand? A hurry. We will take the short
route."

The dismal trek began on July 27. Along the way, another thousand untrained militiamen from Virginia and
North Carolina joined the force, bringing its strength to
approximately 3,500, which should have been ample for its
purpose. But all of them were in poor condition when they
started, ill-prepared, and they grew steadily worse as Gates
drove them petulantly at top speed through the enervating
heat. The meager rations with which they started were
exhausted within a day or two and there was little or
nothing to be found in the country through which they
were passing. The best consisted of a few scrawny cattle,
wholly insufficient for more than three thousand men. The
pangs of hunger grew worse until, half-starved, the weary
marchers ate anything they could pick up which remotely
resembled food. They voraciously devoured unripe corn,
green apples and green peaches. Before the first week of the
march was ended, the whole force was staggering with
dysentery. But Gates showed no mercy and pushed them
forward.

The second week was unspeakable. Cholera morbus
broke out in its most virulent form. Men dropped from the

ranks by the dozen, many to die where they fell by the wayside. Those who succumbed at once were buried hastily. Others, whom Gates considered too ill to carry along, were simply left to perish by the road in abandoned misery.

On August 11, Gates had 3,092 men left, but he was within fifteen miles of Camden and his great opportunity was in his hands. Word came that Rawdon was immediately ahead, his small force spread across the road almost as if he were inviting the fatal blow for which the Continentals had been hurried so desperately. De Kalb urged an immediate attack.

"De men are seeck," he said, with his heavy accent, "but dey can fight. Dey vant to fight. Nodding vill make dem vell so quick as vin right avay vot dey come for. Und it vill be easy."

But Gates went into one of his "granny" flutterings now that an actual grip with the enemy threatened, and he deliberately threw away every tactical advantage he had gained by his suicidal rush over the short road.

"We are not ready for attack," he answered nervously. "I must know more about the disposition of Rawdon's troops. We will wait."

De Kalb's protest was useless and the army waited. Gates gained no new information concerning Rawdon. He did not seek any, since, after all, none was necessary. He simply stopped where he was for two days. Then, on August 13, to the disgusted bewilderment of the officers as well as the men, he suddenly ordered his entire force to march to the right until it reached the westerly road, abandoning the whole purpose for which he had taken the other route! This time he stopped at Clermont, ten miles from Camden, and once more sat down to wait, all his merciless Hillsborough eagerness vanished. He still made no effort to learn what Rawdon was doing and while he waited, he lost forever his glittering opportunity to seize Camden at insignificant cost.

On August 14, Lord Cornwallis arrived to reinforce Rawdon with 1,200 seasoned British regulars from Charleston, bringing the enemy force up to 2,000 highly trained troops. Another day and a night passed and still Gates did not move, nor did he learn about the arrival of Cornwallis. Until the actual moment of encounter with the British, he still believed he had only Rawdon and 800 men to contend with.

He was not yet in full stride, however. On August 15 he heard that the partisan commander, Thomas Sumter, was on a raid to cut off British supplies between Camden and Charleston. Without further ado, at the critical moment when he needed every soldier he could find, Gates detached 400 men and sent them to help Sumter. And these were not some of the militiamen, born and raised in that part of the country and therefore peculiarly equipped to assist the raid, but his best Maryland regulars!

That afternoon the American food situation struck bottom. Gates had nothing to offer his men except raw corn and unripe vegetables. All the rum was gone, too, so the customary ration could not be issued. Instead, each man was given a liberal portion of molasses. The combination had all the effect of an overdose of castor oil.*

With his troops in misery and a weakened condition which was becoming aggravated by the hour, Gates now

* Greene, Maj. Gen. Francis Vinton: *American Revolution.*

suddenly decided to move, on brilliant inspiration. At 10 o'clock that night—August 15—he pushed his force down the road toward Camden, intending to surprise Rawdon before daybreak. Curiously, Cornwallis was coming up the road with exactly the same idea. At 3 o'clock in the morning, the outposts of the two armies met, five miles north of Camden. In the brisk skirmish that followed, the Americans were repulsed, but as the mutual surprises had failed, both armies halted and lay on their arms, waiting for daylight.

A few prisoners taken by the Continentals gave Gates his first stunning intimation of the presence of Cornwallis, and in great haste he called his officers together, nervously asking them what should be done.

The irritable militia general, Stevens, snorted impatiently. "There's only one thing to do now," he exclaimed. "It's too late for anything but to fight."

"Not at all," Baron de Kalb retorted. "Mit Cornvallis in front, it vill be dancherous. His men von't be seeck, wie unser. Ve got time yet to go back by Clermont. Ve shoult take a strong position dere."

De Kalb's sterling advice had been disregarded on all points from the beginning of the compaign. It needed only a word from him to take Gates' mind off his panic now. He stared at the baron coldly. "We will not retreat," he declared. "We will attack at dawn. A swift blow to upset Cornwallis—and victory will be ours." He turned to Stevens. "General, you will place your men on the left. They shall have the honor of launching the attack. You will take the right, Baron de Kalb, and be prepared to crush the enemy in front of you when General Stevens' men have turned their flank."

De Kalb stared at him incredulously. "You vill let de militia make der attack?" he exclaimed. "Men vot are not trained, vot don't efen know vot a bayonet is for, ven you have my regulars to do it?"

Stevens reddened. "You are reflecting on my men, sir," he interposed angrily.

"I am not." De Kalb's voice was gravely courteous. "It is not deir fault dey are not trained. I chust vant to vin."

Gates stopped him with a swift gesture. "You have heard my orders," he barked testily. "They will not be changed. The militia under General Stevens will make the attack."

Gloomy and distracted, De Kalb withdrew from the conference to deploy his troops as ordered, and then lay down to snatch the last hour of sleep he ever was to have.

When the sun arose on August 16, one of the most extraordinary sights in military history was revealed. The two armies were scarcely three hundred yards apart, facing each other on a narrow plain, their flanks hemmed in by deep, impassable swamps. Any sort of strategy in such a position was out of the question. Nothing was possible except direct frontal attack. On the one side were 2,000 healthy, seasoned regulars, some of the best troops in the British army. On the other were 2,700 Americans, so weak and ill that probably no force ever prepared for battle in a worse condition. This body included only 1,000 trained men. The rest were an untrained, undisciplined mob which had never seen action before—and to these General Gates assigned the supremely important task of launching the American attack.

As the first streaks of sunlight crossed the plain, the American commander, seated on his horse well in the rear of his troops, gave the command for the raw militia to advance. The utter imbecility of his plans became manifest at once. The wholly untaught troops did not even know how to move forward. They surged from side to side, entirely without regularity of formation, stumbling over one another's feet. One company intermingled with another until the whole body was in complete confusion. The officers, but little more trained than the men, made frantic efforts to straighten out the ragged lines, but while the disorganization was at its worst the British suddenly seized the initiative on their own behalf and advanced in a furious charge.

Pandemonium instantly swept the garbled militiamen. They milled about desperately as the redcoats swept down upon them, and then broke wildly. The Virginia and North Carolina troops threw down their rifles with one accord and turned to flee in panic without firing a shot. Immediately, the entire American left became a terror-stricken mob, running aimlessly like huddled sheep. While they swept back in a massed tidal wave, entirely out of control, Colonel Banastre Tarleton's British cavalry of savage repute thundered down upon them with sabers swinging to execute a veritable massacre. The militia were cut down by the scores, slashed to death as they ran, or hurled bleeding to the ground to be trampled by the pounding hoofs, their shrieks and groans crushed out as they fell.

As he saw this frightful slaughter being executed before his eyes, General Gates decided the whole affair was entirely too unhealthy for an aging general. He turned and left— at the wildest gallop he could whip from his horse. He did not stop until he reached Clermont and then only long enough to change mounts. In a moment he was on his way again, northward bound, over the hills and far away from Camden.

Back on the battlefield, Tarleton's horsemen were having such an unobstructed carnival of blood that the British infantry abandoned the pursuit and turned against the American regulars. These presented a different picture. Left without support and outnumbered two to one, the Maryland and Delaware men fought with desperate courage. Twice the second Maryland brigade repulsed Rawdon on its immediate front, and followed with a bayonet charge of its own which broke through the British lines and tenaciously held the new position against every attack, until the whole mass of British who had faced the utterly crushed militia turned and stormed them on their flank. With all the rest of the field swept clear of Americans, the Marylanders were faced with capture or complete annihilation. Not until then did they yield. They slowly retired in good order, fighting every inch of the way until they had made their escape over a narrow passageway through the swamp on their right, though only a few of them were left.

Long after the battle was hopelessly lost in every other quarter, the towering De Kalb, his horse shot from under him, fought furiously on foot, leading his men with a heroic desperation which permitted the remnants of his command to retreat safely. But he himself was cut down at last, and when he fell dying he was bleeding from eleven wounds!

The British loss totalled 324. Less than 600 of the American force *escaped*. More than 1,000 were killed and wounded with the almost unexampled condition in modern warfare that the dead outnumbered the injured almost two to one. More than 1,000 Americans were captured. They lost every vestige of their equipment, all their artillery, all their ammunition, 2,000 muskets, all their wagons and all their luggage. The army was not beaten. It was destroyed. It was the worst defeat which ever has been inflicted upon a United States force in the history of the country.

General Gates, meanwhile, was still on his horse. He did not pause the first day until he had covered sixty miles. In fact, returning by the scorned westerly road, he actually made the 210 miles to Hillsborough in less than four days! Then he stopped, feeling fairly safe for a day or two.

At last he reaped the whirlwind he had been sowing for so long. Camden was the epitome of his entire career and the whole country saw him for what he was. His ignominious lone flight brought a storm of scathing ridicule upon him, and he was hooted on all sides as a depraved coward. Even Congress could find no excuse for him this time, and on October 5 humbly asked Washington to suggest a successor to the fallen "Hero." The commander-in-chief immediately named his first choice and, on December 2, General Nathaniel Greene arrived at Charlotte to begin his sensational victory drive through the south. Gates vanished from the scene to be heard from no more, buried deeply beneath the "willows" into which his "laurels" truly had been transformed.

Periodically, Congress screamed loudly against the British use of Indians during the war, and condemnation of this British policy has come ringing down the corridors of time, so to speak, while the proud boast is made that the Americans never stooped to such dastardly and inhuman tactics.

Perhaps Congress conveniently forgot that on May 25, 1776, it decided "that it is highly expedient to engage the Indians in the service of the United States."* And, nine days later, on June 3, it went a step farther with: "Resolved, that the general (Schuyler) be empowered to employ in Canada a number of Indians not exceeding two thousand."** The British never had that many Indians in one force at any time during the entire war. Three days later, on June 6, Congress had become so enthused that it passed another measure, detailing instructions for the recruiting, employment and payment of the Indians shortly to be acquired.***

Be it said to the honor of Washington and Schuyler that they rejected these measures of Congress flatly. The only Indians they ever used were a few who served as guides, and small groups employed only against other Indians. Such few redskins as the Americans had in their ranks never were sent against the British army. But this was not the fault of Congress.

* *Secret Journals of the Acts and Proceedings of Congress.*
** Ibid.
*** Ibid.

7.

The Tragedy of Benedict Arnold

BEYOND question, the most tragic chapter of the Revolutionary War is the career of Benedict Arnold. In this chronicle, which seeks to shed some light on so many long-revered names, it would seem only fitting to speak a word for a name which so long has been universally damned. For more than one hundred and fifty years, "Benedict Arnold" has been a byword, synonymous with the blackest treachery and all that is perfidious in man. Its very mention has been sufficient to send complacent chills of horror up and down all smug, self-righteous spines.

After the fact of his treason, the most extraordinary interpretations were placed upon his every word and deed. Into every previous act of his life, no matter how great or how magnificent, has been read strange evidence that he always was prompted by the heart and mind of a born traitor. No stone has been left unturned to bear out the contention that he was the arch-traitor of all human history, fit company only for Judas Iscariot.

Arnold was a traitor—a deliberate traitor. Of that there is no doubt. But his treason was made a fact only by subsequent history. Arnold thought only that he was saving the future of his country. He did not believe he was betraying it.

He loved his country with a passionate fervor which few of his detractors can emulate. He proved this times without number in his tremendous exertions on its behalf, in his reckless bravery, in the almost unbelievable hardships he endured, in the wounds he suffered and in his refusal to permit those wounds to halt his heroic efforts for his country's cause. Unprejudiced and impersonal consideration of the actual facts cannot but lead to the conviction that he loved his country so much that he was willing to risk all the opprobrium of a branded traitor in order to prevent the fate with which he believed it was threatened.

He was wrong—tragically wrong—but he was sincere. The most popular conception is that Arnold was inspired to treason because of personal spite over the endless injustices of which he was the victim. Such a theory shows only ignorance of his quality and temperament and his character as it is revealed in every indisputable record we have of him. Arnold was no petty, small-souled creature. Fiery, impetuous, violent, yes. But there is no known instance of his ever having committed a rash or regrettable act, even in the heat of anger, in retaliation for any insult or blow to his personal hopes. For him to have planned such a retaliation coldly, over a period of months, for mere personal reasons was so utterly foreign to his nature as to be impossible. He simply was not the type.

All historians who pretend to any semblance of honesty are faced with a difficult *impasse* when they attempt, on the foregoing premise, to reconcile Arnold's previous conduct with his treasonable act. The only explanation offered is the lame assertion that "he changed completely," that his moral fibre was broken down by his wretched treatment at the hands of Congress and his other enemies. This weird hypothesis fails to consider his conduct *after* his treason, when he displayed anything but moral weakness.

The basic character and mental structure of human beings are not subject to revolutionary change. This is a psychological and physical law. The adage that "a leopard cannot change his spots" is not an idle one. It is in tacit admission of this that such desperate efforts have been made to compel all of Arnold's other acts to conform to an accepted fact of treason when it would seem much more to the point to reconcile this single act to everything else he did.

This is not intended as a defense of Arnold nor does it condone his treason. It is an honest attempt to do simple justice to a man who had the qualities of greatness and to whom the United States owes its independence just as definitely as to George Washington, and to seek, from the facts and the facts alone, a dispassionate explanation of the act which eternally blighted his name.

The case against Arnold is predicated upon the assumption that his character was weak, that he was unable to maintain his patriotic equilibrium under the incessant abuse and insults heaped upon him by Congress, that his love for the girl who became his wife, Miss Margaret Shippen, daughter of a Philadelphia loyalist, made him susceptible to Tory per-

suasion, that his extravagance led him into debt which hampered his romance and that all this eventually led him to
negotiate with Sir Henry Clinton for the betrayal of West
Point at a price sufficient to relieve his financial embarrass-
ment. His destruction of the Revolutionary cause was to be
an incidental fillip tossed to his wife and the loyalists of the
circle to which she had introduced him.

His reckless daring in battle is explained on the ground
that he loved fighting for its own sake, a belief which fails
to take cognizance of his strategic brilliance and the fact
that not once in his career did he uselessly sacrifice the life
of a solitary soldier over whom he held command. A man
with an insatiable passion for bloodshed would not have been
so meticulous.

His conduct at the second battle of Saratoga—the most
decisive single engagement of the war—has been described
consistently as that of a man intoxicated or mad. The mendacious James Wilkinson—who was America's real arch-
traitor—in his truthless *Memoirs*, specifically accuses Arnold
with having been "drinking heavily" that day. Perhaps the
liquor of 1777 had a uniquely different effect from that of
the present day. Or perhaps violent insanity, 1777 style, expressed itself differently from modern mental disorders. But
it seems extraordinary that a man who was drunk or crazy
should have led four separate attacks in swift succession, each
of which somehow struck at the exact spot and the exact
moment when it would be most effective and thus won one
of the greatest victories in American history. If Arnold were
drunk or insane or both, it is a tragic pity that the United
States has not had more intoxicated madmen of the same

sort to lead its soldiers. Most of our presumably sane and sober generals have not done quite so well.

For the first two and a half years of the Revolutionary War, until his wounds incapacitated him for further field service, his record was matchless, inspiring Charles Knight to say: "Arnold displayed more real military genius and inspiration than all the generals put together, on both sides, engaged in the war, with the most undaunted personal courage."*

He was one of the first volunteers to report for active service after Lexington and Concord. He suggested the seizure of Crown Point and Ticonderoga. With a handful of men he captured St. John's and its entire garrison. He conceived the brilliant invasion of Canada which failed only because he was wounded. He all but took Quebec. He rehabilitated and then saved his force at Montreal. He performed the miracle of creating the American fleet on Lake Champlain which stopped the British invasion from the north in 1776 and saved the American cause then and there. While on a leave of absence to visit his children, he leaped to arms and routed the British at the Battle of Ridgefield in the spring of 1777, which crushed the enemy raid in Connecticut. He voluntarily led the expedition which shattered St. Leger's campaign against Fort Stanwix and sent him fleeing back to Canada, preventing powerful reinforcements from reaching Burgoyne. He stopped Burgoyne in the first battle of Saratoga and crushed him completely in the second, making the British surrender certain.

His reward? Constant obstruction by Congress when it did not abandon him entirely in every worthy effort he

* Knight, Charles: *History of England,* Vol. I, p. 430.

undertook. A stream of unending calumny behind his back, poured forth by treacherous and jealous incompetents. Although he had the most brilliant record of any brigadier in the army, he was passed by and five junior brigadiers were promoted to major generalships over his head—four of them to be in disgrace or proved utterly incompetent within nine months after their elevation. When his Ridgefield victory forced Congress to promote him, he was insultingly refused restoration to his proper seniority without explanation. He was called before Congress to answer a series of absurd charges concerning his conduct at Montreal, and though he was completely vindicated, he was permitted to suffer because of the charges. Gates flouted him in every conceivable manner and robbed him of his command. His straightforward honesty in handling tangled affairs as commandant at Philadelphia after the British evacuation incurred him nothing but bitter enmity. It won him the venomous hatred of General Joseph Reed of the Executive Council of Pennsylvania, who hounded him for an entire year in the most despicable and cowardly manner before which Congress bowed with pusillanimous groveling.

Yet he wrote Washington that no personal affront could induce him to abandon the service or affect his conduct as long as he could be useful to the common welfare. He wrote Schuyler that his ambition was not to "shine in history" but to "be a good citizen."

He endured a five-year burden of accumulated injustices, all emanating from the same source—Congress—and it did not arouse personal spite in him. But he was filled with despair over the future of his country in such futile, incompetent hands. Even then he would have remained loyal had

Congress not executed the final act which, to Arnold, meant the final destruction of everything for which he had fought. This was the alliance with France.

Too little attention has been given this phase of Arnold's case, which offers the real explanation. It has been so easy to revile him without troubling to go beneath the surface. Arnold hated France—and feared it desperately, a sentiment which was shared by all of New England, of which he was a native. To New Englanders, the shadow of French domination threatened the complete loss of everything they held dear and for which they had struggled since the first Pilgrim landed on American shores—religious and political freedom.

In colonial days, all of New England was violently anti-Catholic, because, to the pioneers of that region, Catholicism represented religious oppression, and France was the outstanding Papist power in the world. Also, France represented the last word in political tyranny—absolute monarchy at its worst, grinding its people into the dust for the benefit of its profligate, dissipated, decadent royalty. To a lesser degree, this distrust of France permeated all the colonies—the supposed American joy over the alliance is just another popular fiction of the historians—but in New England it reached the bitterness of fanaticism.

Arnold heard of the alliance with a dismayed hopelessness. To him—as to many others—it seemed an almost fatal blow to American hopes of real independence, a sentiment he did not hesitate to express repeatedly. He was convinced—and, indeed, history would seem to bear him out—that France's only interest was to strike a blow at England and regain her foothold in America. She had every reason to expect she could entangle the floundering republic in her meshes and soon make it a French protectorate, if not a French possession, to open the way for the recovery of Canada. There is plenty of room for conjecture as to what France would have done about the United States had the ambitions of her royal family not come to a sudden end on the guillotine.

No one knew better than Arnold that within a generation or two no power on earth could prevent the colonies from achieving independence through their own strength if they were not blighted by the royal and oppressive hand of France in the meantime. Thousands of so-called loyalists throughout the country held precisely the same view. They favored independence but believed 1776 was not the time for it, that the country was too weak to stand on its own. The French alliance certainly did nothing to dissipate this conception. Arnold felt that under anything like the Continental Congress he had come to know so well, the country had nothing to offer against French importunity, and that the one guarantee of future independence, an independence which would be genuine, lay in keeping the colonies under the wing of the country which had given them birth and which had generated their principles of political freedom, despite the current misrule, until they were strong enough to go their own way.

He was not a Washington. He did not have the balance, the calm serenity, the clarity of vision nor the superb forbearance of the commander-in-chief, who could see the possibilities of the new nation in spite of its existing weak condition. But he was sincere. Every other act of his life attests his sincerity.

In his first letter to Clinton he described himself as a high-ranking American officer open to persuasion to join the British *because of his complete disgust with the French alliance* and "other recent proceedings of Congress." A man who simply wished to be a traitor for a price would not so carefully emphasize the French alliance as the primary cause of his willingness to change his allegiance. As to the "recent proceedings of Congress," they need no comment.

It is unnecessary to detail the actual facts of Arnold's treason, the plan to surrender West Point, the capture of Major John André and Arnold's own narrow escape.

Curiously, the greatest proof of his sincerity of purpose is offered by his conduct *after* he joined the English. When he heard André had been condemned to hang as a spy, he went to Clinton and offered to surrender himself as a ransom for the unfortunate major.* This would have meant certain death for Arnold—ignominious execution. It was not the act of a traitorous blackguard. But this is not all the evidence in his favor. He received 6,000 pounds sterling—about $30,000—for his efforts. Had he been simply a traitor, bargaining to sell his country for a price, he would have taken the money and retired to some safe place to live. The sum was not a mean one in the eighteenth century and would have provided Arnold, always a good business man, with plenty of capital to start a new fortune for himself.

Instead, having failed to insure British victory in the matter of West Point, Arnold asked for and received the opportunity to help England win in the field. He was made a brigadier general and fought vigorously to the end of the war. He was taking his life in his hands every time he took the field, as desperate efforts were constantly made to capture

* *London Morning Herald,* February 19, 1782. The story was told by Captain Louis Battersby of the 29th regiment, who was in New York in September, 1780, and was on terms of intimacy with members of Clinton's staff.

him—a fact of which he was well aware. A treacherous scoundrel would not have taken such risks.

After the war Arnold so conducted himself that he became an honored citizen of England and his four sons all served in the British army for many years with distinction.

There is no question that Mrs. Arnold knew nothing whatever of the West Point plot, despite some writers' insinuations. But her loyalty to her husband never wavered. Through all the shadows of his troubled life, she showered him with tender affection and unchanged admiration. Arnold repaid her with the same loyalty. No one ever has been able to find a solitary stain upon his personal conduct nor his domestic life in the twenty-one years he lived after his treason.

The great tragedy for him came in the later years when he realized how mistaken and how utterly unnecessary his treason had been. As the struggling republic became the United States in fact and his beloved former friend, Washington, became its first president, he saw at last how wholly wrong he had been, and then his real punishment began. His latter years were not happy. He wished always to return to the land he had so mistakenly betrayed and he was eternally barred from seeing its shores again. In June, 1801, when he knew he had only a few hours to live, his last act was to don once more the uniform of a major general in the Continental Army which he had always preserved.

"Let me die," he said, "in this old uniform in which I fought my battles. May God forgive me for ever putting on any other."

8.

St. Clair Leads the Death March

IN SPITE of Gates, Sullivan, Lee, Wilkinson and the rest of the wolf-pack; above all, in spite of the Continental Congress, Washington fought through to Yorktown and to victory, and the Republic of the United States came into being. It was not a very impressive republic in 1783. The states glared at one another with unabated jealousy and hatred. They had no coördinated central government. The country was overwhelmed with a mountain of debt. To meet its obligations it had nothing except bales and bales of money, worth slightly less than the paper it was printed on—the paper being soiled by the ink. And it still had its Old Man of the Sea, the Continental Congress, stumbling and fumbling along to complete collapse.

One of the more serious problems was offered by the disbanded soldiers of Washington's army who were inconsiderate enough to want their back pay. They became so insistent that the country at large was annoyed—now that the war was over—and grew violently anti-militaristic. "No standing army!" was the battle cry of peace.

The response was sweeping. The "regular army" of the United States, at the moment the weakest and most defenseless nation in the world, was reduced to exactly 80 men! Of these, twenty-five were assigned to guard the military stores at Pittsburgh and the rest were assigned chiefly to West Point, with a few at minor munitions depots. Not an officer was retained above the rank of captain.

By 1787, the Continental Congress had fallen to such depths that it had practically ceased to function, the meetings often lacking a quorum. During this last gasp its president was Major General Arthur St. Clair. It was not quite so brisk a St. Clair as the colonel who had paced through Camp Sorel with such purposeful strides. The general was more portly than he had been eleven years before and he suffered from frequent attacks of the gout. But his duties were not particularly exacting as the head of the dying Congress.

During the summer of 1787, it did perform one notable act. It passed an ordinance creating the "Territory of the United States Northwest of the Ohio." Many ambitious spirits had been gazing toward the Ohio country, waiting only for its legal organization. Within a few months more than 20,000 white settlers invaded the region.

As a pleasant gesture, Congress appointed its president as the first governor of the new territory. St. Clair accepted with considerable reluctance and later insisted the post had been forced upon him. He was inclined to regret he had not been more absolute in voicing his disinclination when he reached his new domain. He made his headquarters at the midget settlement of Marietta, O. (named for Marie Antoinette), and soon found plenty of trouble on his hands.

Smarting under defeat in the Revolutionary War and hoping to speed the collapse of the unstable republic, the

British were inciting the Indians of the country to harass the American settlers. The redskins, resentful at the white invasion on their own account, needed only this encouragement. Open war was not declared but every white man who ventured beyond the palisaded settlements risked the scalp knife.

For three years St. Clair was in constant hot water, failing alike in curbing the Indians with whose methods he was unfamiliar, and in governing his unruly pioneers, whose temperament he could not understand. Increasingly ambitious military drives against the Indians continued wholly unsuccessful, and finally, in the early summer of 1791, the gouty governor went to Philadelphia to take up the matter with President Washington in person. He found the executive ear sympathetic. Washington procured Congressional authority for St. Clair to establish a strong military post in the heart of the Miami country at the present site of Fort Wayne, Ind., and gave him full power to raise sufficient troops to adequately protect the inhabitants of the Northwest Territory.

Just before St. Clair left with his official documents, Washington emphasized the dangerous tactics of the Indians and repeatedly urged him to take every precaution in his campaign. Assuring the President of his prospective watchfulness, the governor limped away.

Raising an army proved difficult. The repeated failures of previous military efforts had made the frontiersmen skeptical. By September only 2,000 men had been recruited, but St. Clair decided to wait no longer and, though he was fifty-seven years old at the time, he groaningly mounted his horse and took the field himself as the commander-in-chief.

The "army" moved toward its destination slowly, stopping to build two forts on the way. Hostile Indians were not encountered until October 24, but thereafter the soldiers were continually under the sniping fire of small bands of redskin scouts, who lingered near the flanks of St. Clair's force and took an occasional scalp whenever a careless soldier wandered too far from his lines.

St. Clair either forgot or chose to ignore Washington's final advice. Making no effort to learn how large a force threatened him nor where it was, he moved forward, oblivious to the increasing number of hostiles who flitted through the forest around him.

On the night of November 3, 1791, he had reached a point 97 miles due west of Fort Washington (Cincinnati), deep in the heart of the wilderness. In pitching camp, he was guilty of stationing 350 half-insubordinate militia several hundred yards in advance of the main force. The rest of the troops he placed in a neat, orderly and compact mass arranged in two lines about forty yards apart with the small quantity of artillery between them. With the exception of the untrained militia, he had no outposts. The customary sentinels remained within a stride of the camp.

Through half the night, Indians were appearing constantly around the camp, singly or in small groups, so numerous that the guards were kept busy taking pot-shots at them, but St. Clair made no concession to prudence other than to order his troops to sleep on their arms.

In the early morning, the hostiles had disappeared and the general was sure all fears were groundless. At dawn the men were mustered for roll call and dismissed to prepare breakfast. Fifteen minutes later, while the fires were blazing merrily, the air was rent with a blood-curdling whoop and more than two thousand Indians swooped upon the militia. At the first alarm, the militia fled wildly back into the main camp and threw the entire force into confusion while the redskin horde came leaping ahead.

Completely disorganized and massed so closely they could not keep out of one another's way, the troops were caught like rats in a trap. The artillerymen dashed for their guns, but the Indians' best marksmen soon took care of them. Every artillery officer was killed or wounded and the crews so quickly destroyed that the guns were silenced in less than five minutes.

The cannoneers were the only members of the army who attempted any sort of organized resistance. The rest floundered about helplessly while the Indians swarmed over the camp, braining the soldiers with tomahawks and gunstocks, pausing only long enough to rip off the scalp before leaping to the next victim.

St. Clair tried desperately to undo the results of his negligence but the effort was hopeless. His gout prevented him from mounting a horse without help—and he had to be helped three times during the fight, as three animals were shot under him. Rallying the troops was impossible. Their only thought was escape and so completely were they ringed by their savage foes that only after two hours of overwhelming slaughter did the remnants of the army force their way through.

Even then, all that saved any of them from death was the exultant avarice of the savages. These found such a wealth of loot in their hands at the camp that they abandoned the massacre of the whites to fight among themselves over the spoils. As it was, more than 1,000 soldiers were killed, fully one half of St. Clair's force. Not a wounded man at the camp escaped. All were tomahawked and scalped.

"The conduct of the army after quitting the camp was disgraceful," says Lossing.* "Arms, ammunition and accoutrements were almost all thrown away; and even officers, in some instances, threw away their arms, thus setting an example for the most precipitate and ignominious flight. They left the camp at nine o'clock in the morning and at seven o'clock that evening they were in Fort Jefferson, twenty-nine miles distant."

Though he lost three horses and eight bullets passed through his clothing, St. Clair miraculously escaped unwounded. His horse difficulties almost proved his undoing, however. He finally was reduced to a decrepit pack animal, but he managed to follow the retreat on this beast, although it scarcely could be spurred into a trot.

The disaster sent a wave of depression over the entire country. For a time all emigration to the Ohio country ceased and St. Clair was condemned everywhere. Washington, whose temper went out of bounds on several historical occasions, went red with fury when he received the news.

"Here," he shouted to his secretary, Tobias Lear, "yes, on this very spot I took leave of him. I wished him success and honor. 'You have your instructions,' I said, 'from the Secretary of War. I had a strict eye to them and will add but one word—beware of a surprise! I repeat it—*beware of a surprise*! You know how the Indians fight us.' He went off with that, as my last solemn warning, thrown into his ears. And yet, to suffer that army to be cut to pieces, hacked,

* Lossing: *Pictorial Field Book of the War of 1812.*

butchered, tomahawked, by a surprise—the very thing I guarded him against!" In his rage, Washington's clenched hands were thrust into the air. "Oh, God! Oh, God! He is worse than a murderer! How can he answer it to his country? The blood of the slain is upon him—the curse of widows and orphans—the curse of Heaven!"

Washington's volcanic outbursts always subsided almost as quickly as they had begun. A few minutes later he said to Lear in an altered tone, "This must not go beyond this room." He sat down again and, after another lengthy pause, "General St. Clair shall have justice. I looked hastily through the dispatches—saw the whole disaster, not all the particulars. I will hear him without prejudice."*

The general received more than justice. When he reached Philadelphia and hobbled into the executive office, Washington treated him with kindly consideration though he did not condone the massacre. That was taken care of by Congress, which investigated the conduct of the campaign and acquitted its leader. It was the end of St. Clair's trail, however. He resigned his commission and went back to Ohio simply as governor. He found nothing but grief and open antagonism awaiting him there and he soon retired from public life. His declining years were clouded by ever-darkening failure and he died in abject poverty at Laurel Hill, Pa., in 1818.

* Lossing: *Pictorial Field Book of the War of 1812.* Lear did not observe the injunction to silence and so this intimate glimpse of Washington has been preserved.

9.

A Traitor Takes Command

WHEN St. Clair went back to Ohio, a familiar figure stepped into the national scene. As the new military commander for the territory, the government appointed Brigadier General James Wilkinson, the "Wilkie" of Saratoga days and the most sinister character in American history.

Although he was only 35 years old at the time, "Wilkie's" career already had gone through many kaleidoscopic changes. During the Revolutionary War, his rise in rank had been unbelievably rapid. A private in August, 1775, he was a captain in March, 1776, and a major in June. In January, 1777, he was a lieutenant colonel and, in November, at the fulsome recommendation of Gates, Congress made him a brevet brigadier general—at the age of 20! Likewise, he became secretary of the Board of War when Gates was made its president. When the odoriferous bubble of the Conway Cabal burst, "Wilkie" was the first to leap for safety by publicly denouncing Gates as a treacherous scoundrel. However, he could not entirely shed the unpleasant aroma of the conspiracy and he resigned his commission. Two years later, in 1780, he popped up again as the clothier-general of the army and, judging by the prevailing ragged condition of Washington's troops, not a very good one.

Prosperity eluded him in Maryland after the war. He went to Kentucky in 1783, where he launched an extremely successful merchandise business at Lexington. He later built the city of Frankfort and is credited with introducing the tobacco industry to Kentucky.

Then troubles came. New Orleans was the only practical outlet for Kentucky products and the Spanish, in possession there, were inclined to be hostile. They closed the port to the upriver American merchants whenever the mood inspired them and often confiscated entire shipments. Wilkinson pondered the situation for some months and finally solved it very simply.

In the spring of 1787 he went to New Orleans and visited the Spanish officials with agreeable results. The Spanish governor and the intendant agreed to open the market for *el brigadier americano*. In return Wilkinson took the oath of allegiance to the King of Spain and became a Spanish spy at a high salary. Thereafter, he worked unceasingly to dismember the western territories of the United States and turn them over to Spain. Naturally, he did not make his arrangements public. The unexpected affluence he displayed upon his return to Kentucky aroused some deep suspicions and his conduct thereafter intensified them, but the truth was long in coming to the surface. As a matter of fact, the convincing proof lay hidden for more than one hundred years. The Spanish officials at New Orleans sent their secret documents to Havana, where they remained until 1898. During the Spanish-American War, when the American troops occupied the Cuban metropolis, the ancient papers were discovered and among them was Wilkinson's oath of allegiance to Spain and sundry other documents revealing many of his plots.

For two years after he returned from his first trip south, Wilkinson worked tirelessly to segregate Kentucky from the United States—and almost succeeded. But, in 1790, he was overruled and Kentucky became a state. This put a temporary check on his Spanish enterprise and damaged his prestige at a moment when his business was sagging toward bankruptcy. Searching for a way out of his difficulties, he applied to President Washington and received a new commission as a lieutenant colonel in the army. He immediately went on two forays against the Indians of the northwest, one as a subordinate officer, the other as the leader. Both were barren of real result, but Wilkinson reported his own expedition in such glowing terms that he was rewarded with his old rank of brigadier general and sent to command the Ohio forces in 1792.

Washington, weary of the continued failures to subdue the Indians, finally turned to a commander upon whom he knew he could rely, "Mad Anthony" Wayne. This fighter was given the rank of major general, made commander-in-chief of the regular army—now to be increased to 5,000 —and sent to Ohio, where Wilkinson was to remain as his second in command.

"Wilkie" did not like this. He wanted to be commander-in-chief himself. Besides, he had cause to fear the presence of Wayne. The new leader came within an ace of trapping Wilkinson, when messengers of the Spanish authorities came to visit him, well supplied with pieces-of-eight to pay his regular spy salary. A bitter animosity developed between the two generals, but Wayne did not waste much time on the personal feud. He set about developing an army which really could cope with the Indians. He refused to move until his "Legion of the West" was ready—in sharp contrast to the previous commanders—and when he did march into the Indian country, he advanced with such stealthy caution that the hostiles themselves called him the "Rattlesnake." He proved his right to the title on August 20, 1794, when he struck.

The Battle of Fallen Timbers was short but deadly. Within an hour Wayne had completely routed the largest force of redskins ever assembled in the territory, with a total loss to himself of only 133 men killed and wounded. The single blow forced the Indians to sign a treaty which brought uninterrupted peace to the northwest for nearly twenty years.

General Wilkinson had command of the right wing at Fallen Timbers but he did not cover himself with glory. Some accounts say Wayne had to drive him into the fight under penalty of removing him from command unless he showed a little more courage. Wilkinson retaliated after the battle by writing to Washington, to Congress and to General Henry Knox, the Secretary of War, denouncing Wayne's conduct of the entire campaign and particularly the Fallen Timbers fight.

Wayne replied caustically and, for more than a year and a half, the charges and countercharges flew thick and fast. They reached so serious a stage that Washington finally decided to place the matter before the proper departmental heads and summoned the two officers to Philadelphia to thrash the matter out. But Fate intervened when Wayne died suddenly in 1796 at Presque Isle (Erie).

As a result, Brigadier General James Wilkinson, citizen of Spain, automatically became the commander-in-chief of the armies of the United States—a position he was to hold for seventeen years! The pupil of Gates had put his mentor to everlasting shame. With scarcely a wave of his hand he attained all the "Hero" of Saratoga had struggled for so futilely.

In the light of the facts which have gradually emerged from the shadows of his dark trail, Wilkinson is an almost incredible figure. For decades he commanded the respect, confidence and intimate friendship of leading characters in the national drama, including the first four Presidents, under all of whom he commanded the army. All the while, he was conducting an endless series of traitorous intrigues, utterly without honor, betraying friend and foe alike, oath-bound citizen of two inimical countries, both of whom he tried to betray to still other nations.

At the trial of Aaron Burr, in 1807, Andrew Jackson, who knew Wilkinson well—to his own sorrow—branded, him the paid spy of Spain, "a double traitor, the man who betrayed his country and perjured himself afterward."

Vehement John Randolph of Roanoke, who became Wilkinson's nemesis and tried desperately to bring him to justice, declared: "Human nature never appeared in so degraded a form—the double traitor—the most finished scoundrel that ever lived—the only man I ever knew who, from bark to core, is a villain."

Three times he was brought to trial on an amazing array of charges of which he was guilty and three times, he was thoroughly white-washed, chiefly because too many people—some of them revered historic idols—would have been tarred with the same brush which convicted him.

His every imprint in history makes more ironic his early association with Benedict Arnold. Arnold went down to an infamy he did not deserve, while the real arch-traitor went on, high in the favor of the mighty, so protected and shielded by them that his name and his deeds have been kept practically unknown through the years.

He first betrayed Arnold, then Schuyler, then Washington, then Gates, then his country to Spain and, after a year or two, both his own country and Spain to England and France in turn. In the midst of this, he reverted to more personal efforts by playing the traitor to Aaron Burr.

The deeper one goes into the evidence, the more certain it becomes that in his southwestern project of 1805 and 1806, Burr was as completely guiltless of treasonable intent as the court held him. There is every reason to believe his only purpose was a possible conquest of Mexico for which he had the unexpressed but definitely implied sanction of President Jefferson and his administration. There is even greater reason to believe that whatever of treason existed in the so-called Burr Conspiracy was almost entirely on the part of Wilkinson. And it was Wilkinson who betrayed Burr as he betrayed everyone else.

During the seventeen years Wilkinson was at the head of the army, the military organization of the United States fell into the worst condition it ever knew. The country was fortunate in that it was involved in no major wars until the very end of the period. To Wilkinson, more even than to the inept War Department, was due the wretched state of the army at the beginning of the War of 1812. It led directly to the miserable record made by the American military forces in that war to which he contributed no little himself.

He is the real stench in American history.

He needed no war to butcher men as he proved shortly after he received his first coat of white-wash following the Burr trial. He was still in Washington in the latter part of 1808, when the growing threat of war with England led Congress to vote an increase in the regular army. Wilkinson pointed out that the British would be most likely to strike first at New Orleans, which had been in American possession for the five years since the Louisiana Purchase, and it was decided to send 2,000 men there.

The new troops were to march to Pittsburgh and float down the rivers to New Orleans, while the general took the sea route. His orders were dated December 2, 1808. The day before Christmas, he finally embarked—taking with him a load of flour and apples, products expressly banned by the Embargo Acts then in force. It took him 110 days to reach New Orleans. But then, he had been busy disposing of his forbidden cargo in Havana, just turning a dishonest dollar or two while on his way to the army.

When he reached New Orleans in April, 1809, he "found a body of two thousand undisciplined recruits, men and officers, with few exceptions sunk in indolence and dissipation, without subordination, discipline or police and nearly a third sick; medical assistance dependent upon two surgeons and two surgeon's mates, one of the former confined to his bed; without paymaster; men deserting in squads; the military agent without a cent in his chest; his bills protested; a great deficiency in camp equipage; medicines and hospital supplies scarcely sufficient for a private practitioner."*

Wilkinson tried to blame the War Department but the country chose to believe if he had been at his post instead of peddling apples, the troops would not have reached such a sorry condition.

The state of affairs made it imperative to move the force at once and the commander started in search of a barracks site. After six weeks, during which the army continued in a situation which grew steadily worse, he chose a location 12 miles from New Orleans, known as Terre aux Boeufs. The hundred-odd acres of the place were covered with a heavy growth of palmetto scrub which had to be cleared by fever-stricken soldiers before the camp could be made habitable. So it was June 10, two months after Wilkinson found his soldiers in their desperate plight, before he settled them in their new home.

The reason for the long delay found its way into ready rumor. It was said the owner of the camp site had agreed to accept the clearing of the scrub as compensation for the use of his land, that the rental the government was to pay was transferred into the general's own pocket, and that Wilkinson had refused to close for a camp site until he could find an owner ready to make such an agreement.

Shortly after the camp was established, torrential rains came and converted it into a swamp. The tents were leaky. The blankets were soaked. Sickness increased by leaps and bounds. Clouds of mosquitoes drove the men close to madness and the general had provided no nets, although these were indispensable against the pests in Louisiana. The ra-

* Wilkinson: *Memoirs of My Own Times.*

tions consisted of maggoty flour, worm-eaten beans and peas and rotten meat.

Terre aux Boeufs became another Sorel. Men died in squads and by August 1, Wilkinson had only 1,574 soldiers. Of these, 963 were bedridden—sixty per cent of the entire force. The remaining 600 were so weak they were incapable of policing the camp or taking care of the bedridden.

The indictment against Wilkinson goes far beyond the incompetence which permitted these conditions. President James Madison's first Secretary of War was Dr. William Eustis, former army surgeon. He was a bad war secretary but a good doctor. As early as April, Eustis, having heard of the condition of the recruits at New Orleans, wisely ordered them removed from the water-logged country to the hills near Fort Adams and Natchez. In 1809, there was only one mail a week from Washington to New Orleans and the mail boats required nineteen days for the trip. At the latest, the order would have left on May 6, reaching Wilkinson on May 25—16 days before he settled his army at Terre aux Boeufs. Of course, this would have eliminated the rent graft and he later claimed that he did not receive the order until June 14—a convenient date—but "no one believed him," says Henry Adams. "Wilkinson's reputation warranted the belief that he suppressed the order."

Even after receiving it, Wilkinson wrote Eustis, refusing to obey the removal instructions, saying the men were in no condition to be moved so far, that transport was not available and that he could not defend New Orleans if his force was at Natchez. Just how he would defend the city with 60 percent of his force in bed, he did not explain.

Eustis now issued a peremptory order for the abandonment of the camp and accompanied the message with an order from the Secretary of the Navy, placing every ship and boat at New Orleans at the disposal of Wilkinson. This order arrived on July 19. Wilkinson kept it a secret for six weeks and then waited two more weeks before he obeyed it. The camp was not abandoned until September 14.

At this final severance of his rent graft, Wilkinson inflicted his resentment on his men. In weather which was abnormally hot and humid, the boats were heavily overcrowded and the men were permitted to swelter while the entire affair was conducted with unbelievable sloth. During the shameful trip, 250 men died on the transports and the force was so completely shattered that the death list mounted to nearly 800 after the hill country was reached. In five months Wilkinson had caused the deaths of 1,200 men—60 percent of his entire original force!

A wave of horrified revulsion swept the country as the scandal was revealed. When Wilkinson reached Natchez, he found orders awaiting him to turn over the command to General Wade Hampton and proceed to Washington to account for his conduct. Coincident with this, more ugly rumors arose. Wilkinson was charged with having had a deal for a share of the profits with the contractor who provided the rotten food for the sick troops. As proof—difficult to dispute—it was pointed out that all the contractor's bills had been approved by the general and paid, without a solitary protest over the condition of the rations.

Sick himself now—the people considered it a Divine visitation—Wilkinson did not reach Washington until April 14, 1810, where he faced two Congressional investigation committees—one to "inquire into the cases of the mortality of the troops on the Mississippi," the other into his "private life, character and conduct."

The investigation stumbled along for more than a year. On July 7, 1811, Wilkinson was ordered to appear before a court-martial at Frederick, Md. He was faced with eight general charges under which were listed twenty-six specific crimes of which the government believed him guilty. These included ten allegations of receiving money as a pensioner of Spain, conspiring to dismember the United States, helping treasonable conspiracies, disobedience of orders, neglect of duty and misappropriation and waste of public funds and supplies: theft, graft, conspiracy, embezzlement and treason. The situation looked hopeless but the white-wash brush was ready. He was acquitted on every count on the grounds of insufficient evidence! Then he was sent back to New Orleans, still commander-in-chief, with a major war only a few months distant.

10.

The Poltroon Carnival

WHEN the War of 1812 became official, months after it actually had begun, something like spontaneous combustion happened in the War Department and Brigadier General Wilkinson suddenly ceased to be commander-in-chief of the United States Army. He was not superseded precisely. The position simply vanished in the general turmoil. Squads of new generals were created in the best 1776 manner, but their duties were hazy and no one was placed in supreme command. The situation offered a fair glimmering of how the war was to be conducted.

The outbreak of war was a trifle overwhelming for the milk-and-water President Madison and good Dr. Eustis. A glance at the map revealed that the country was vastly greater than it had been in Revolutionary days, which offered the only precedent for them. It presented the possibility of action on many fronts which meant that lots of generals would be needed. To the minds of the President and the Secretary of War it also meant that there was no room for a single commander-in-chief. The nation should be divided into departments, each to operate under its own directing head, with subordinate generals to fight the battles. It also seemed the part of simple political wisdom to commission good administration men as far as possible.

So the whirlwind of appointments began. Henry Dearborn, collector of the port at Boston, former Secretary of War under Jefferson, veteran of the Revolution, aged 61, was made first major general and given command of the Northern Department which was to take care of the conquest of Canada. Thomas Pinckney, venerable South Carolinian, veteran of the Revolution, was commissioned as second major general to command the Southern Department. James Wilkinson, heretofore commander-in-chief, was considered for a major generalship but was passed by. He was in bad odor at the moment. His recent acquittal in court-martial had lacked something of the robust vindication which might have been wished for. Besides, Eustis did not like him. It was decided to leave him where he was, at New Orleans, with rank unchanged, to command the Department of the Southwest. With him, too, was left Brigadier General Wade Hampton, a self-satisfied, violent-tempered and wholly incompetent Louisianan. It was a combination with all the possibilities of a volcano. Hampton had superseded Wilkinson before the latter's court-martial. Now Wilkinson, in turn, had superseded Hampton, to the latter's wrath. The two hated each other with undisguised venom.

Colonel Alexander Smyth of Virginia and the regular army, one of the most pompous windbags the service ever saw—but a good follower of the administration and in high favor at Washington—was made a brigadier general. Another good Madisonian, Major John Armstrong, aide-de-camp to Horatio Gates at Saratoga during the Revolution and intimate friend of Wilkinson, also was made a brigadier general. But the quality of even these sterling appointments was surpassed when the white-haired William Hull, governor of Michigan, aged 59, was made a brigadier general and entrusted with the opening campaign of the war, the invasion of Canada from Detroit.

These were the leaders of the country's youth in arms at the outset of the war, an array of incompetence scarcely equalled in the world's history, certainly never surpassed. If the Revolutionary War was marred by stupid vanity and treacherous self-seeking, the War of 1812 was a veritable carnival of poltroons in high command. From the outset their presence guaranteed a continual flood of needless bloodshed. There is little in the military record of the war to make Americans point with pride. For more than two years it was marked by disaster after disaster, openly invited and shamefully incurred. That the war was won on land at all was due only to the fact that three commanders—Andrew Jackson, William Henry Harrison and Jacob Brown —finally forced their way through the bonds of governmental prejudice.

Jackson was deliberately kept out of action for nearly half of the war because of the personal antagonism of the President and the Secretary of War. The same administrational spite hounded the victorious Harrison out of the service before the war was over. Brown was suppressed until the last six months of the war because he was "too aggressive."

The war was a curious one in many respects. Natural conditions and governmental incompetence made of it a panorama of small engagements scattered far and wide. Small detachments of troops dotted the map in all directions. Only once was a sizable army assembled under the American flag and then it was divided almost immediately. Actually there was but one major field battle in the entire war and that was fought after the peace treaty had been signed. At no time were there as many troops engaged in a single fight as in such battles of the Revolutionary War as Brandywine or Monmouth.

This reduced the size of the bloodstains on the commanders, but the war was marked by a continual sequence of small butcheries which swelled a tragic total of lives futilely tossed away. North, west and south, they were spread democratically over the entire field of operations, convincing proof of the universal degradation of the army system. To cite them all would mean but the dreary monotone of endless repetition, except for the few which stand out as gory blotches of particular note.

Bad as they were, the generals alone were not at fault. The régime of Wilkinson as commander-in-chief had permeated the army organization with wretched incompetents from top to bottom. As a result of the manner in which the army was distributed in small units, many junior officers—colonels, majors, captains—were given the opportunity to add to the crimson toll. In fact, it was a captain who inaugurated the war's festival of needless carnage.

In the spring of 1812, the coming of hostilities between the United States and England once more sent the Indians on the warpath. Throughout the Northwest Territory, the savages roamed the country, searching for victims so they might collect the bounty offered by the British authorities for each American scalp presented them. The farthest west and most exposed post was Fort Dearborn on the shores of Lake Michigan, where Chicago now stands.

The garrison under Captain John Heald was a small one, scarcely numbering a hundred. In addition, the inhabitants of the fort included the wives and children of the soldiers. But their danger was slight. The fort was so strong and so thoroughly equipped that Heald was in a position to withstand any redskin attacks for at least six months. In addition, reinforcements were promised before summer came. For a frontier post in time of war, the position was nearly ideal. In April, however, came a message from Brigadier General William Hull, the white-haired governor of Michigan:

"Captain Heald: Pursuant to the orders of the President, I am preparing to move on Canada. For this purpose, all possible troops in the northwest are to be concentrated to march for Detroit. If feasible, you will please take your command to Fort Wayne and there await further orders."

Heald was elated with the promise of welcome relief from the monotony of garrison duty in the wilderness and ignored every other consideration. Particularly, he ignored the discretionary powers the order gave him. His route would lie through the heart of hostile Indian country, with massacre threatening every step of the way. To make the journey at all was not feasible. To make it with the women and children who must accompany the troops was unspeakable.

Over the protests of his subordinates and every inhabitant of the fort, he stripped the post of its defenses and prepared for departure. Over their greater protests, he accepted the escort of 500 supposedly friendly Pottawattomies whose loyalty he had every reason to suspect.

With considerable trepidation the soldiers, women and children started down the shore of the lake, but their suspense was brief. A few miles from the fort they entered the barren region of the Sand Hills along the beach and had scarcely moved into the midst of these when, with a sudden whoop, the Pottawattomies made a concerted rush and threw themselves behind the protection of the dunes. The next instant, as the whites stopped in startled uncertainty, redskin muskets blazed. While the shrill, terrified cries of children and the screams of bleeding women rose above the first shock of conflict, the soldiers swung their rifles into action.

The fight, short and desperate, was not a battle. It was a massacre. As the fire of the whites slackened, the whoops of the savages sounded again and they rushed down from the hills to complete their grisly work. All but twenty-eight of the men were slaughtered, seventeen of the women were tomahawked as they stood cowering against the wagons, and twelve of the children were murdered. Without exception, every wounded victim was scalped, regardless of sex. Not a Dearborn soldier joined General Hull.

This was only a minor beginning. The pace quickened rapidly. The aged Hull reached Detroit on July 6, with 2,000 men. Next day, he began his Canadian invasion by sending most of his force across the Detroit River, presumably to attack the only British post in Upper Canada, the weakly held Fort Malden, which stood some miles down the shore. But he did not make the attack. He halted his force on the river bank, immediately opposite Detroit, and stopped there. For the next month he offered a demonstration of generalship which is unique in American history. Almost every day he issued orders to prepare for a march against Malden, and his eager troops leaped up for action. Every day he as faithfully rescinded his orders before the troops had marched a step. Late in July he gave *positive* orders for the attack. But word was brought to him that Malden had been reinforced with a thousand men. This made the British total 1,400. Hull still outnumbered them, but he hastily cancelled the attack once more.

Each day he became more timid and each day his enraged troops approached nearer to mutiny. By August 7 their antagonistic spirit was so pronounced that he called a council of war and ordered a *definite* attack on Fort Malden. This time the men reached the point of being lined up in full marching order when the new order came from the commanding general—to recross the river to Detroit.

Hull's weird conduct now led his sullen army to believe he either was an imbecile or a traitor. He shut himself in his room for hours on end. At other times he was abstracted and confused, giving the most ordinary instructions with a wavering uncertainty when he did not grumble them sullenly. His chief officers banded together to displace him, but before they could act it was too late.

The British were bewildered by the curious operations of the Americans. They had expected to be attacked and overwhelmed. Now as Hull continued to go around in circles they suddenly took the aggressive themselves, marched their inferior force before Detroit and demanded its surrender. When Hull refused, they began a brief bombardment. Several shells struck the stockade harmlessly, but one—just one —went over the side and killed several men. This was the end. Without consulting anyone, Hull ran up the white flag and surrendered. More than 2,000 men, eager for battle, were condemned to rot in British prison hulks without being permitted to strike a blow. Thus ended the first campaign of the War of 1812. Hull was later tried by court-martial, found guilty of cowardice and neglect of duty and condemned to be shot. But President Madison pardoned him.

The farce went on. On the Lake Ontario-St. Lawrence frontier, the British forces were weak and other American plans were made for invasion. Brigadier General Solomon Van Renssalaer, sincere and quite capable head of the New York militia, was to attack on the Niagara frontier. Major General Dearborn was instructed to provide Van Renssalaer with 5,000 men, but General Dearborn was busy with other matters. Hearing a rumor that the United States had sent commissioners to England to discuss peace, he promptly negotiated an armistice with Sir George Prevost, British commander in Canada. He did not trouble to consult the government about it. Two weeks later he received angry instructions from Washington to cancel his unauthorized interruption of hostilities at once. But he continued his armistice for two weeks more and the thirty days' grace was all that Prevost had needed. During that time his forces had been increased materially and, thanks to Dearborn's graciousness, he was in a much better position to resist attack.

Van Renssalaer was then ordered by the War Department to attack at once with his 5,000 men, received from Dearborn, but this he found a trifle difficult as his force, on September 1, totalled exactly 691 men, all of whom he had provided himself. Some help came shortly afterward, with the arrival of 1,200 soldiers headed by Brigadier General Alexander Smyth, and several hundred recruits joined Van Renssalaer's own force. But Smyth was contemptuous of militia officers and said so and did not even deign to report in person to his superior. Instead, he wrote Van Renssalaer an insulting letter telling him how to conduct the campaign, although he had never been in the north before and Van Renssalaer knew every inch of the country. When his suggestions were rejected, Smyth huffily refused to attend a council of war and declined to coöperate in the proposed attack. In desperation, Van Renssalaer launched the drive without his assistance. Part of his command crossed the Niagara River from Lewiston and began a vigorous assault on Queenston Heights. Given proper support, it promised an easy success. But the support did not come.

The New York militia, still at Lewiston waiting to embark, turned cowards. While Van Renssalaer begged and pleaded with them to assist their comrades who faced destruction unless reinforced immediately, they refused to go, on the grounds that as militia, under the constitution, they could not be taken out of the state! So they stood and watched while the force on Queenston Heights was cut to pieces and the few survivors were compelled to surrender. In disgust, Van Renssalaer resigned his commission and Smyth rose to the supreme command on the Niagara frontier.

Now came a touch of sorry comedy as Smyth entered upon a fierce offensive—of proclamations. These were classics in their way. Certainly, nothing like them is to be found elsewhere in American records. The first was issued November 10, to the public at large.

"One army," it said, "has been disgracefully surrendered and lost. Another has been sacrificed by a precipitate attempt to pass it over at the strongest point of the enemy's lines with most incompetent means. The cause of these miscarriages is apparent. The commanders were popular men, destitute alike of theory and experience in the art of war. In a few days the troops under my command will plant the American Standard in Canada. They will conquer or they will die. Will you stand with arms folded and look on this interesting struggle? Must I turn from you and ask men of the Six Nations to support the government of the United States? *Shame, where is thy blush?* No. Where I command, the vanquished and the peaceful man, the child, the maid and the matron shall be secure from wrong. The present is the hour of renown. . . ."

This was but a start. Shortly came another, this one directed to the troops:

"Companions in Arms! The time is at hand when you will cross the stream of Niagara to conquer Canada and to secure the peace of the American frontier. Whatever is booty by the usages of war shall be yours." And, after offering $200 apiece for horses which might be captured and used for artillery, he proudly proclaimed his soldiers as the mightiest in the world.

A few days later he took a deep breath and burst forth once more:

"Soldiers of every corps! It is in your power to retrieve the honor of your country and to cover yourselves with glory. Rewards and honors await the brave, infamy and contempt are reserved for cowards. Companions in arms! You come to vanquish a valiant foe. I know the choice you will make. *Come on, my heroes!* And, when you attack the enemy's batteries, let your rallying word be, 'The cannon lost at Detroit or death!' "

In three weeks his multifarious effusions, which were

greeted with gales of laughter in both Canada and the United States, had so completely revealed his plans that the British were prepared to meet his every move anywhere along the frontier. At length he ordered the embarkation at 3 o'clock of a cold November morning, when 400 men actually started across the river in 21 boats. When they reached midstream they were greeted with such heavy fire from the calmly waiting British that six boats were compelled to turn back. The rest of the men landed and began a vigorous attack, but when no more troops came to their support, they were forced to return, after suffering serious losses.

More plans for embarkation were launched. In one instance, Smyth kept his men sitting in the half-frozen boats all day, then majestically ordered them to "disembark and dine!" The climax came on November 30 when the embarkation was ordered for eight o'clock in the morning via a typical Smyth ukase.

"The general will be on board," he promised thrillingly. "Neither rain, snow or frost will prevent the embarkation. While embarking, the music will play martial airs. 'Yankee Doodle' will be the signal to get under way. The landing will be effected in despite of cannon. The whole army has seen that cannon is to be little dreaded. *Hearts of War!* Tomorrow will be memorable in the annals of the United States!"

The "Hearts of War" protested violently. They were beginning to entertain a deep distrust of their commander. The embarkation was once more postponed but when it finally was attempted again, the soldiers made so much noise that the startled British sounded the alarm all the way from Fort Erie to Chippewa. In the midst of the furor, Smyth hastily called another council of war. Troops already a quarter of a mile from shore were frantically recalled. Then the whole army was ordered to disembark and General Smyth announced that the invasion of Canada must be abandoned.

A wild riot broke out among the infuriated troops. They began firing muskets in all directions and the camp became a bedlam. Proposals were made to hang Smyth as a traitor. As the wave of fury against him mounted, he was forced to place double guards around his tent and he was fired upon half a dozen times when he ventured outside. The War Department finally put an end to the affair. In the terminology of the Army Register, Smyth was "disbanded." That is, he was deposed without a trial and excluded from further army service. Thus ended the second Canadian campaign of 1812.

★ ★ ★ ★ ★ ★ ★ ★ ★

11.

Murder on All Fronts

WITHIN a month, the farce on the lake frontier had brought grim horror to the west. Released from immediate danger by the successive fiascos of Hull, Dearborn, Van Renssalaer and Smyth, the British joined active hands with the northwest Indians under the inhuman command of General Proctor. They swept across Michigan, leaving a smoking trail of ruin and death behind them and as the year ended, they were nearing Frenchtown (now Monroe) on the Raisin River, one of the largest settlements in the territory.

In January, 1813, the small body of troops and frontiersmen there were hard pressed and sent an urgent appeal for help. It reached Brigadier General James Winchester, in camp with 1,000 men on the Maumee, thirty-five miles to the south. Winchester was a man with deeply humane instincts and not much else. His kindly heart was touched by the cry of distress. He at once set his troops in motion toward Frenchtown. He was in such a hurry, that he did not bother to consult his superior, Major General William Henry Harrison, who was sixty miles away. In fact, he was in such a hurry, he did not even take time to distribute his new supply of ammunition which had arrived the previous day and he refused to be hampered by his artillery. So he sent his thousand men forward to certain battle, lightly armed, with less than ten rounds of ammunition apiece.

On the way he refused to take primary precautions and when he finally sent out a group of five scouts who returned with the news that Proctor's already strong force was being reinforced by a large body of troops from Fort Malden and at least 400 Indians, he bluntly told them they were lying!

Without further hesitation he rushed his force ahead, rushed it on without advance scouts, rushed it directly into the savage arms of Proctor's overwhelming force which swarmed over Frenchtown in a resistless attack just as Winchester arrived. Within a few minutes the Americans, their meager ammunition gone, were surrounded and hopelessly overpowered.

The butchery which followed is indescribable. The merciless Proctor released his painted fiends without restraint. Here were scalps for bounty and the howling redskins set out to collect. Surrender meant nothing. In one small space, one hundred Kentuckians of Winchester's force were tomahawked and scalped in less than five minutes. Every rule of warfare was disregarded as the screeching savages, thirsting for blood, swept through the helpless defenders, killing and mutilating every American they could grasp. Even death did not save them from the maddened blood-lust of their slayers. Arms, legs, even heads were chopped from the bodies of the victims. The redskins literally bathed in blood, stabbing, hacking and leaping upon the dead and living alike. With the arrival of Winchester's force there had been 1,200 Americans in Frenchtown. When Proctor finally called a halt on the carnage, less than one hundred remained alive to be taken prisoners. Among this handful was the humane Winchester.

With this victory as their inspiration, the Indians, prodded and aided directly by the British, arose in a savage drive from Canada to the Gulf of Mexico. In the south, the long-smouldering Creek War burst in a wave of horror. The red scourge swept through the gulf states in such fury that the white settlers were forced to flee for their lives. As spring gave way to summer, every day saw the number of refugees growing in the stockades which extended in a long chain through the terrorized country.

One of the largest of these was Fort Mims, in southern Alabama, under the unfortunate command of Major Daniel Beasley, a blustering, self-sufficient martinet who was supremely contemptuous of the Indian menace and refused to take any steps to insure safety for the increasing swarm of settlers who came to him for protection. The fort became so overcrowded that Beasley finally condescended to enlarge the stockade by driving a new row of pickets beyond the east end.

The work went on slowly and carelessly. No guards were posted outside the stockade. The fields immediately around the fort were tilled freely by unarmed men. The cows and horses were permitted to graze at considerable distances. The main gate of the fort was left wide open at all hours, day and night. In fact, it had been unclosed for so long that the sand had drifted against it and held it immovably ajar.

On August 29, 1813, Fort Mims contained 553 persons, a great many of them women and children. During the morning of that day, two negro slaves, one the property of John Randon, the other owned by a man named Fletcher, came running into the fort from the grazing field, crying that they had seen two dozen savages on the edge of the near-by swamp. The alarm aroused Beasley sufficiently to make him send three mounted men to reconnoiter. When they returned at sunset without having seen an Indian, the major charged the negroes with lying, and ordered them whipped for raising a false alarm.

Randon's negro was lashed but Fletcher, inclined to believe his slave's story, refused to permit him to be flogged. This enraged Beasley and he ordered Fletcher to leave the fort with his entire family by 10 o'clock next day. In the morning the alarm had subsided and Fletcher decided he would rather have his negro beaten than be driven from the fort. So the slave was tied up for a noon-day castigation, and 10 o'clock found Beasley sending a message to Major F. L. Claiborne, the commander of the district, assuring him of his perfect safety and his "ability to maintain the post against any number of Indians."

At noon the women in the stockade were preparing dinner, the soldiers were loafing about playing cards or lounging half-asleep, and almost a hundred children were playing about the cabins and tents, while older boys and girls were dancing to the tune of a wailing fiddle. The only jarring note in the scene was Fletcher's poor negro, tied to a post, his back bared for the whip. And at that moment, less than 400 yards away, more than a thousand Creek warriors were crouched in a ravine, awaiting the signal to attack.

It came from the fort itself. Just at noon the garrison drum beat for dinner. At its first roll the redskins swarmed up from the ravine and charged for the open gate, filling the air with their hideous yells. All that may be said for Beasley is that he was the first to die. When the alarm sounded he rushed in a futile effort to close the gate and he was pawing desperately at the drifted sand when the savages leaped upon him. A tomahawk was buried in his brain, clubs beat him to the ground and, over his dying body, the blood-thirsty Creeks poured into the enclosure.

The pitiful force inside made a desperate defense, but they were overwhelmed in the first mad rush. Fletcher's slave, still hanging in his bonds, was shot dead on the spot where he was to have been punished for trying to prevent the tragedy which now had begun. Maddened by the sight and smell of blood, the savages gorged themselves in an inhuman orgy of slaughter. The bodies of men were ripped from head to heel before the death blow was given. Children were seized by their legs and their heads battered to pulp against the stockades. Pregnant women were disemboweled and their unborn children hurled high in the air.

The ravaging, torturous butchery continued for hours. The British agent at Pensacola had offered five dollars apiece for American scalps. That day's harvest cost him more than $2,000. By sunset, more than four hundred refugees and soldiers were dead. Not a solitary white woman or child escaped. Only the negroes were spared, these to become the slaves of their savage captors. In all, thirteen human beings broke from the slaughter-pen. Twelve soldiers of the garrison and one negro woman managed to cut their way through the pickets and found refuge in the neighboring swamp.

Terrible vengeance overtook the Creeks. At long last the government summoned Major General Andrew Jackson to the service, after having coldly rejected him before, and he swept through the Creek country with a studied ferocity which beat the savages to death and all but wiped them out.

The tide of useless bloodshed was not ended, however. In April, 1813, the inept Eustis—whom Jackson had called "an old granny"—left Madison's cabinet and Brigadier General John Armstrong became the new Secretary of War.

Armstrong began planning big things at once, among others the most pretentious campaign of the war on the northern frontier, thus far only a graveyard of several generals' hopes. It was but natural, too, that he should give a thought or two to his old friend, Wilkinson, for whom he immediately recommended a major generalship. The promotion was authorized duly enough, but Wilkinson was not happy. Neither were the men who had lain in idleness under his commands since the war began. With the promotion of his friend, Armstrong received a flood of mail from New Orleans, all letters from Wilkinson's subordinate officers, unanimously proclaiming that they would refuse to serve under him in any active campaign, particularly if he were assigned to lead them against the Creeks.

Armstrong bowed before the barrage and, casting about for a post worthy of his friend's talents, determined to place the great Canadian campaign in his hands. There was one phase of the matter he overlooked. General Hampton had been transferred to the north some time before. It was a situation fraught with possibilities. Wilkinson was ordered to report at Washington and by the time he reached the capital city, Armstrong had matters well under way in the north. He gathered there the largest American army assembled during the war and the ambitious campaign included the capture of Montreal and Kingston with the prospective conquest of all Canada.

Three great obstacles stood in the way of success—Wilkinson, Hampton and Armstrong—a formidable combination. Wilkinson disputed so vigorously with Armstrong concerning the campaign that he finally started north without any definite plan of operations. When he attempted to give orders to Hampton, the latter wrote to Armstrong that he would not serve under Wilkinson and demanded that his command be recognized as a separate one.

Wilkinson arrived in August at Sackett's Harbor, N. Y., near the junction of Lake Ontario and the St. Lawrence. He found himself nominally in command of about 16,000 men, 4,000 under Hampton at Burlington, 6,000 at Sackett's Harbor and 6,000 under Brigadier General Jacob Brown at Fort George. Against this force were only about 8,000 British, spread out thinly from Montreal to the western end of Lake Ontario.

The Wilkinsonian genius began operating immediately. He called a council of war—which Hampton refused to attend—and announced his intention of concentrating most of the troops at Sackett's Harbor for the expressed purpose of striking "a deadly blow *somewhere*!" Hampton scoffed, Wilkinson retorted and Armstrong decided only his personal presence could save matters. He left Washington and proceeded to Sackett's Harbor.

Within two weeks the three presiding geniuses of the

campaign were fighting like mongrels and so much time was consumed with the quarreling that the summer passed before any action was launched. In hasty desperation it was finally decreed that Hampton should move directly north from Burlington with 5,000 men, clearing the path toward Montreal. Brown, the only capable officer in the lot, was to drive for Cornwell, halfway between Montreal and Kingston. Wilkinson was to capture Kingston. A smaller force was to move into Canada at the Niagara frontier and keep the British right wing busy while the other three bodies shattered the center and left.

The campaign opened with Hampton's positive refusal to obey orders, either of Wilkinson or Armstrong. Instead he went on an independent expedition to capture Montreal by himself. He was trapped by an overwhelming force of British and his command was cut to pieces. Nearly three-fourths of his men were killed, wounded or captured.

The Niagara troops fared almost as badly. A diminutive advance was made into Canada but was driven back. In the retreat, a subordinate American officer wantonly set fire to the town of Newark. The pursuing British and Indians flew into a rage and their vengeance was swift. They drove the Americans headlong before them, captured Buffalo, completely destroyed it by fire, leaving only four stone buildings standing, and went on a massacrous raid through north-western New York in which hundreds of non-combatants were slaughtered.

Taking personal command of the Kingston expedition, Wilkinson embarked on a dark night with a storm brewing, at a time of the year when the violence of lake storms, perilous enough to large vessels, could mean nothing but disaster to the small boats into which the soldiers were packed, together with ordnance, hospital stores, ammunition, baggage, camp equipage and two months' provisions. The storm came with the inevitable result. For thirty-six hours, the boats were driven before a terrific gale, accompanied by rain and sleet, against which the troops had no protection. The boats were scattered. Dozens of them were wrecked. Many men were drowned. Practically all the supplies were lost or ruined by the water. When the storm finally subsided, the drenched, exhausted troops were scattered over the islands, without food or shelter. By the time Wilkinson could assemble them and make feeble efforts to start again, the British were upon him. On November 10, he met them in the Battle of Chrysler's Field. It was the first battle ever directed by the man who had been commander-in-chief of the United States army for 17 years—and he forgot to bring any reserve ammunition! As a result, after the battle had raged for five hours with the losses heavy, the Americans were forced to beat a swift retreat to escape annihilation.

Completely disheartened and dispirited, the troops finally reached Cornwell, far down the St. Lawrence. Here they were met by General Brown, the one commander who had carried out his assigned task.

After a few days of dawdling, Wilkinson gave up the whole enterprise. The troops were sent up the Salmon River to French Mills, the boats were scuttled and the army went into winter quarters. There was one marked difference in the army. Wilkinson had begun with 16,000 men. Three months later only 8,000 were left. The entire campaign had ended in disaster and disgrace.

It had one good result. It ended the military careers of

Wilkinson and Hampton. The latter resigned his commission and returned to his sugar plantations in Louisiana, followed by the nation's contempt. Wilkinson was called before another court-martial, but the third coat of whitewash was forthcoming and he was acquitted once more. So much opprobrium was heaped upon him, however, that he resigned his commission, never again to hold official position in the United States.

Armstrong returned to Washington and for the next nine months demonstrated his right to the title of the worst Secretary of War that the nation ever had. But the war staggered on in spite of him. Brown, assisted by the young brigadier, Winfield Scott, began winning victories in the north, the first victories the country had gained there, while Jackson destroyed the Creeks and swept the Mississippi valley clear of the enemy.

Then came the denouement. The end of the Peninsular Wars and the exile of Napoleon to Elba, released many of Wellington's veterans for service in America and 4,000 of them came to drive against New Orleans. All that Jackson, Harrison and Brown finally had accomplished promised to be undone.

Wounded and ill, Jackson leaped into the breach. With a puny force, he threw up the cotton-bale defenses before New Orleans. In desperation, he threw open the Louisiana prisons and placed convicts in his ranks. He drafted hundreds of negro slaves and added them to his force. And so at last came January 8, 1815, and the British host under Sir Edward Pakenham drew up in battle array to crush Jackson. No need to retell the story of the fight. It was a holocaust. Rarely in all the world's history has there been such a discrepancy in losses. Only tattered fragments of the British force escaped. They left 2,600 of their number behind them, 700 killed outright, including General Pakenham, 1,400 wounded and 500 prisoners. And Jackson's loss was 8 killed and 13 wounded.

A wave of hysterical rejoicing swept the country. The news that the peace treaty had been signed at Ghent two weeks before the battle did not matter. It mattered even less that the treaty was a farce, a document which said nothing, and wiped out none of the causes of the war. The Battle of New Orleans had proved that the nation had nothing to fear from the military best of Europe, that under capable leaders, its soldiers could achieve all and more that might be asked of them. New Orleans was unquestionably the decisive battle of the war, irrespective of when it was fought. It gave the country as a whole the vision of its right to stand before the world as a power equal to any. And the world saw, too. The attempts to badger the still youthful republic ceased. It had passed the crisis.

ANDREW JACKSON

12.

The "Perfect" Generals

PEACE returned in 1815, with the seeds of another war already planted, although years passed before they bore fruit. The trouble with Mexico started with the Lousi-ana Purchase of 1803. Spain began a boundary dispute im-mediately. When Mexico won her independence in 1821 she continued the argument. There were other grievances, too, complaints on both sides, arising from the growing tide of pioneers who were elbowing their way westward.

By the end of 1835, the Nordics in Texas were in re-volt. They conducted their efforts in the muddled manner of revolutionists. The newly chosen Governor Henry Smith was at continual loggerheads with his Council. They agreed only upon the choice of Sam Houston as com-mander-in-chief of the Texas forces. The forces themselves felt differently about the matter. They approved heartily of Houston but, in a cantankerous demonstration of their own independence, refused to accept him, merely because they had not been consulted in the appointment.

Those loosely concentrated at San Antonio took matters into their own hands. Hearing that Santa Anna was leading an army into Texas, all but 150 of them marched away to make a surprise flank attack on the Mexican dictator's troops. The 150 were left behind, under Lieutenant Colonel William Barrett Travis, to hold the Alamo, a fortified mission near San Antonio.

The Executive Council not only approved the flanking expedition but authorized another similar one of its own under James W. Fannin. Houston protested vigorously. He declared the defense of San Antonio was all-important, and for weeks he and Smith exerted every effort to have both expeditions recalled. But the Council ignored them and the stage was set for the Alamo tragedy.

Unfortunately, Santa Anna did not take the route the "flankers" had planned for him. On February 24, 1836, Travis suddenly found his post surrounded by 3,000 Mexicans. Immediately, he sent out his famous call for help.

"The enemy has demanded a surrender . . . otherwise the garrison are to be put to the sword if the fort is taken. I shall never surrender. I call on you, in the name of Liberty, or patriotism & everything dear to the American character, to come to our aid with all dispatch. If this call is neglected, I am determined to sustain myself as long as possible & die like a soldier who never forgets what is due to his honor & that of his country—victory or death."

The call *was* neglected—by all except a band of 38 men who heroically cut their way through the Mexican line and joined Travis on March 1. The "flanking" forces were motionless until a detachment of Santa Anna's army fell suddenly on the first one and annihilated it. Even after news of this disaster reached him, Fannin did nothing. As soon as the desperate Houston heard of Travis' plight, he forced recognition of his leadership and on March 7, finally accepted as the commander-in-chief, he leaped into action. He gathered such troops as he could himself, ordered Fannin to join him at all speed and started for San Antonio. But it was already too late. On Sunday, March 6, every man in the Alamo was butchered.

What actually happened inside the fortified mission on that day will never be known fully. The only available accounts are the reports of Mexican officers who took part in the assault and the horrified recollections of the one woman in the garrison, the wife of Lieutenant James Dickinson. She and her little daughter were the only human beings who escaped the slaughter.

It is known that before the final attack began Santa Anna told one of his generals, "You know that in this war there are no prisoners." When his waves of cutthroats swarmed over the walls, they lived up to the letter of that admonition. Even so, the desperate garrison, outnumbered 16 to one, held them at bay for a full hour and exacted a fearful toll before bullet and bayonet cut them down. The heroic 188 fought to the last gasp of their lives and for every American who died three Mexicans lay in the shambles.

Mrs. Dickinson and her daughter took refuge in the church, while her husband fought to the death against the savage horde. Once, for just an instant, he came to her, only to be called away by the cry that the Mexicans were within the walls. Then, with a parting kiss, he rushed back to his doom, sword in hand.

"Soon after he left me," said Mrs. Dickinson, "three unarmed gunners came into the church and were shot down at my side. Just then a Mexican officer came in and asked me in English, 'Are you Mrs. Dickinson?' I answered, 'Yes.' 'Then,' said he, 'if you wish to save your life, follow me.' I followed him and, although shot at and wounded, was spared."

So the lives of the courageous 188 were tossed away but it cannot be said they died in vain. The massacre aroused the Texans in united fury. Six weeks later, on April 21, at San Jacinto, Houston with 800 men attacked Santa Anna's greatly superior army. With the raging battle cry of "Remember the Alamo!" Houston's grim little force swarmed over the Mexicans with a savage fury which nothing could withstand. In the first rush the Mexicans broke, but the Texans were not content with mere victory. Every man a sharpshooter, they shot down their fleeing foes like sheep. More than 600 Mexicans were killed in that vengeful slaughter and of their whole force only 40 escaped. Santa Anna himself was brought in, a bedraggled prisoner. The total Texan loss was 2 killed and 23 wounded.

San Jacinto brought both revenge and independence. The United States recognized the Lone Star republic. Mexico refused and notified this country that a move to annex Texas would be looked upon as a declaration of war.

It is not the province of this narrative to deal with the causes of wars and that with Mexico is shrouded in many complexities. Stripped of all its camouflage, it appears to have been chiefly an experiment in imperialism on the part of President Franklin K. Polk and his administration.

Polk's eyes wandered far beyond Texas to New Mexico and California. The glory of expanding the United States from the Atlantic to the Pacific by the simple expedient of a little war with Mexico was too great a goal to quibble at the means employed. The jaundiced sentiment of the nation at large was eager to support him, despite the protests of the anti-slave party that the project's only objective was to increase slave territory. So Texas was annexed in 1845 and the threatened consequences were invited.

As a result of the extraordinary success of the American armies during the war the campaigns have been paraded as masterpieces of generalship on the part of the two American commanders, Winfield Scott and Zachary Taylor. As a matter of fact, with the exception of one brief period, the generalship was unqualifiedly atrocious, winning both Scott and Taylor eminent rank among the "fatal generals."

The American soldiers won in spite of their leaders, won because their native fighting ability shattered the Mexicans' morale and overcame the monumental blunders of their commanders.

When the war clouds thickened Scott was general-in-chief of the United States Army, but he was a Whig with presidential aspirations, so Democratic President Polk first sent Major General Zachary Taylor into the field. Later in the summer of 1845 he was ordered to Texas to defend the borders of the new addition to the country. In order to keep American skirts as clean as possible, he was instructed to wait until the Mexicans became irritated enough to strike an aggressive blow, thus placing on them the onus for starting hostilities. They obliged on April 25, 1846, when General Arista's force crossed the Rio Grande into Texas and captured a detachment of 60 dragoons under Captain Thornton. The war was declared under way immediately; Polk called for 50,000 volunteers, reinforcements were sent to Taylor and the drive began.

Zachary Taylor was an interesting son of destiny, thick-set as to figure with remarkably short legs and possessed of tremendous physical strength and endurance. He was 62 years old and had behind him 40 years of service, chiefly against the Indians. He had no education, was coarse and ungrammatical in speech and unkempt about his person and clothes to the point of being dirty. He delighted in his title of "Old Rough and Ready."

When he started for Texas, he had never seen a real battle, nor, for that matter, a real army. With a boundless, rough-hewn courage adapted only to rough-and-tumble fighting, he had no strategic sense whatever. He was almost wholly immune to suggestion, particularly from trained, educated officers, a class for which he had a species of contempt, and he never displayed the slightest ability to handle any reasonable body of soldiers.

He established his first camp at Corpus Christi, Texas, while waiting for Mexican passions to rise, and reported his troops as "healthy, remarkably well-behaved and very comfortable."* Actually, more than 20 percent of his force was on the sick list and more than half the rest were nearly ill. His camp was so poorly located that the water was three or four feet deep in some of the tents much of the time. He was so neglectful of fundamental necessities that the cooks often had too little firewood to prepare the meals and camp-fires usually were impossible, in a region where

* Stephenson, Nathaniel W.: *Texas and the Mexican War.*

temperatures varied from torrid to freezing within a few hours.

Taylor's military knowledge was so limited that he did not know how to get his men into line, an ignorance shared by most of his officers. This condition was so pronounced that all drills were abandoned and the men were left to idle their days and nights away. As conditions grew worse, many deserted and the majority of the rest spent their time in carousals. A host of gamblers and liquor dealers opened booths near the camp without restriction. Drugs were easy to obtain. Drunken orgies, narcotic stupors and continual brawling were the rule.

Ordered by the War Department to move toward Matamoros on the Rio Grande, in February, 1846, Taylor was so ignorant of the country in which he already had spent six months that he had to make extensive inquiries as to the road, and he was not ready to move for a month. Finally, after much laborious and poorly conducted maneuvering on his part, the first actual battle of the war was fought at Palo Alto, Texas, on May 8, a puny affair in which the opposing forces simply lined up and indulged in some miscellaneous gun-fire with little effect. Neither army was victorious. But the Taylor publicity began at once back home. An American triumph was reported because the Mexicans next day retreated a few miles to a ravine called Resaca de la Palma, a good defensive position helpfully protected by heavy growths of chaparral—a tangled type of brushwood covered with thorny spines.

Taylor sent his men against the ravine by a frontal movement. In the trying chaparral, the fighting was desperate, but he had no ideas to offer and simply told his troops to keep going. By sheer luck, Captain Charles May of the regular cavalry ran across a cleared path through the chaparral which led around the end of the ravine. Without instructions he followed it. When he emerged he discovered he was on the Mexican flank. On his own responsibility he ordered a charge which struck the Mexicans such a staggering blow, they were thrown into panic and fled in a wild stampede across the Rio Grande. Taylor had won his first accidental victory.

He was so astonished, he scarcely knew what to do but finally crossed the river and took possession of Matamoros. Arista's army was completely demoralized and could have been crushed by an immediate blow. Instead, Taylor stopped at Matamoros and made no further aggressive move for four months. Meanwhile, volunteers poured into his army but he was incapable of devising means of providing for them. The conditions of Corpus Christi were repeated with the added aggravation of a devastating fever which swept the camp and for which his medical facilities were entirely unequipped.

"The mortality in our camp," wrote one soldier, "was appalling. The dead march was ever wailing in our ears and I can scarcely look back to our stay there without a shudder. Large hospital tents were constantly full—the dead being removed at sunrise and sunset but to make room for the dying. The groans and lamentations of the poor sufferers during those sickly, sultry nights were heartrending."*

* Stephenson: *Texas and the Mexican War.*

Another eye-witness said the funeral dirge was heard so continually that even the birds could whistle it.*

In September Taylor decided to move again and set out for Monterey with about 6,000 effectives. This stronghold was on a plain surrounded on three sides by mountains and offered strong defensive possibilities of which General Ampudia, the new Mexican commander, took full advantage. To overcome him, Taylor's only plan was to divide his force.

The drive began on September 21 and continued uninterruptedly for three days. Few battles in history have been marked by more bungling. The two American forces acted independently without coördination or communication. At times Taylor was wholly out of touch with most of his army, while all his chief subordinates also piled blunder on blunder. But the conduct of the men in the ranks was above all praise. In the face of heavy fire they fought their way into the city, street by street, until they had Ampudia and his troops entirely surrounded in the center of the town.

Then, at one stroke, Taylor destroyed all the results for which his men had been sacrificed. Instead of demanding an unconditional surrender, he decreed an armistice and permitted the Mexican commander to march out of the city with his troops unmolested. In the three days' fighting, Ampudia's casualties were 367 killed and wounded while Taylor lost more than 1,000. But the American public was not told the truth. Even Taylor's official report of his casualties was a deliberate lie. The capture of Monterey

* Smith, Justin H.: *The War With Mexico*, Vol. I.

was hailed as a titanic achievement. Taylor was the hero of the hour and his presidential boom was launched.

But Polk, infuriated by Taylor's armistice fiasco, had lost all faith in this commander who was going nowhere except into the hearts of his countrymen. He became more disgruntled when Taylor now proceeded to indulge in an endless series of meaningless little attacks for which he scattered his army in small, exposed units over a 500-mile front. Back in Washington an entirely new plan was developed to invade Mexico from the eastern seacoast, and the President reluctantly ordered the ambitious Whig, General Scott, to take charge of this campaign, leaving Taylor where he was.

The new field commander, then 60 years old, was a curious composite of excellent and reprehensible qualities. In vivid contrast to Taylor, he was well-educated, something of a writer, an avid student of military tactics and had a brilliant mind which endowed him with unquestioned talent. To counteract this seriously, he was ruthlessly ambitious and vain as a peacock—an elderly fop. He loved resplendent uniforms and he appeared on horseback at every opportunity because he, too, had short legs and could not "tower" except in the saddle.

When he started south in January, 1847, he directed Taylor to send him a considerable portion of his force and take the rest back to Monterey, in a defensive position. The hero of the hour went into a rage at his subordination. He had to send the troops Scott demanded, but the retreat order he flatly refused to obey. Instead, with his force reduced to 4,718 men, he pig-headedly pushed far into the interior, despite reports that Santa Anna—once more at the head of Mexican affairs—was moving rapidly to attack him with 15,000 men. On February 21, Santa Anna almost trapped him, and he was forced to make a precipitate 12-mile retreat to the hacienda of Buena Vista, so hard pressed that he was able to remove only part of his supplies.

Buena Vista lay at the head of a mountain pass in the midst of a region of ravines and crevasses. Here Taylor made his only flight into grand strategy. He placed his force in a position where he could slaughter the Mexicans if they attacked him along the high road as he decided they should. But Santa Anna declined the invitation. To Taylor's complete chagrin, he swung his army through a series of shallow, lateral depressions which the American commander had left unguarded. Only the slothfulness of the Mexicans prevented disaster. While they were maneuvering into position on February 22, Taylor just managed to throw a slender line of men across the exposed quarter before night fell. He was far from safe but he left the field and rode to his base at Saltillo that night. He had not returned when Santa Anna attacked next morning.

The thin defensive line was hurled back, barely saved from annihilation and the Mexicans rushed on victoriously. At the moment when the battle seemed hopelessly lost, Taylor reappeared and found the one situation he was qualified to handle. Nothing remained now but a slam-bang fight for life and in this he gloried. Santa Anna helped him, foolishly confining his efforts to futile cavalry charges until Taylor had mustered his reserves. When the Mexicans finally attacked in force again, it was too late and they were pushed back.

When night came to end the day's fighting, the two

armies stood in almost exactly the same positions they had held twenty-four hours before. The net result had been nothing except dead and wounded men. Taylor had lost 673 killed and wounded, and nearly 1,800 of his men had quit the field during the first attacks when defeat seemed certain. He now had scarcely 2,500 men left, while Santa Anna still had more than 12,000. But once more the fighting qualities of the American soldiers had broken the Mexican nerve. Instead of renewing the attack next day, Santa Anna withdrew his force and returned to Mexico City, saving Taylor from the complete consequences of his folly which had cost so many lives in a battle which never should have been fought.

The hero worshippers back home knew nothing of this, however. When Taylor, to his dumfounded amazement, discovered his enemy was gone, he immediately sent dispatches announcing a tremendous victory. The country went wild with rejoicing and there was no question as to the presidential boom. It was Taylor's last appearance in the war. Somewhat chastened, he retired to Monterey and remained there.

On the eastern front, Scott's expedition began brilliantly. On March 9, he landed his force near Vera Cruz. By August 20, he had passed over the rugged, ever-rising mountain passes, had destroyed one Mexican army at Cerro Gordo and had driven another behind the fortifications of Churubusco, the last of the outer defenses of Mexico City itself, all with less than 650 battle casualties. Then, for no apparent reason, he suddenly abandoned his consistently successful and economic flanking methods and sent his army into a frontal attack. On the afternoon of August

20, in four hours' fighting, 1,000 men fell, almost twice as many as had been lost in the previous four and a half months. But the Americans won in spite of Scott's blunder and captured Churubusco and the 3,000 Mexicans who had been unable to escape.

Scott had Santa Anna at his mercy. Churubusco should have ended the war. Had it done so, the American commander's record would have been almost stainless. But now his political aspirations and his vanity overcame him and he attempted to demonstrate his ability in diplomatic fields.

Santa Anna applied for an armistice, reiterating his frequently voiced assertion that the Mexican people wanted immediate peace and he wished only the opportunity to take the matter up with them directly. In spite of the Mexican dictator's record for duplicity, Scott granted the armistice, instead of occupying Mexico City at once. During the two weeks of "negotiation," Santa Anna stealthily reconstructed his defenses and reorganized his beaten army. On September 7, he suddenly dropped his mask; Scott was exposed to the world as his dupe, and the Americans were forced to fight three more bitter engagements, the bloodiest of the war.

Furious over the position in which he had placed himself, Scott lost his head. At the foot of the hill of Chapultapec was Molino del Rey, a group of stone buildings occupied by a Mexican force. Hearing the place was used as a cannon foundry, Scott peevishly ordered its destruction at any cost.

Nearly 4,000 American men were hurled into this unpardonable attack against almost impregnable defenses.

They encountered desperate opposition. Assault after assault was repulsed and as the Americans fell back, one of the most savage incidents of the war occurred. Sallying from their position, the Mexicans rushed over the battle-field and ruthlessly murdered every wounded man they were able to reach. The sight drove the Americans to frenzy. They leaped into a wild forward rush which ignored all cost and swept forward until the Mexicans broke and fled. Then came the tragic revelation. The hard-won stone buildings were only stone buildings. There was no cannon foundry. One third of all the American officers and nearly 1,000 men were killed and wounded in the ghastly affair, their sacrifice entirely fruitless.

Its futility maddened Scott. Five days later, against every advice of his engineers, he ordered his army to storm the fortified heights of Chapultapec. The battle developed into a furious hand-to-hand struggle with tremendous losses, while the terraces literally ran with blood. But the Americans plunged eagerly into the fight. Thirsting for revenge for the murder of their comrades at Molino del Rey, they swarmed up the hill in the most desperate bayonet charge in American history, never equalled before or since, even in the World War. In their fury, they burst all bonds. The shouted commands of their officers were ignored. Every Mexican they saw was marked for slaughter. For a time the charging host gave no quarter, and every foe met was spitted again and again until his death was certain. The savagery of five days before was repaid with heavy interest. But again the Americans lost nearly a thousand men in a fight which was unnecessary.

In his mounting rage Scott now hurled his troops directly on, past conquered Chapultapec, and drove two columns through the gates of Mexico City itself. The next day, September 14, 1847, the whole capital was taken, and Santa Anna fled with the remnants of his force, to fight no more.

The peace treaty was signed February 2, 1848, establishing the southern boundary of the United States almost as it is today. Texas, Arizona, New Mexico and Upper California were lost to Mexico forever, and the United States extended from the Atlantic to the Pacific in fact. The experiment in imperialism had been an unqualified success.

The war had other effects. Once the lure of empire had been satisfied, the old schisms within the country were intensified. The quarrel which followed over the division of the Mexican spoils between the "slave" and "free" elements was the greatest single factor in solidifying the North and South into two distinct sections, violently opposed to each other.

By the irony of fate, it was the boorish, incompetent Taylor who was hoisted into the presidency on the tidal wave of Mexican war-hero worship and Scott, much more worthy, whatever his faults, had to swallow the bitter pill of ruined hopes. He returned to his post as general-in-chief of the United States Army. He still was there on the April day in 1861 when a gun was fired at Charleston, S. C., and the shell exploded against the walls of an island fort called Sumter, to launch the holocaust for which his Mexican victories had paved the way. It was a holocaust whose rivers of blood had never been equalled, whose fatal generals were so many and whose fatal blunders were so constant that only the most flagrant can be cited here.

13.

The Man Who Lost Bull Run

AN OLD MAN—a very old man—in a uniform was sitting in a tent, a few miles south of the Potomac River. He was not, as might have been imagined, decked out for a veterans' reunion. At the sprightly age of 69, he was a major general in the Army of the United States, commanding 15,000 men in the field. At the moment he was reading a message:

> "Washington, D. C.,
> "July 13, 1861.

"Major General Robert Patterson,
> "Commanding U. S. Forces at Martinsburg, Va.

"Sir—If not strong enough to beat the enemy early next week, make demonstrations so as to detain him in the valley of Winchester; but, if he retreats in force toward Manassas and it be too hazardous to follow him, then consider the route via Key's Ferry, Leesburg, etc.

> "WINFIELD SCOTT,
> "Lieutenant General."*

* Official Records of the Civil War.

The aged general shifted uneasily and passed the dispatch to the bushy-haired cavalry officer who sat across the table.

"I don't like that, Colonel Thomas," he said, in the thin voice of years. "I've told him the superiority of Johnston's force against us. I've told him the three-months enlistments of half my men will expire within ten days. Yet he sounds as if he expects me to attack or else rush this army to McDowell. He appears to think we have no obstacles in our path."

Colonel George H. Thomas read the message with thoughtful deliberation, his short, rather scraggly beard sunk on his chest. When he had finished he returned it to the general, his broad face utterly impassive.

"If I may be permitted to say so, general," he said quietly, "I don't think they are as serious as you believe. I am certain Johnston is not so strong as you think. My scouts are very reliable. They tell me there are no more than 10,000 of the enemy at Winchester. That means we are superior now and will be for another week at least. Much can be done in a week. I believe we can defeat Johnston. Certainly, we can keep him here in the valley until McDowell attacks Beauregarde."

General Patterson looked at him almost aghast. "And what would we do at the end of the week, after half our force is gone?" he exclaimed. "It would be suicide."

The deep-set eyes of Colonel Thomas gleamed curiously for a moment as he stared at Patterson, but there was no change in his tone as he replied, "If I may be pardoned for saying so, general, I believe a blow now would inspire most of the three-months men to reënlist." He leaned forward, slightly. "We can force Johnston to fight or submit to being held in the valley and keep ourselves in position to join McDowell in one move, sir. Johnston must go through Ashby's Gap. Well, so can we. If we extend our left sufficiently to bar the road to the Gap, we will accomplish our every purpose."

Patterson drummed nervously on the table. "The risk is entirely too great," he finally said with a touch of asperity. "We would only invite destruction. A demonstration we can make safely. We will move on Charlestown tomorrow. Farther we cannot go until we are heavily reinforced. You will prepare to advance your cavalry tomorrow morning."

Thomas arose, his stolid expression unaltered as he saluted, though his eyes were troubled. Then he turned and walked out at his never-varying leisurely gait, a stocky figure, just above medium height, wholly unimpressive, unconsciously masking the greatness which was to go unrecognized so long.

Outside Patterson's quarters, he untied his horse and mounted with the same deliberation, and set off at the jog which was his ultimate pace on horseback and won him the name of "Slow Trot" Thomas. He was never known to make a rapid physical movement in his life—an illusory slowness which often made others fail to note that he arrived everywhere and did everything on time.

He was more deeply perturbed than he cared to admit. He knew a priceless opportunity was being tossed to the winds, though he had no choice but to obey orders. The situation seemed so simple and clear. Major General Irvin McDowell had about 35,000 men at Washington, nearly all of them raw recruits, but they had been drilling for

more than two months and they were eager to fight. For the
Confederates, Brigadier General G. T. Beauregarde had
about 22,000 at Manassas Junction. General Joseph E. Johnston had 10,000 more at Winchester—Thomas would have
sworn there were no more than 10,000. If he were to join
Beauregarde before the approaching battle, the forces would
be almost equal but the Southerners were in better fighting
trim and, taking defensive positions, the odds would be
heavily in their favor. The godsend for the Union was
Johnston's presence in the Shenandoah Valley, when Patterson had 15,000 men on hand to keep him there, certainly long enough to prevent his joining Beauregarde. Patterson held the entire fate of the coming battle in his
hands—if he would only see and act while there was yet
time.

He did not. Since he had ventured across the Potomac,
a radical change had come over Patterson, which would
have been ludicrous had it not been so tragic in its poten-
tialities. He was a veteran of the War of 1812 and the
Mexican War. A Pennsylvanian, at the outset of the Civil
War he had leaped to arms once more, a bit creakily, but
he had been made major general of the Pennsylvania
volunteers. His force had increased so rapidly that, within
a few weeks, he notified Scott he had an army sufficient
to recapture Harper's Ferry then occupied by Johnston.

Scott not only took him at his word but sent him reinforcements, including the 5th U. S. Cavalry commanded
by Thomas, whereupon Patterson began writing prolific
letters to the general-in-chief as to the general demolition
of the enemy he was about to execute. Finally arrived at
Hagerstown, Md., enroute to the Shenandoah Valley—

after Johnston already had evacuated Harper's Ferry—he wrote, typically, on June 23:

"I shall not avoid the contest they may invite—indeed, if it meet with the approval of the general-in-chief, I would march my whole force upon the enemy and drive him step by step to Winchester. I believe this force can, in ten days, rid the adjoining portion of Virginia of its oppressors. I may be forced to this course. My fear is that I may inter- fere with the general plan of the general-in-chief and drive the enemy to the aid of the main body. *They would, how- ever, go as fugitives to aid in its demoralization!*"

There were many more such—until the army finally crossed the Potomac. Then all of the antique major gen- eral's optimism seemed to vanish. He made one or two feeble demonstrations and then stopped. When Thomas made a sudden cavalry attack and inflicted a smart defeat on a Confederate detachment, Patterson was proud but horrified—for fear a real battle might result.

Johnston retired comfortably to Winchester and made a great show of force and activity via the cavalry under Brig- adier General Thomas J. (not yet "Stonewall") Jackson. Patterson began wailing anew and exuded volumes of grief concerning the imminent departure of his three-months troops, moaning that he would not be able to keep them a day beyond their enlistment and completely forgetting that McDowell was faced with precisely the same situation.

On July 14 he finally did push on with the utmost cau- tion toward Charlestown. Thomas's cavalry caused him a great deal of worry. Thomas was trying desperately to keep in touch with Johnston's movements, though he was play- ing practically a lone hand, and every time he became encouragingly venturesome Patterson called him back in wild dismay for fear he would bring on a fight—which Scott had all but ordered him directly to do.

Back in Washington Scott was assuring McDowell that he had nothing to worry about so far as Johnston's joining Beauregarde was concerned. Patterson not only would force him into a fight or cut off his exit from the valley, but would be in a position to reinforce McDowell himself. But Scott became a bit worried. His general in the valley was still writing long letters, but each of them dealt almost exclusively with the impossibility of making an attack with an army whose enlistments would expire in a week. On July 17, the day before McDowell started his battle march, he wired Patterson rather curtly:

"Do not let the enemy amuse you and delay you with a small force in front whilst he reinforces the Junction with his main body."

Patterson was in the midst of his irritation over this message when Thomas came to him again, graver than usual, if possible.

"I beg of you, general," he said, "let us extend our line toward Ashby's Gap, now, before it is too late. I am certain Johnston is planning to leave at the earliest possible moment to join Beauregarde."

"Impossible," Patterson snapped. "His whole force is still before us and will stay there."

"Then will you permit me to make an extended reconnaisance toward the Gap, sir? I am convinced it is most important."

Patterson clasped his head and gestured wearily. "Oh, all

right, all right," he exclaimed. "But if you are trapped and annihilated, the fault will be yours."

"I will accept the responsibility, sir." Thomas saluted and went out. Before dark he was well on his way.

Patterson had an unhappy evening of it. Finally, at 1:30 in the morning, he sent another dispatch to Colonel E. D. Townsend, Scott's adjutant, repeating his distress over expiring enlistments and adding, "Some regiments have given warning they will not serve an hour overtime. To attack under such conditions against the greatly superior force is most hazardous."*

That ended Scott's patience. Back came a sizzling reply:

"I have certainly been expecting you to beat the enemy. If not, to hear that you have felt him strongly and at least have occupied him by threats and demonstrations. You have been at least his equal and, I suppose, superior, in numbers. Has he not stolen a march and sent reinforcements toward Manassas Junction? A week is enough to win victories. The time of volunteers counts from the day of muster into service. You must not retreat across the Potomac.

"WINFIELD SCOTT."

Patterson petulantly replied that no marches had been stolen and that he had done extraordinarily effective work in the valley. But he had scarcely sent it when a somber-eyed Thomas returned.

"We are too late, general," he said, a dreary note in his voice. "Johnston's whole force is pouring through Ashby's

* Official Records, Vol. II.

Gap at this moment. He is on his way to join Beauregarde."

The general stared at him glassy-eyed. "But that's impossible," he cried. "My scouts tell me he is still at Winchester."

"A handful of men—decoys," Thomas returned briefly.

"But there's nothing else we could do," Patterson protested. "Our men already are leaving as rapidly as their enlistments expire. We could not risk a battle."

Thomas gazed at him steadily for a moment. "I suppose not, sir," he said heavily. His pace was slower than usual as he walked away. Then he turned and came back. "Do you plan pushing on to join McDowell, sir?" he asked. "I fear this force will be needed."

"Certainly not," Patterson retorted. "This army is in no condition to move until it is reinforced itself."

Thomas bowed and said no more.

Patterson made no move to inform Scott of Johnston's escape until July 20, two days after the Confederate troops had left. Then he said, "With a *portion* of his force, Johnston left Winchester by the road to Millwood on the afternoon of the 18th. His whole force was *about 35,200*."*

But the angry Scott already knew and on July 19, he issued General Order No. 46, relieving Patterson of his command, to take effect July 27, although Patterson did not learn of this until after the Battle of Bull Run. The senile general fidgeted in his quarters for two days. Then, unable to think of anything else to do, he suddenly ordered his whole command to retire to Harper's Ferry. He arrived there July 21.

* Official Records.

July 21! Bull Run! Through all that blistering hot Sunday, the raw, untried troops of General McDowell had been giving a notable account of themselves—men fresh from offices, schools, factories and farms, hastily gathered, hastily drilled and armed, and as hastily sent into battle because the North demanded a battle. They had fought unflinchingly through all the hell of their first day under fire, under a blazing sun which sapped the strength of every man on the field, blue or gray. The tide had swayed back and forth, but the raw men of the North were pushing forward steadily. It needed only an extra ounce of strength, the encouragement of only a small reinforcement of fresh troops, to give them a sweeping victory.

A cloud of dust arose from the Shenandoah Valley road. McDowell watched it anxiously. If that were Patterson's force, coming at last, he could sweep the field. Beauregarde and Johnston, the latter having arrived alone a day earlier, also watched the dust cloud with strained eyes.

The grim fight went on, and then suddenly a wave of thundering cheers came from the Confederate ranks. McDowell stared and his soul went sick, as rank on rank of gray soldiers, dusty but unwearied, swept forward in a veritable flood and with them came Stuart's cavalry.

The tired Union men already had done more than anyone had dared hope. Utterly exhausted now, they could do no more. They fell back and back before this storm of fresh men. They did not break and run from the field in panic. History has done brave men no graver injustice than in the repetition of the oft-told tale of an army which fled from the heart of battle. The famous Bull Run panic began back among the supply trains. Here a throng of lighthearted congressmen and their gay feminine friends had ridden in carriages as though on a picnic to watch the crushing of the Confederacy.

When the tide of Stuart's cavalry was seen in the distance, it was these who went wild with fear and started on a screeching dash back toward Washington. Their fright was infectious. It spread to the supply soldiers who joined in the wild flight, many cutting the horses from their wagons and mounting them to hasten their escape. This maniacal confusion was at its height when the worn fighting men stumbled to the rear. Weary, disheartened at the loss of all they had struggled for through the day, they, too, were caught by the panic fever. But not until then did they fall into the disorder of the mad retreat to Washington.

Not many knew the real cause of the failure. But Scott, old as he was, knew, and in his fury he could wait no longer. At 1:30 on the morning of July 22, less than nine hours after the retreat from Bull Run had begun, he sent a peremptory message to Brigadier General Nathaniel P. Banks, at Baltimore:

"Proceed to Harper's Ferry and relieve General Patterson."

He could not wait until the 27th, when his general order would take effect. So General Patterson stepped out, three months and two weeks after the first shot had been fired. He was in the Civil War just long enough to change the entire course of events and chalk beside his name a mark that was not entirely black. It was tinged with dripping blood.

14.

The Napoleon of Fort Donelson

A LONG breathing spell followed Bull Run, with most of the fighting confined to small, unimportant engagements throughout the balance of 1861. The time was spent in a general girding for the real struggle. One of the least noticed events of the year, destined to have important results, was the promotion on August 17, 1861, of Colonel George H. Thomas of the 5th U. S. Cavalry to a Brigadier Generalship and his assignment to Kentucky. More conspicuous was the retirement of the aged General Scott on November 1, at his own request. His place was taken by the young, ambitious and extraordinarily popular George Brinton McClellan. In the South, General Robert E. Lee became the supreme director of military operations.

Curiously, during the first year of the war, the popular idol of the Confederacy was not Lee, Beauregarde or Joseph E. Johnston, but General Albert Sidney Johnston. He was a dashing figure, handsome, debonair, above six feet in height, with an active military bearing. With no par-

GEORGE H. THOMAS

ticular achievement to his credit, his intriguing personality had won him great adulation. As a result, when the western field of operations began to develop major importance at the end of 1861, he was placed in command there.

His first move was an attempt to seize control of Kentucky before the might of the northern forces had fully gathered, and he was making distinct progress when he received a sudden setback of major significance. On January 18, 1862, Brigadier General G. B. Crittenden, with 4,000 Confederates, staged a sudden attack on 2,500 Union men under the command of General Thomas at Mill Springs. He was on the verge of overwhelming them when Thomas appeared on the field. Trotting leisurely from regiment to regiment under a storm of fire, the Union commander deployed his heavily outnumbered force into more favorable positions and in less than two hours the whole state of affairs was reversed. Thomas beat back all attacks, then turned and struck hard. Three hours after the fight began, the Confederates were crushed and in full flight. Thomas pursued relentlessly and did not halt until Crittenden's entire force had been driven out of Kentucky.

At one blow Johnston's whole line of operations had been broken. He was forced to abandon Kentucky entirely and Nashville, Tenn., was endangered. Fearful that the Union forces would attempt to take the water route to that city, Johnston determined to make Fort Donelson on the Cumberland his first line of defense, while he shifted his base from Bowling Green, Ky., to the Tennessee capital. He had about 32,000 men under his immediate command. Early in February he sent 18,000 of them to the fort and assigned their operations to three brigade chiefs—John B. Floyd, Gideon J. Pillow and Simon B. Buckner.

It was an extraordinary combination. Floyd, the ranking brigadier, was a thick-lipped, heavy-featured individual, under indictment at Washington for corrupt practice as Secretary of War under President James Buchanan and for complicity in the embezzlement of public funds. Pillow was hawk-faced and narrow-eyed, by nature jealous, quarrelsome and insubordinate, and he had a bitter and long-standing personal animosity toward Buckner. Buckner himself was a striking contrast to the others, infinitely superior to them in every respect, character, personality, military knowledge and the ability to inspire confidence in his troops.

With this incongruous trio in command, Johnston optimistically expected his 18,000 to beat back all attacks and close the Cumberland pathway to the Union forces. Instead, they walked into an obvious wide-open trap. Even while the contingents were arriving, General Grant was only a few miles away advancing against them with 23,000 men.

When General Floyd arrived by boat on February 13, Grant's army already was closing around the three land sides of the stronghold, while Commodore Andrew Hull Foote's gunboat flotilla was approaching to cut off escape by the river. By morning of February 14, the fort was completely invested. During the afternoon the Confederate artillery defeated Foote's gunboats and wrecked two of them, but this was of little help to the garrison, as no boats were available for escape. In the evening Floyd called a council of war and expressed his belief that the fort could not be held successfully by less than 50,000 men.

"If we remain we are trapped," he declared. "Our only chance lies in cutting our way through Grant's army before he improves his position. His right wing is weak now. It may not be so a day or two hence. I propose that we drive through that wing tomorrow morning with a force sufficient to open the road to Charlotte and Nashville. That is our only hope of escaping to rejoin General Johnston."

The suggestion met with general approval. By the plan finally adopted, 10,000 men were to make the sortie. General Pillow was to take his entire division directly against the right wing, while Buckner held back the right of the Union center. If the dash was successful, Buckner was to cover the retreat of all the other forces in the fort and act as rearguard for the march to Charlotte.

The weather came to the sudden aid of the Confederates. During the day the temperature had dropped abruptly below the freezing point, accompanied by snow flurries which worked a severe hardship on the Union troops, many of whom were without tents. Early in the night a weird gale of terrific velocity began to blow, driving the temperature steadily downward while the dismal howling of the wind through the trees drowned all sound of the Confederate preparations. Even the rumbling of the heavy gun carriages went unheard. The entire 10,000 were lined up and ready for the attack, without an alarm having been raised.

At dawn, when Pillow advanced, the ground was covered with ice and snow, but this was much less inclined to hamper the assailants who were prepared for it than the unsuspecting men who were to be attacked. More luck came to the help of the Confederates. At five o'clock in the

morning Grant had gone six miles down the river to consult with Foote on one of the gunboats and his army was
temporarily without a chief. Moreover, the Union right was
weaker than Floyd had imagined. Brigadier General
John J. McClernand, holding that portion of the line, had
found it necessary to extend his lines until they were spread
out thinly and his troops were short of ammunition. Numb
with cold and wholly unsuspecting, the Union soldiers were
just rising from ice-caked beds. Not a company had fallen
in when the attack began.

Favored with all these auspicious circumstances, Pillow
began his drive. Shortly after six he struck McClernand's
advance line and rolled it back with the first rush. At the
second line the resistance began to stiffen, but the sheer
weight of the concentrated assailants carried them on.
They were halted again and again, but each time they renewed the attack and each assault found them nearer success. It was bitter, costly business. The Confederates could
only plunge directly forward in the face of a galling fire.
Men fell by the score, by the hundreds, their blood freezing
almost as quickly as it reddened the snow. But every moment made their sacrifice more worth while. The sallying
force was moving forward steadily, irresistibly. McClernand's men were cut to pieces, and when their ammunition
ran out they were helpless. Appeals for more cartridges
brought only the discouraging order to take the boxes from
the dead and wounded as no others were available. When
this meager supply was gone, the whole brigade was rolled
back. By eleven o'clock, the sortie was a complete success.
McClernand's shattered brigade was gone, Buckner was

holding back the Federal center according to schedule, and the road to Charlotte was open for the entire garrison.

Pillow was intoxicated by his success. In the exaltation of his vanity, he believed he had not merely done a workmanlike job of smashing through one brigade as planned, but had administered a crushing defeat to Grant's whole army. He felt himself a Napoleon who had executed a marvelous coup and must not pause until he had driven the enemy from the field.

Disdaining to consult Floyd, his superior officer, he took full command and spurred toward his old enemy, Buckner, who was firmly holding his position.

"What is the meaning of this shameful conduct?" he shouted. "Why do you stand here, doing nothing? We have the enemy at our mercy, while you waste precious minutes like a poltroon. Attack!"

Buckner reddened but kept his temper under control. "Attack?" he exclaimed. "I don't understand you, sir."

"I said 'Attack,'" Pillow bawled. "You have the opportunity to roll back the entire Yankee line. Attack! Now!"

"We are not here to do more than we have done," Buckner retorted angrily, "nor have we the right to do so until the garrison has safely left the fort."

"Garrison?" Pillow's face went purple. "You speak of saving a garrison when we can crush Grant's army. I order you to attack at once."

Buckner stared at Pillow incredulously. Then with his jaw set he saluted. "You are my superior officer, sir," he said curtly. "Yours is the responsibility." He whirled and set his force into motion.

Pillow galloped back to his own division, swung his

troops into line and ordered them forward. Then as the new attack began he called an aide to his side. Taking a slip of paper from his pocket, he rested it on his knee and wrote:

"General A. S. Johnston,
    "Nashville, Tenn.
"I have defeated Grant overwhelmingly. On the honor of a soldier the day is ours.

"Gideon J. Pillow
"Brigadier General."

He handed the message to the aide.

"Find the nearest telegraph station and send this at once," he ordered. He swung his horse about once more and hurried after his troops. He did not have to hurry far. His men were hurling themselves against fresh troops who had taken no part in the early-morning fight, and these stood like a stone wall. While the wearying Confederates beat futilely against them, the Union general, Lew Wallace, gathered some of McClernand's scattered forces and swung far to the right. By two o'clock in the afternoon the Charlotte road gap had been closed and the whole purpose of the sortie had been ruined. At three o'clock the whole Federal line was making a furious counter-attack, and half an hour later the Confederate force had been pushed behind the breastworks of the fort again. There were 3,000 men in gray who did not go back, 3,000 whose life-blood was pouring in the snow, their bodies freezing in the icy air, all fallen in vain.

The garrison was completely disheartened and lounged

about in gloomy silence waiting for the inevitable end. As night fell the officers began an even more somber council of war. Buckner was justifiably bitter.

"We have thrown away our chance," he declared. "We cannot escape now, nor are we strong enough to resist the assault which is certain to be made tomorrow by a force twice as large as our own."

"A little more aggressiveness by yourself," Pillow answered harshly, "and the attack would not have failed."

"It did not fail," Buckner retorted. "We opened the road. But—" he gestured futilely and turned to Floyd. "If General Johnston has not yet reached Nashville, I think we should continue our defense at the risk of complete destruction. His force, at least, must be saved."

"It is saved," Floyd said. "I received word today that all his troops have arrived at Nashville."

Buckner arose and paced the room for a moment or two, finally stopping before Floyd again, his face solemn. "Then, sir, it would be wrong to subject the army to a virtual massacre, when no good could result from the sacrifice. As general officers, when further resistance is unavailing, we owe it to our men to obtain the best terms of capitulation possible for them."*

Floyd moved uncertainly. "I think you're right, General Buckner," he said at last, "but I don't propose to surrender myself. You know what faces me in Washington. I can't afford to be taken prisoner. Two steamers will be here at daylight. I am going to leave on one of them and take aboard as many men of my division as possible."

"An excellent idea," Pillow interjected with a leer. "There

* *Battles and Leaders of the Civil War*, Vol. I.

aren't two persons in the Confederacy the Yankees would rather get their hands on than you and me. What do you think of my going with you?"

Floyd eyed him. "That's a question every man must decide for himself," he said coldly. "As for me, I consider it my duty to save as many of my troops as I can."

"And your own skin as well." Pillow laughed unpleasantly. "Well, I'll just save mine."

Buckner glared at them both with contempt. "You may do as you choose," he declared hotly, "but I conceive it my duty to stay with my men and share their fate, whatever it may be."

Pillow shrugged. "As you like. I'm going."

Shortly before dawn the expected steamers arrived and the two senior brigadiers left. For reasons never explained, Floyd calmly appropriated all the available transportation for his own particular command and crowded about 1,000 of his men aboard.

The next day Buckner surrendered unconditionally, and 14,000 men were sent to prison camps who might have been safe in Nashville.

15.

Grant Opens the Blood Gates

FORCED out of Kentucky by the Battle of Mill Springs, Johnston now found himself driven out of Tennessee by the disaster at Fort Donelson. While he had displayed little genius thus far, his subsequent actions were marked by real wisdom. He accepted the full consequences of his previous debacles at once, abandoned Nashville, gathered up all the scattered detachments of his force, and retreated rapidly until he reached Corinth, Miss., where he was sure he was safe.

While he was rehabilitating his army there, the Union chieftains made further plans to annihilate him. After the fall of Donelson, Major General Don Carlos Buell, commander of the Department of the Ohio, occupied Nashville with 25,000 men. Grant's Army of the Tennessee, about 20,000 strong, moved along the river for which it was named, until it reached Savannah, where headquarters were established. Most of the army went nine miles farther to Pittsburg Landing, only twenty miles from Corinth,

to establish a base for operations against the Memphis &
Charleston Railroad, Johnston's chief means of transport
for soldiers and supplies. It then was decided to use Savannah as the concentration point for a new drive against
Johnston. Buell was to bring his army from Nashville,
while Grant's force was to be greatly enlarged by the addition of newly recruited regiments. When the combined
armies totalled approximately 70,000 men, Johnston was to
be crushed.

This noteworthy plan appears to have been made without
consulting General Johnston who had been doing rather
well since he reached Corinth. He started with some soldiers of his own. Then General Beauregarde was sent as
his second in command and immediately began scouring
the country for some more soldiers. He found them. Next
General Braxton Bragg arrived with 10,000 reinforcements.
By the end of March Johnston had about 41,000 effectives
under his command. Also, he was thoroughly awake.

Among the other things which Buell and Grant apparently failed to consult in the grand plan for demolishing
Johnston, were a map and a clock. One glance would have
shown that the distance between the Confederate army of
41,000 and Grant's much smaller force was only twenty
miles, while Grant's only reinforcements at Nashville were
120 miles distant as the crow flies and considerably more
as the soldier walks. Likewise that it would take Buell six
times longer than Johnston to reach Grant. Nor does it
seem to have occurred to any of the Union leaders that
Johnston might not wait to be crushed, but might attempt
some crushing of his own before the opposing army was
too large.

Everything about the Federal plan and its execution appears to have been done without considering Johnston as anything except a prospective and passive victim. No one feared anything. No one was in a hurry.

Buell started to leave Nashville on March 15. With his divisions spaced six miles apart, his army extended over forty miles of highway. It took him eight days to cover the fifty miles to Columbia. Here he found that the bridge over the Duck River had been burned, so he stopped to rebuild it, the work being entrusted to the vanguard division of Major General A. D. McCook. After four days it still was unfinished, and McCook ordered a pontoon bridge constructed. Two days later this had not been finished, either.

Only one man in Buell's army was perturbed by this dilatoriness. The fiery giant, Major General William Nelson, commanding the second division in the line, was restlessly uneasy. Never an equable soul, he chafed with impatience under the continued delay. An intimate friend of Buell's, he daily pleaded for more haste, and finally received permission to take the advance with his own division.

On the morning of March 29, he forded the river and started for Savannah by forced marches. Behind him, Buell took matters casually. The bridges were finished on March 30, and the leisurely forward movement was resumed.

The activities at Pittsburg Landing were much more extraordinary. Grant was serenely indifferent to the possible actions of the Confederates. The fixation in his mind was that he was to be the aggressor, regardless of circumstances or comparative strength, and this conception governed his every move.

His first curious decision was to concentrate at Pittsburg Landing rather than Savannah. The latter town was on the east side of the Tennessee River, Pittsburg Landing was on the west. That is, at Savannah he would have had the river between himself and any sudden movement of the enemy. At the Landing he had the river at his back, a situation with disconcerting possibilities if anything unpleasant happened. Then when he began to assemble his growing army there, he made no provisions whatever to protect it. No breastworks were built, no trenches dug. The soldiers simply pitched their tents and spent their days drilling. That the soldiers needed drill there was no question. All the incoming regiments were absolutely raw. Many of them had started for Pittsburg Landing with no equipment whatever, and received their guns while on the way.

In the face of this, Grant's disposition of his troops was peculiar. His army faced to the south and west, in the general direction of Corinth and was distributed between the river and Shiloh Church, about two miles west of Pittsburg Landing.

The church was considered the key position, and this was given to General Sherman, but Grant sent only his rawest troops to make up Sherman's division. On the extreme left wing, farthest south and therefore most exposed, he placed the division of Brigadier General Benjamin M. Prentiss. Not only were Prentiss' troops entirely untrained, but Prentiss himself was wholly inexperienced. He had been in the service only a month or two and had never seen a battle. Back nearer the river was McClernand and his well-tried division, with Brigadier General Stephen Hurlbut's semi-experienced troops and the battle-tested division of General C. F. Smith in reserve. The hardy veterans of Lew Wallace were stationed at Crump's Landing, five miles north of Pittsburg. In other words, Grant's most exposed troops were his least trained and least disciplined. His tried and proved veterans were farthest from the front line. It was a troop disposition worthy of Horatio Gates.

Grant conducted his personal efforts on a "day labor" schedule. Although his troops were at Pittsburg Landing, he continued his headquarters at Savannah, nine miles away, where more comforts were to be had. Each morning his dispatch boat carried him to Pittsburg landing. Each night, the day's work finished, he steamed back to Savannah.

Grant paid little attention to Johnston's activities. He did some perfunctory scouting which only increased his confidence. Johnston was not so indifferent. He knew the lay of the land, Grant's strength and the movements of Buell. He decided to strike before Buell could arrive.

On April 2 he started his army on its way, but when a portion of his advance troops became entangled in some vigorous skirmishing with reconnoitering troops which had ventured far from the Shiloh camp, he almost lost hope of a surprise attack. He need not have worried. Both Grant and Sherman were sublimely immune to the warnings received.

While this splendid serenity continued, Nelson was making his furious dash to the rescue, but on April 4 he began to wonder if he was not making a fool of himself, for he received the following dispatch:

"To The Officer Commanding Buell's Advance:
 "There is no need of haste; come on by easy stages.
     "U. S. Grant,
                    "Major General, Commanding."

Nelson momentarily regretted his headlong drive, but his latent uneasiness returned and he decided to pay no attention to the message. He pushed on, and at noon of April 5, Colonel Jacob Ammen's brigade marched into Savannah. Nelson immediately sought out Grant and expressed his fears, but the commander was extremely deprecating.

"There's nothing to worry about," he said. "Give your men a good night's rest. Get a guide tomorrow morning and march your division up the east bank of the river. You can cross over as soon as Sherman picks out a place for you. There will be no fight at Pittsburg Landing. The battle will be at Corinth."

Dissatisfied, Nelson went to his own quarters. A little later General Buell appeared, having ridden ahead to prepare the way for his oncoming divisions. But he was tired and so was Grant. The two commanders did not meet that evening. However, before he went to bed, Grant took time to write to Major General Halleck, at St. Louis, "I have scarcely the faintest idea of an attack."

At the same hour General Sherman at Shiloh Church was writing to Grant in the same cheerful vein:

"The enemy is saucy, but got the worst of it yesterday

and will not press our pickets far. He has some cavalry in front; I think there are two regiments of infantry and one battery of artillery about two miles out. I will not be drawn out far unless with certainty of advantage and I do not apprehend anything like an attack on our position."*

Sherman was right about the two regiments of infantry and the battery of artillery, but it was a slight understatement. There were several other Confederates about. Johnston had his entire 41,000 drawn up in battle array and no one in the Union camp knew anything about it!

But, just as Buell had one uneasy general, so too did Grant—the wholly inexperienced Prentiss, who felt an uncanny foreboding and could not subdue his restlessness. On Saturday, April 5, he saw a curious phenomenon which set him thinking deeply. All during the day he noted an unusual number of squirrels and rabbits flitting through the woods, all moving in one direction—away from Corinth and toward Pittsburg Landing. He could not help thinking that this single-hearted migration might be caused by the advance of a large body of men.

In his vague unrest Prentiss determined to take every possible measure against surprise. That night he ordered his pickets to take their posts a mile and a half in front of his lines, an almost unheard-of distance. Still he was not satisfied. He could not sleep. At three o'clock on Sunday morning, April 6, he came to a sudden decision and sent Colonel David Moore with three companies of the 21st Missouri regiment on a reconnoitering expedition.

* *Official Records.*

At a quarter past five, while his widely spread men were moving forward cautiously, Colonel Moore heard the sharp sound of firing at the extended picket line. Pulling his force together, he hurried forward. The firing became more brisk, and ten minutes later he met the retreating pickets carrying their wounded, pursued by a wave of gray-clad men. Throwing themselves behind trees and bushes, Moore's men opened fire instantly—and the Battle of Shiloh was on.

Only three hundred strong, the Missouri men held back the enemy for a full hour, yielding ground stubbornly and putting up such a furious defense that Major James Hardcastle, commanding the Confederate vanguard, reported that he had battled more than a thousand men. Then they slowly fell back, but they and Prentiss had done their work well. Johnston's hoped-for surprise had been averted, and Grant's army was given a slender chance for life.

More elements of Prentiss' division came up, and their obstinate resistance slowed down Johnston's entire attack. Not until eight o'clock was he crashing against the whole Federal line, and by that time portions of the Prentiss division had been fighting savagely for nearly three hours.

Despite the delay, Johnston struck with terrific force and Grant's curious choice of his front-line troops bore immediate fruit. Prentiss' raw men displayed exceptional staying power in the face of murderous fire, but Sherman's regiments failed miserably. While their general raged, whole companies threw down their arms at the first shot and raced madly for the river, where they took trembling shelter below the high bank at Pittsburg Landing.

Others joined them as the day wore on, but the majority

of the Federals fought desperately. Caught in the trap of Grant's blundersome devising, they battled for their lives, forced back and ever back. They lost their tent lines, artillery, supplies—but they kept on fighting with a wild fury that drenched the field in slaughter such as the nation had never seen.

The commanding general reached the field late. He was having a quiet breakfast at Savannah when the roar of distant firing jolted him from his usual complacency. Jumping up from the table, he boarded his dispatch boat at once and went steaming up the river. Still convinced that a general engagement was impossible, he thought Wallace's isolated division at Crump's Landing had been attacked, but when he stopped there, all was quiet. Wallace had his men ready to move, but Grant still was unperturbed.

"I don't think it's a general fight," he said. "I don't see how it could be. Johnston's at Corinth. Just some heavy skirmishing, I imagine. However, keep your men ready. If it's anything serious, I'll let you know."

His first violent jolt came when he approached Pittsburg and saw thousands of men cowering behind the bank. All doubt as to the real nature of the situation was gone. He leaped on horseback, galloped to the front, and after his first glimpse of the action sent an order to Lew Wallace to bring up his division at once.

With Wallace and Nelson both at hand, Grant felt confident he could turn the tide. But Wallace and Nelson did not come. Throughout the day the murderous fight went on, with the Union men falling back, always back. As the afternoon passed Grant sent officer after officer to learn what had happened to Wallace, and finally one galloped back with the word that Grant's order had not been conveyed clearly to the divisional chief, that he had taken the wrong road, had counter-marched and now was advancing so slowly he could not reach the field before night.*

Grant looked at the courier stolidly. "He counter-marched—he's coming slowly," he muttered as if unable to credit his ears. "Great God, what does he think this is?" Turning to Colonel J. D. Webster, his staff artillery commander, he ordered, "Station all your siege guns before the Landing. Surround them with every piece of artillery you can gather."

Webster hastened to execute the command, and as sunset approached these field pieces were all that stood between Grant's army and annihilation.

Tragedy struck the gray army when General Johnston was killed during the afternoon, but Beauregarde took immediate command and drove on relentlessly. By a desperate rush the Confederates finally broke through the Union left late in the day and surrounded the remnants of the courageous Prentiss division. They fought to the last, but at 5:30 were compelled to surrender, and 2,000 more men had been lost to Grant.**

* The bitter dispute concerning the order to Wallace raged violently for more than twenty years after the war and it never has been settled satisfactorily. The various versions offered by the principles—Grant, Wallace, Grant's adjutant and the dispatch bearer himself—are most conflicting on essential points. The only possible conclusion is that the whole matter was handled very badly.

** As a reward for his heroic salvation of Grant's army, Prentiss was subjected to a cruel libel. After the battle newspapers every-

ULYSSES S. GRANT

Just before sundown, when the situation of Grant's army seemed utterly hopeless, Colonel Ammen's brigade of Nelson's division suddenly arrived and hurried across the river, with Nelson himself in command. They threw themselves into line just as the Confederates swept forward in a final assault which seemed certain of success. But Nelson's limited force held. The Confederates crashed against it futilely and fell back broken. It was their last attempt.

Nelson was entirely blameless for his delay in reaching the field. In the absence of a direct road from Savannah, his men had been forced to slosh their way through swampy areas. Only by pushing desperately did they reach the battle of April 6 at all.

The day had been a horrible one for Grant. He had begun with 38,000 men, but Wallace's division of 5,000 had no part in the battle at all. Of the remaining 33,000, more than 10,000 raw recruits had fled from the field and taken shelter at the river bank. Against Johnston's 40,000, the great part of the battle was fought by less than 25,000 Union soldiers. And, of these, Grant lost 11,000—almost fifty per cent. More than 2,000 had been captured. Nearly 9,000 others lay on the field.

The night which followed was one of horror. Early in the evening a terrific downpour of rain began. The scattered fragments of Grant's division drooped over their arms without tents, shelters or supplies of any kind. And all through the hours of darkness the wails and moans of the

---

where throughout the North announced that Prentiss' men had been captured in their beds in the first Confederate rush of the morning. No amount of refutation wiped out the persistent calumny, and Prentiss was forced to submit to the stigma for decades.

wounded, lying helpless under the drenching storm, made the night hideous.

Shortly after dark Lew Wallace came up with his division. During the night A. D. McCook's division of Buell's army arrived, and General Thomas L. Crittenden's division came in the early morning. The fresh troops gave the Federals the upper hand. His own decimated ranks restored to a semblance of order, Grant struck back with every soldier at hand on the morning of April 7. For hours the battle continued, but by three o'clock the Confederates had been driven back past the farthest Union outposts of the previous day and were in full retreat.

Johnston had 40,000 men on the field at the beginning of the fight. Grant had 33,000. Wallace's 5,000 and the 20,000 from Buell's army raised the total Federal forces in the two days' fight to 58,000. Of the 98,000 men engaged on both sides, 23,746 were lost in the bloody shambles. The casualties of the Union forces were 13,047 in killed, wounded, captured or missing. The Confederate loss was 10,699 in killed, wounded and missing.

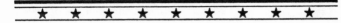

★ ★ ★ ★ ★ ★ ★ ★ ★

16.

Gun Fodder Heaped High

AN INCREDIBLE farce now began in the Federal army. A few days after the Battle of Shiloh Major General Henry W. Halleck, department commander of all the western troops, arrived to take personal command of future operations. Halleck, an elderly, arrogant lump of self-esteem, had been directing matters in a general way from his headquarters in St. Louis, and undoubtedly he was the greatest "paper" general on the northern side. During the entire war he was in the field for only two and a half months, the period upon which he now entered.

Beauregarde had retreated swiftly to Corinth, to begin a rapid rebuilding of his force until it numbered 60,000. In keeping with his own showy plans, Halleck waited to begin his pursuit until he had the largest army of the war to date, 120,000 men. Then he began his "drive" on Corinth —a foot at a time. A dozen shots in front would make him stop for hours, even days. He had a nightmare fear of a Confederate attack—by a force he outnumbered two to one.

It took him a month to advance twenty miles and when he finally "assaulted" Corinth he found it empty. The entire Confederate army had escaped. Halleck reported a tremendous victory.

Curiously enough, on paper, his own favorite medium, Halleck appeared to have done great things in the west. Within a few months the Confederates had been driven out of Missouri, Kentucky and western Tennessee, and had been compelled to abandon a considerable portion of Mississippi. It looked impressive. But Halleck had had little to do with the victories in Missouri and Arkansas. He had had nothing to do with the Kentucky campaign which had been conducted by Buell before he was under Halleck's domination. He had violently opposed Grant's plans to capture Forts Henry and Donelson which drove the Confederates out of Tennessee. He had contributed his share to the near disaster at Shiloh and had permitted Beauregarde's army to escape from Corinth.

As a reward Halleck was summoned to Washington to become general-in-chief of all the Union armies! He took the post on July 11, 1862, and held it until March 12, 1864, when Grant became the Union overlord. In the interim Halleck was the consistent evil genius behind the blundering Union movements which cost countless thousands of lives.

When he took command the eastern situation was in the doldrums, so far as the Union was concerned. McClellan's long Peninsular Campaign against Richmond had floundered through to failure and the Army of the Potomac was resting on its heels. Then Lee sent "Stonewall" Jackson with 24,000 men into the Shenandoah Valley and Halleck decided to dispose of him.

His first move was to organize a new Army of Virginia and place Major General John Pope in command. Halleck increased the force by drawing heavily on McClellan, until Pope had nearly 70,000 men. When Lee saw McClellan's efforts thus brought to a stand-still he took the bulk of his army and joined Jackson in the valley, assuming personal command. His total force numbered about 50,000.

General Pope signalized his rise to power by issuing a proclamation which was strangely reminiscent of those of General Alexander Smyth in the War of 1812. Said he:

"I have come to you from the west, where we have always seen the backs of our enemies; from an army whose business it has been to seek the adversary and to beat him when he was found; whose policy has been attack and not defense. I presume I have been called here to pursue the same system. . . . It is my purpose to do so and that speedily. I desire to dismiss from your minds certain phrases which I am sorry to find so much in vogue amongst you. I hear constantly of 'taking strong positions and holding them,' of 'lines of retreat' and of 'bases of supplies.' Let us study the probable lines of retreat of our opponents and leave our own to take care of themselves. Let us look before us and not behind. Success and glory are in the advance, disaster and shame lurk in the rear. . . . Your banners shall be inscribed with many a glorious deed and your names will be dear to your countrymen forever."

The army was greatly heartened by this effusion—the

Confederate army, that is. When he heard of it Lee had the measure of his opponent and acted accordingly. Pope's campaign began on July 14. It continued until September 1, when his army was disbanded—by General Lee. From the start Pope was like a child in the hands of Lee and Jackson. They outmaneuvered him at every turn, and he floundered about frantically, making worse blunders with each move, while Halleck's constant confusing orders helped to keep him in continuous hot water. He had no complaint to make of his troops.

Six battles were fought. The first was at Cedar Mountain on August 9. In the next twenty days four more engagements occurred, each finding Pope in a worse position, forced to scramble for escape from an enemy he outnumbered by 20,000, and on August 29 he was back on the old battleground of Bull Run with the opportunity to redeem the first debacle of the war. Here was staged the sixth and last battle of the campaign.

It lasted for two days and developed from a battle into a slaughter. By evening of August 30, Pope's entire army was crushed in one of the worst Union defeats of the war, his troops scattered to the four winds. In twenty-one days he had lost 14,462 men.

The tide of futile bloodshed for 1862 was rising, but there was more to come. After Pope's disaster the harassed man in the White House told Halleck to restore McClellan to command in the east, since there seemed no one else in sight, and in less than three weeks the idolized general was given the great opportunity of his career.

Encouraged by his startling success against Pope, Lee made his first daring attempt to invade the North. He swooped down on Harper's Ferry, and in two days had captured it and 12,500 prisoners. Then with less than 37,000 men he dashed over into Maryland. McClellan advanced with 87,000, threw himself across the Confederate path, and met his foe at Antietam on September 17.

Lee seemed in a hopeless position. His ragged army was hemmed in on one side by Antietam Creek, on another by the broad Potomac, and before him lay a powerful army more than twice the size of his own. He determined to fight for his army's life, and when McClellan hurled his forces into the attack there followed one of the bloodiest days in American history. But it was war—legitimate war. Lee cannot be blamed for attempting to move the battleground from the South to enemy territory, and McClellan was there to stop and crush him.

McClellan failed. After a day of savagery the best he could do was to retain possession of the battlefield, after losing 12,000 men. Lee had lost the same number, more than 30 percent of his entire troops.

McClellan's opportunity still lay before him. He had the enemy trapped with a force which now outnumbered Lee's three to one. The stage was set to wipe out the Confederate army, a stroke which unquestionably would have ended the war and the sacrifice of 12,000 men would have been worth while. Instead, McClellan transformed his loss into futile waste. After the battle he did not move—he did nothing while Lee extricated himself from his dangerous position, crossed the Potomac and dashed back into Virginia without the loss of a man.

McClellan's apologists have insisted his army was tired and needed a rest. That Lee's force might have been weary,

too, seems not to be considered. As a matter of fact, Mc-
Clellan's huge army came to the battlefield fresh, while
Lee's men had been maneuvering at top speed for more
than two months, at one time so footsore and lacking in
shoes that two brigades were unable to drag themselves
into battle during the latter days of Pope's campaign.
Through the threads of McClellan's own explanation there
is the obvious display of a small-mindedness which pre-
ferred to take no risks for a coup whose failure might
endanger his own command. He had won the semblance
of a victory and demanded that this be satisfactory. Actually, he had chosen the one course of action which did lose
him the command. His titanic failure blotted him abruptly
out of the war picture. Lincoln ordered him relieved of
command, and Major General Ambrose E. Burnside was
elevated to his place.

The appointment of Burnside was one of the ghastliest
blunders of the war. He appealed to officialdom because
he had demonstrated great aggressiveness in subordinate
positions. He contrasted McClellan's super-caution with
utter recklessness.

His army was reorganized. New troops were added. His
force was raised to 122,000 men and he started in pursuit
of Lee. Through October and November of 1862, he undertook to outmaneuver the greatest maneuvering genius
of the war. Then he decided to make a flank movement
toward Fredericksburg. He was on the wrong side of the
Rappahannock River, but Halleck had promised to send
him plenty of pontoons. Halleck failed—as usual—and
the pontoons did not arrive.

Burnside still could have crossed by the fords, as the

water was low, and, once in possession of the heights beyond Fredericksburg, he could have afforded to wait. But his recklessness did not include this particular type of precipitation. He sat down and waited for Halleck's pontoons. While he still was waiting Lee grasped the golden opportunity. By forced marches he, instead of Burnside, rushed across the Rappahannock, and it was he who occupied the heights. He gathered 74,000 men, erected impregnable defenses, and then he took his turn at waiting, justifiably content to do so.

Burnside suddenly awoke to the necessity for action and sent out his engineers to build bridges for the crossing of the river. The work required three days, during which Lee poured an incessant hail of fire upon the engineering force, killing and wounding hundreds of men engaged in a task which could have been performed without a single casualty a week or two before.

Now Burnside went mad. He knew the fighting qualities of Lee's troops in open battle, to say nothing of their power behind breastworks. He knew Lee's position was impregnable. But he had plenty of men to waste in a desperate effort to undo the costly results of his dallying, even though the effort smacked of nothing but murderous insanity. He listened to no one's advice, though his corps commanders, Joseph Hooker, Edwin V. Sumner, George G. Meade and William B. Franklin, protested violently against the assault he planned. He sent his army across the river—the largest single army ever gathered on American soil—and on the morning of December 13 ordered it to commit suicide by driving against the Confederate works.

The horror which followed had no precedent and it was

to have only one parallel—destined to come eighteen
months later. The Confederates simply awaited the uphill
charge of the blue lines until they were within two hundred yards of the breastworks, then unleashed a hail of
death which no force in the world could withstand. Thousands were mowed down like grass. The fragments of the
Union line rushed the outer works of the Confederates,
clung there desperately for a few moments and then went
reeling back.

The Union men re-formed, new men came to join them,
and once more they were hurled against the heights, while
fallen men blanketed the hills. Once more they were
thrown back, but Burnside was not content. He had 50,000
more pieces of gun fodder than the gray leader on the
heights above. He determined to use them.

Four times he ordered his might against the unbreak-
able barriers, and four times it rolled back through crimson rivers of blood. A fifth attack was ordered, but it moved
slowly, slowly because the slopes were so thick with the
dead and dying that the advancing men could not move
without treading on the mangled bodies of those who had
already been cut down. Not a man reached the line of
fire whose shoes were not red with the life-blood of the
bodies over which he stumbled.

There was no yielding on the hilltops. The lines of blue
staggered back again to the banks of the Rappahannock,
while Burnside fumed. A fierce winter wind suddenly arose
from the north, sweeping the field of death with its bitter chill. And still the lines of blue stood in battle array,
shivering in the cold.

Burnside refused to admit defeat—and he still had plenty

of men. He sent more troops to the vanguard, and late in the afternoon he ordered the sixth assault. Once more the soldiers by the river advanced into the mouth of hell.

They found the bodies of their fallen comrades frozen stiff as they plunged over them, and grisly inspiration came—a ghoulish move for self-preservation. They snatched up the dead men from the ground, carried the bodies before them, stacked them in long piles. Behind these ghastly breastworks of human flesh they fought with the desperation of madmen, but there was no escape. Lee's flanks swung out and poured death into their ranks no matter how high the corpses were piled. The crescent hills blazed and roared with unceasing fury and only darkness at last brought an end to the unspeakable carnage.

The macabre drama was not yet ended. As dusk came the Union men still on the slopes raised the frozen bodies of their dead comrades, stood them erect as dummy sentries all along the outer battle line, left them leaning against the piles of their fellow cadavers. Then under cover of night the living slipped back down the hill, through Fredericksburg, across the Rappahannock, broken, crushed, in horror and defeat.

History records that Burnside spent a terrible night of remorse, that he stood in his quarters wringing his hands and crying, "Oh, those men over there, all those dead men!" Yet next morning he called his generals together and sent a new chill through them by ordering that the assault be renewed. It was the only suggestion he had to offer for undoing the previous day's slaughter.

The sharp-faced slender Hooker, always Burnside's jealous antagonist, exploded in fury.

"Are you utterly mad?" he shouted. "Do you want to wipe out the entire army?"

Burnside's chubby features flamed. "The enemy has been weakened," he retorted. "And we still outnumber him by more than 30,000."

"You wish to equalize the forces, no doubt," Hooker exclaimed bitingly. "We left 13,000 men on those hills yesterday. Lee lost only a fraction of that number. Why not? He was on the hilltops where we should have been two weeks ago."

"This is no time to regret the past," Burnside thundered, his long side whiskers quivering. "We are here to win now."

But even the calm, steady-eyed Meade protested vigorously. "A renewed assault today would be an even more disastrous mistake than that of yesterday."

Burnside whirled on him. "Then you, too, consider yesterday's affair a mistake," he barked with asperity. "You seem to forget we are here to wipe out the enemy."

"But not to be wiped out ourselves," Meade replied evenly. "I do consider the attack a tragic error. I thought so before we undertook it and told you so. But I am not in command of this army."

"You are right—you are not." Burnside leaned forward. "I am, and it is my will that we renew the attack."

At this, the elderly gray-bearded Sumner leaped to his feet. His was a tall, spare figure and every line of it, to the seams in his wrinkled face, was taut, while his eyes flashed as he exclaimed, "Issue that order and you find not only the men in the ranks but their generals refusing to obey."

A. E. BURNSIDE

Burnside looked at him in startled amazement. His jaw dropped. He drummed nervously on the table as he looked about the group before him, every face a picture of hostility. At last he cleared his throat.

"Your assertion, General Sumner, sounds dangerously insubordinate," he said, "but I am going to overlook it. Your corps suffered greatly." He hesitated, then went on. "The sentiment seems to be unanimous against the plan which I believe offers the only means of redeeming our defeat. Very well. The attack will not be renewed."

The depression of the Union camp was overwhelming in the days which followed. Burnside sank into deep melancholy while his generals divided into warring factions, and the rank and file of the fighting men fell into a discouraged hopelessness. Burnside finally wrote to Halleck asking to be relieved of command. At the same time he assumed full responsibility for the slaughter at Fredericksburg. But the generous assumption was of comparatively little help to the men who had died on the heights.

17.

Even General Lee

FREDERICKSBURG came in December, 1862, but the butchery was not ended for the year. Since the troops in the east were exhausted, it remained for those in the west to round out the year's crimson record. There had been changes since Halleck left the western front. Beauregarde had given way to the obstreperous Braxton Bragg in command of the Confederate forces, and Bragg had indulged in his prolonged race over the landscape with Don Carlos Buell, a race which covered 1,400 miles and accomplished nothing except the mutual exhaustion of the armies.

Through it all, the quiet figure of General Thomas had moved on steadily, entirely unassuming, performing brilliant feats and apparently distressed if anyone mentioned them conspicuously. Unquestionably, the greatest single obstacle to Thomas's advancement was his excessive modesty. His passion for shunning the limelight was almost an obsession. In council he was consistently self-effacing.

His voice had the soft modulation of his native Virginia, but so great was his reticence that it was seldom heard. He never spoke unless he had something to say, and then voiced his opinions so quietly that their excellence was rarely realized except in retrospect.

His temperament was beyond compare. He had the patience of a saint, and even under the most violent provocation he was never known to lose his temper. Utterly imperturbable, he went on from achievement to achievement, not caring who received the glory so long as the end was accomplished.

He commanded a boundless affection from his troops to whom he was universally known as "Pap" Thomas, and his care of their welfare did demonstrate considerable parental solicitude. In his personal relationships he held the deep admiration and respect of all who were privileged to know him well, and his own loyalty to his friends was almost a fault at times, as he showed in the fall of 1862.

Whatever Buell's qualities, and he had many which were excellent, he was not a success and had completely lost the confidence of his army. In September Halleck decided on a change. He wired Thomas, directing him to relieve Buell of his command.

Thomas was greatly distressed. He was extremely fond of Buell and believed in his ability, convinced that circumstances and the eternal hampering hand of Halleck had been the chief instruments in his lack of success. Therefore, he went directly to Buell and told him what had happened, adding, "I am refusing the command."

Buell was touched but said, "If you are doing this because of your friendship for me, I cannot permit it for a moment, General Thomas."

"I will let you judge for yourself," Thomas replied. "Here is the answer I am sending to General Halleck." He extended the dispatch and Buell read:

"Major General Henry W. Halleck,
    "General-in-Chief, U. S. Armies.

"Sir—Col. McKibbin handed me your dispatch placing me in command of the Department of Tennessee. General Buell's preparations have been completed to march against the enemy, and I, therefore, respectfully ask that he may be retained in command. My position is very embarrassing, not being as well informed as I should be as the commander of this army and on the assumption of such a responsibility.

"GEORGE H. THOMAS,
    "Major General."

Buell eyed Thomas steadily after he had finished. "Do you really mean that?" he demanded.

Thomas nodded and Buell returned the dispatch. "On those grounds, I can accept your action," he said. He suddenly grasped Thomas by the hand. "I think you know my sentiments, general."

The record of Thomas is practically flawless, but this refusal to take command of the army must be charged against him as a mistake. The Union cause would have profited by his acceptance. He had saved Buell's position, but only momentarily. After the Battle of Perryville Halleck, planning another of his elaborate paper campaigns, directed Buell to launch a vigorous offensive in eastern Tennessee, which was suicidal. Buell was dumfounded and informed Halleck such a campaign could invite nothing but disaster, owing to the impossibility of maintaining communications with his base at Nashville or receiving continual necessary supplies and ammunition. Halleck replied by immediately relieving Buell of command without recourse.

Obviously, Thomas was the only logical man for the place, but Halleck, lamely offering the excuse that since Thomas had refused the command once he could not well offer it again, appointed Major General William S. Rosecrans as Buell's successor.

Rosecrans was a peculiar general. By turn, he had bursts of genius and monumental stupidity, which kept his generals, his soldiers and the country at large continually guessing as to which he would demonstrate next. In appearance, he was of medium height and well-proportioned, and he had the carelessness of dress which seemed almost universal among the Union generals. It extended to his person. His long, straight hair was rarely well combed and his beard, while worn short, was infrequently trimmed with any degree of neatness. His features were rather sharp. He had a high forehead, a long, hooked nose, and his eyes were set close together. In military ability, despite his flashes of brilliance, he was far below Thomas's standard and even below that of several other generals under his command.

When he took command he immediately began concentrating his forces around Nashville to attack Bragg who was at Murfreesborough, only thirty-two miles away. Bragg had lodged himself in comfortable winter quarters and did not dream Rosecrans seriously contemplated an attack. But on Christmas day, 1862, the Union commander put his army in motion. On December 30, he had reached Stone River and his army was opposite Bragg's in complete battle array, prepared to attack in the morning. His plan of battle was comparatively simple. His right wing was simply to hold the Confederates in check while he struck in force with his left, intending to roll back Bragg's right flank by the sheer weight and intensity of his attack.

Rosecrans' outstanding blunder was in the disposition of his force. Wholly unappreciative of the abilities of Thomas, he had relegated that master warrior to the center with the smallest command of any corps leader and the slightest prospect of taking active part in the fight. His left he assigned to Crittenden, who was to carry the burden of the assault. The right was entrusted to McCook, with orders to stand firm until Crittenden forced back Bragg's flank, when the whole Union army was to sweep the field.

Finding his position precarious, Bragg made hasty efforts to extricate himself and decided to launch an attack of his own on the comparatively weak right of the Federals. To do this he extended his own left well beyond the end of the Union line. When McCook was warned of this on the evening of December 30, he ordered General Richard Johnson to take his division to the extreme right to prevent any possibility of being flanked.

Johnson could not arouse any serious interest in the matter. He moved leisurely to the right and established his headquarters a mile and a half to the rear of the lines, so far back, that if anything went wrong it would take almost an hour to reach him through the wooded area. In addition, he halted his reserve brigade near his headquarters, a point from which it could not possibly reach the front in time to be of assistance in an emergency. General E. N. Kirk, commanding one of the advance brigades, made his way through the dark woods to Johnson's headquarters during the night and begged him to send the reserve brigade within supporting distance. Johnson peremptorily refused.

Early in the morning of December 31 Rosecrans ordered Crittenden to advance. General Horatio P. Van Cleve's division crossed the river without opposition, and General Thomas J. Wood was preparing to follow when the sound of battle came from the right. Momentarily, Rosecrans was elated. He had reason to believe McCook was strong enough and sufficiently well placed to hold, and if Bragg attacked there, Crittenden's task would be much easier. But he had scarcely begun to vision a decisive victory when one of McCook's aides rode up to him and told him the right had been attacked by an overwhelming force.

"Tell McCook to hold his ground," Rosecrans replied. "Tell him, if he holds an hour, we will have won. By that time Bragg will have more than he can attend to on his own right."

Twenty minutes later another McCook aide came galloping furiously and cried, "Our right is completely crushed. General McCook is falling back."

"Impossible!" Rosecrans shouted. He spurred his horse toward McCook's position only to meet wave on wave of soldiers in blue pouring through the woods in wild disorder. The worst had happened. Back in his headquarters Johnson had paid no attention to his division. General August Willich, another of his brigade commanders, had galloped back to implore Johnson to send up the reserve at once. Before he reached his destination the Confederate attack had come, so swift and overwhelming as to be almost a surprise. In five minutes the slender, unsupported lines were crushed. General Kirk was mortally wounded, and, with Willich away, the right wing was without a general in command. At the first onset both the Kirk and Willich brigades were shattered. Willich, spurring desperately to rejoin his command, was caught in the wave of advancing Confederates and captured.

Instead of winning a great victory, Rosecrans suddenly discovered he would have to fight for the very existence of his army. But as the right collapsed, the center and Thomas came into action and the story changed abruptly.

Rosecrans ordered a new line formed, but it was apparent the Confederates would overrun it before it could be organized, unless they were stopped at once. The salvation of the army suddenly rested upon Thomas. Turning to an aide, he said quietly, "Tell General Rousseau to change front to the right, throw his division between our retreating troops and the enemy, and hold his position until ordered back, if every man falls."

Rousseau, one of the grimmest fighters in the northern armies, smiled when he received the order and sent his men into their new position at the double. They reached it just in time to block the path of the exultant men in gray who came yelling through the cedars, confident of an easy victory. For twenty minutes the fight raged savagely, but the torrent of Confederates was held back. Then Thomas sent another message to Rousseau: "Splendidly done. Fall back. Our new line is formed."

Facing the enemy, the remnants of Rousseau's division retreated, leaving half their number dead and wounded, but the tide of disaster had turned. There was no more retreating. Bragg flung his forces fruitlessly against the Union Army, but when the short winter day drew to a close the blue line still stood adamant.

So terrific had been the struggle that neither army was able to renew the fight next day and both stood motionless. On January 2, Bragg flung General John C. Breckenridge's division into a desperate charge against the Union center, but fifty field guns tore the gray ranks to shreds and sent them back in stumbling fragments. The next day Bragg retreated and Rosecrans took Murfreesborough, but his only trophies were two thousand Confederate wounded.

For the number of men engaged, Stone River was one of the bloodiest battles of modern times. The combined strength of the opposing armies actually in the fight numbered 85,000. Of these, more than 20,000 were killed and wounded, 25 percent of the total. Besides his proportion of these casualties, Rosecrans lost 4,000 prisoners, and General Joseph B. Wheeler raided his rear, destroying nearly 1,000 wagons and thousands of horses and mules. In all, Rosecrans lost 31 percent of his entire force. It was a fitting close to the year. From Donelson to Murfreesborough more than 100,000 men had been tossed away in battles which were wholly in vain, a record which takes no account of the fighting which might be termed legitimate.

With the new year the tide of wasted blood swept back to the east again. General Hooker had taken the place of

Burnside and spent the winter preparing for a blow which would undo the errors of his predecessors. By the middle of April his reorganized and rejuvenated army had been increased to 130,000 men. Lee was in the Wilderness near the Rappahannock with 62,000. Again the Union had more than twice as many soldiers in one sphere of action as the South. But the Confederates had Lee and Jackson. The Federals had only Hooker.

On April 27, 1863, Hooker launched his determined effort to envelop Lee. He started with a flash of encouraging brilliance. He sent General John Sedgwick to make a feint below Fredericksburg, and for once the great Lee was completely deceived. He turned against Sedgwick, and while his attention was distracted Hooker swept up the Rappahannock. In four days he had 40,000 men on Lee's left flank at Chancellorsville. Lee was caught, if Hooker moved swiftly. But Hooker had exhausted the fountain of his generalship. Once he had arrived in position for a spectacularly successful attack, he was seized with indecision. He frittered away an entire day, and by the time he did move Lee had recovered himself and was ready. So the Battle of Chancellorsville was fought in the manner which Lee, and not Hooker, decided upon.

Lee never flashed more brilliantly than during the four days from May 2 to May 5, and few generals ever looked worse than did Hooker in the same period. Lee was a flashing rapier. Hooker was a ponderous, slow-moving broadsword. So swiftly did the gray commander juggle his limited forces back and forth that he actually outnumbered his foes at the precise point of contact whenever they engaged and had Hooker clumsily trying to catch up with him. When the

bloody farce was ended he had driven the tremendous Union
army back across the Rappahannock in disorderly retreat.
He had lost 12,281 men, but Hooker had wasted 16,080.
Yet the victory was blighted by disaster for Lee. No success
in the field of this nature could compensate him for the loss
of "Stonewall" Jackson, who was killed, his death the more
tragic because he had been felled by a blundering volley of
his own men.

So, to McClellan, Pope and Burnside, the name of
Hooker was added on the list of Union commanders who
had gone down before Lee, and now Major General George
G. Meade was elevated to Hooker's post, just as the Confederate leader swung with lightning rapidity and swept
into his spectacular invasion of the North. He sent General
Halleck into the doddering jitters. While Lee moved his
forces in sensational feints to cover his real intentions, the
Federal general-in-chief plunged into a ludicrous frenzy of
blind, frantic efforts to stop him. While he still was trying
to decide whether to give the command to Meade he par-
celled out the Union forces all over the map from West Virginia to the Peninsula, and could not shake from his mind
the one idea of saving Harper's Ferry, whose possession
meant nothing.

Then Meade was chosen. In some strange manner this
good business-like general had won Halleck's favor, so he
was permitted to operate without interference. He swiftly
pulled the scattered army together, and though he was
unable by this time to prevent Lee's advance into Pennsylvania, he was able to throw his army of 103,000 across the
Confederate path.

It is needless to retell the story of Gettysburg. Its only

place in this narrative lies in the fact that it imposed the
only real blemish of unwarranted slaughter which stains the
record of General Lee. But it is a serious blot. The battle
raged for three days, July 1, 2 and 3, 1863. By the end of
the second day Lee's last hope was gone and he must have
known it. The losses on both sides already had been appalling, but Lee could not resist one last throw of the dice
in the hope that a miracle would come to pass. When he
sent General George Pickett's division against the Union
center on the third day, it was as hopeless and futile as
Burnside's mad assaults at Fredericksburg. Lee was too wise
not to know it was hopeless. That he wished to rescind the
order for the charge after he had given it and actually tried
to do so, seems well borne out. But when Pickett told him
his men were eager to make the attempt and would be disheartened if denied the chance, Lee yielded.

So the waves of gray went hurtling into the mouths of
the Federal artillery. It was a fearful revenge for Fredericksburg which the blue exacted. Pickett sent 15,000 men into
the hopeless assault. Exact figures of his losses were never
revealed, but it is certain that he lost more than half his men,
and that the most decimating loss sustained by any single
unit in the entire war occurred in the charge. One of Brigadier General Pettigrew's regiments started on the tragic
advance with 800 men. Only 80 came back. More than 90
percent were wiped out. And the 720 who fell were less than
10 percent of the total.

No other battle of the war saw such tremendous slaughter.
In the three days Meade lost 23,186 men, among them 17
generals. With the black weight of Pickett's charge, Lee's

loss became much greater than this. It totalled 31,277, with 14 generals on the casualty list.

Except for the fatal third day attack of Lee's, these losses were the unavoidable toll of an unavoidable battle in which the fate of a nation was at stake. But once more a Union general nullified all the sacrifice of his men into futility.

Defeated, Lee was in his most desperate position since the war began, much more precarious than it had been after Antietam or at Chancellorsville. The Potomac River was at his back again, and this time at the flood stage, impossible for a hard-pressed army to cross. Before him was Meade's army, still more than 80,000 strong. Escape seemed impossible. Everyone—including Lee—took it for granted that Meade would follow up his tremendous victory immediately and wipe out the Confederate army. So sure of it was Secretary of War Stanton that he declared to Lincoln:

"If a single regiment of Lee's army ever gets back into Virginia in an organized condition, it will prove that I am totally unfit to be Secretary of War."

For the first time since the war began, Lincoln himself was confident, certain of an immediate end to the drawn-out holocaust. With Lee captured, his army gone and the road to Richmond open, the South was crushed. But the dream of peace faded.

With Lee in his grasp, Meade did exactly what McClellan had done in the same situation—nothing. It took him days to launch a stodgy, lumbering forward movement, and by that time Lee had taken not only "a single regiment" but every one of his regiments across the Potomac, safe once more. The whole North was enraged, and a wave of violent criticism was showered upon the Union commander. The vitriolic war secretary, for months, could not hear Meade's name mentioned without growing purple.

Meade himself became bitterly resentful at the criticism. Petulant and indignant, he tendered his resignation and was a trifle surprised, not to say a little more indignant, when it was accepted instantly.

Despairingly, the sorrowful President looked about for a new leader and in the west he saw the man who had just captured Vicksburg. So he sent for Grant—and elevated to the chieftainship the greatest butcher of them all.

18.

The Chickamauga Flows Red

W HEN Lee's invasion failed and Vicksburg surrendered simultaneously, the South was desperate. It had to have a victory and it determined to concentrate on winning it in the Valley of the Cumberland. In that region Bragg and Rosecrans had been continuing their duel ever since the Battle of Stone River. During the early summer it appeared as if the choice of Rosecrans to lead the Union army had been vindicated despite his failure at Murfreesborough. He executed a series of master strokes, completely outwitted Bragg for a time, and forced him to withdraw from Chattanooga. But with the capture of that city Rosecrans was burned out, so far as the fires of military genius were concerned. From that time his record became consistently worse.

It was an auspicious time for a counter-stroke. To give Bragg all the necessary preponderance of strength he could wish, 15,000 men were sent him from Mississippi and Longstreet's corps from Lee's Army of Virginia was ordered to join him as well. With his Mississippi men on hand and knowing Longstreet was on his way, Bragg now turned subtle. Shortly after he lost Chattanooga, he practically broadcast that he was retreating precipitately toward Rome, Ga. Many deserters came into the Union lines and all told the same story—that Bragg was completely demoralized and in headlong flight.

Rosecrans believed every word of it. Overjoyed by his "success," he divided his command, sending his three corps commanders, McCook, Crittenden and Thomas, on independent advances. By September 10, 1863, his army was scattered over a fifty-mile front with the various corps widely separated and entirely out of supporting distance of one another. Bragg's strategy had succeeded beyond his wildest hopes. With his entire army concentrated at Lafayette, Ga., only 25 miles from Chattanooga, he prepared to destroy the Union army piecemeal, while Rosecrans, utterly oblivious of danger, continued ordering his scattered generals to hurry or Bragg would escape.

There was only one serious flaw in Bragg's scheme. He had his army at Lafayette and the man whom Rosecrans had assigned to take Lafayette was George H. Thomas. Thomas had been extremely dubious of Rosecrans' plans and the segregation of the army's units worried him, so he advanced with extreme care and deliberation. The impatient "Rosey" became exasperated by his delay and finally sent him peremptory orders to occupy Lafayette at once, as Bragg was in full retreat.

Thomas sent Major General James S. Negley's division ahead in response to this command, for the purpose of feeling out the territory before he obeyed Rosecrans completely. He became increasingly perturbed when he heard the sound of heavy firing in the vicinity of Negley's advancing line some hours later and his qualms were not greatly allayed when the distant thunder ceased. When a pair of deserters were brought to him and they eagerly reiterated the story of Bragg's demoralization, he dismissed them almost immediately.

"Those men are lying," he said positively to his fellow officers. "And if they're lying, so have a lot of the others been lying. It's a little too remarkable that every deserter tells exactly the same story and in almost exactly the same words. Instead of retreating, Bragg's whole army may be ahead of us. If I obey Rosecrans' orders, I may be going to destruction."

When he received word from Negley that he had met surprising resistance to his advance, he sent back orders for the division commander to move no step farther toward Lafayette. Then he sent out several strong scouting parties to determine the enemy position before he moved. The next day he received a biting reprimand from Rosecrans for his failure to go forward. But late in the afternoon his scouts returned and, for the first and only time in the war, General Thomas almost broke into physical speed. He sent messengers on wild gallops to Negley, ordering the division to retreat at top speed, he dashed off the most desperate message to Rosecrans he had ever sent and he shot swift orders to every unit in his corps to prepare both for instant action and instant movement. For he knew the truth at last and saw immediately that the whole Federal army was facing destruction.

"Nothing but the most stupendous blunders on the part

of Bragg can save our army from total defeat," he told his staff. "With Negley on his way back, this corps is safe for the present but Bragg can strike McCook or Crittenden before they have a chance to extricate themselves."

Rosecrans was appalled when Thomas's message reached him.

"Great God," he cried to Brigadier General James A. Garfield, his chief of staff, "we've made an awful mistake. Our only chance is to pull the army together and fall back on Chattanooga. And neither Thomas nor Crittenden can be moved until McCook is safely drawn in. I'm afraid Bragg won't wait for Longstreet before he strikes."

"He has tried to strike," Garfield answered, "but Thomas was too smart for him. Instead of reprimanding him you should have given him a medal."

"I know, I know," Rosecrans said nervously. "I should lean on Thomas more. He's my right arm in this crisis."

He sent orders to McCook to join Thomas; to Thomas to hold his position until joined by McCook; to Crittenden to defend the roads to Chattanooga to the last man until the other two corps joined him on the way there. This done, there was nothing for Rosecrans to do but wait, and, waiting, he gradually became a nervous wreck.

On the other side of the mountains Bragg was having his troubles, too. When the blow against Negley failed through Thomas's quick withdrawal he gave General Leonidas Polk strict orders to turn to the north and attack Crittenden in force. Ignorant of his danger, since he had not yet received Rosecrans' warning dispatch, Crittenden chanced to order General Samuel Beatty to make a reconnaisance with his brigade at the time Polk was approaching his position. Beatty's skirmishers stumbled into Polk's advance corps and by brisk action drove it back on the main body. Frightened, Polk decided to disobey Bragg's orders. He drew back to a strong position, started to fortify it, and sent word to Bragg that he was about to be attacked by a vastly superior force and would wait reinforcements. Before he awoke to the truth, Crittenden was gone, saved by a miracle.

So Crittenden and Thomas both escaped, and Bragg went into a fury over this second miscarriage of his plans. But now he became vacillating, instead of striking decisively while he still held his extraordinary advantage. He considered attacking Crittenden again, then Thomas, then McCook—and wound up by attacking nobody and waiting for Longstreet. The "stupendous blunders" for which Thomas had not even dared hope were coming to Rosecrans' rescue.

It took McCook three days to reach Thomas, days during which Rosecrans in his overwrought state neither slept nor ate. At the end of this period of suspense he was in a nerve-shattered condition from which he did not emerge until it was too late, and undoubtedly his subsequent actions were influenced seriously by this.

On September 17 McCook reached Thomas and reported that he had left three brigades at Valley Head under the command of General William H. Lytle. For a moment Thomas was so amazed, he was speechless. Then he said heavily, "And you did this, knowing it was a matter of life and death that the army be united as soon as possible."

"The safety of my trains depended upon leaving Lytle behind," McCook replied flushing.

"And yet you knew," Thomas continued coldly, as near to open anger as he ever had been, "that Longstreet was coming, that Bragg is in our front and might strike at any moment. This means three more days of waiting. The battle will be lost or won before that time."

Reprieve came from an unexpected quarter. One of Thomas's young officers declared he knew a short-cut over the mountains with which he was familiar, and volunteered to lead Lytle's brigade by this route. Thus it was that Lytle's three priceless brigades were able to reach McCook and Thomas the night before Bragg finally struck. Tragically, it was Lytle's last move. He was the first general officer and one of the first men of any rank to be killed the next morning.

All during September 18 the great clouds of dust opposite them warned the Union forces that Bragg was moving up to give battle, and they prepared for action. Crittenden, too, was now on hand. Rosecrans, miraculously, had been able to assemble his entire command, and when night fell all that separated the two armies was the sluggish current of the Chickamauga.

During the night, after pondering the situation seriously for some time, Thomas suddenly roused his force and moved far to the left. Once more he saved the Federal force. His move took Bragg completely by surprise. He had expected to roll up the Federal left here as he had destroyed the other wing at Stone River, but Thomas firmly blocked his path. Rather, instead of crushing the Union left flank, Bragg found his own right being turned when Thomas abruptly attacked on the morning of September 19. It was a brilliant defensive offensive, and it threw Bragg's plans out of gear for the entire day. He had to adjust all his positions, and it was mid-afternoon before he was able to attack along the whole line. When night fell the Union army had yielded a little before Bragg's superior force, but in actuality the two armies held almost the same positions they had had in the morning.

That night Rosecrans called a council of his generals, during which Thomas simply said, "Watch the left." But he did not stop with saying it once. He reiterated it again and again. "Watch the left." Rosecrans finally listened and ordered Negley's division to be withdrawn from the center to the extreme left to give Thomas the strength he needed. Then Rosecrans made another move which was to have fateful consequences. He ordered General Thomas J. Wood's division of Crittenden's corps to take Negley's place in the center.

At that meeting Rosecrans was not the leader who had captured Chattanooga. The strain of the preceding week had had a telling effect upon him. He was nervous and distrait, listening anxiously to every rumor, influenced by every comment to such a degree that it was difficult to hold his attention. He seemed unable to take a comprehensive view of the situation, and before the meeting was over it was obvious that he did not have his army well in hand. It was a situation not calculated to instill confidence in his subordinates.

In the morning, knowing the army was facing a desperate struggle for existence, Thomas waited anxiously for Negley, who had been ordered to move at dawn. On the Confederate side, Polk had been ordered to attack Thomas at the same hour. By a curious freak of fate both Polk and

Negley failed to obey their orders. It was Polk's second offense during the campaign. He did not charge until nine
o'clock, a fact which saved Thomas, for Negley had not
yet moved.

Negley was not entirely responsible. He had failed to
leave his position because General Wood also had neglected to obey orders and had not relieved Negley. Learning this, Rosecrans commanded Wood to take Negley's
place in the line at once, and at the same time sent Negley's
reserve brigade to join Thomas—a move which Negley
could have made earlier. The brigade arrived just in time.
When Polk finally moved forward he hurled a terrific assault against Thomas, but the arrival of Negley's supporting troops enabled the Union corps commander to resist
the first onslaught and stand firm.

Other assaults were coming, however, more powerful
than those of the day before. In the early morning Longstreet finally had arrived, bringing 15,000 men, and Bragg
was at the maximum of his power. He placed Longstreet
in the center of his line and greatly strengthened his attacking forces on the flanks, particularly those sent against
the Federal left.

Thomas looked and waited in vain for the main body of
Negley's division. Finally he sent another urgent appeal to
Rosecrans, who in turn communicated with Negley only
to find Wood still had not relieved him. Overwrought as
he was, Rosecrans went red with fury. He spurred his
horse up to General Wood, and, before all the divisional
officer's staff, shouted:

"What is the meaning of this, sir? You have disobeyed
my specific orders. By your damnable negligence you are

endangering the safety of the entire army, and, by God, I will not tolerate it. Move your division at once, as I have instructed, or the consequences will not be pleasant for yourself."

Wood's face went white, so enraged he could not speak. Without a word, he saluted and swiftly set his division in motion. Fifteen minutes later he had relieved Negley. But Negley never reached Thomas. His soldiers went to the rear and stayed there! The conduct of the division in the crisis of the battle was to be the subject of an official inquiry later. Negley was exonerated of blame but the strange action of the division never was satisfactorily explained.

The battle was now raging along the entire front in all its fury. The thundering roar of the field guns and the rattling crack of the rifle fire were incessant, while a pall of smoke gathered heavily above the bloodiest single day's fighting of the war in the west. Thomas's entire position was an inferno. He was bearing the brunt of the morning attack, grimly holding with his limited force against assault after assault, still waiting and calling for the reinforcements which never came.

In his distracted state Rosecrans had become little more than a futile bystander. In the midst of the heaviest fighting of the morning, word was brought to him that there was a gap in the center of the line between Wood and General Joseph J. Reynolds. This was untrue. The division of Major General John M. Brannon, one of the best in the army, held the line solidly between Wood and Reynolds. Rosecrans should have known this, but apparently he had lost track of his divisions. Without investigating the report, he immediately wrote an order to Wood to "close up *on Reynolds*" and support him.

When Wood received the order he stared at it incredulously for a moment. Then his eyes narrowed and he smiled grimly. He carefully folded the order and put it into his pocket book which he returned to his coat with the comment, "I am certainly happy to have this in writing." He turned to a staff brigadier. "Get the division in motion."

The staff officer looked at him aghast. "But you can't close up on Reynolds," he protested. "Brannon is between us."

"I know it," Wood returned, with a laugh. "Still it's very simple. *We'll move to the rear of Brannon.* Orders are orders, I've been informed—very recently, at that."

"Great God, general," the shocked brigadier cried, "you can't do that. It will leave a gap in the line and the attack is coming on our center any moment."

Wood turned on him savagely. "I can't help that," he exclaimed, his eyes gleaming with fury. "I shall obey my orders. General Rosecrans will never have another opportunity to speak to me as he did this morning. I have my order here—in writing"—his hand rose to his breast pocket —"and I couldn't think of disobeying an order in writing— not when it comes from General Rosecrans."

"But what about the break in the line, general? The army can be crushed."

The skin across Wood's high cheek bones and thin jaws seemed to tighten. "I shall send word to both McCook and Davis that I am moving out of the line," he said grimly. "Let them fill the gap as best they can. I repeat, I am obeying my orders."

He kept his word. He withdrew at once and left a break in the Union line, half a mile wide, just as Longstreet, at the head of 25,000 men, prepared to attack at the very spot Wood had abandoned. General Jefferson C. Davis made frantic efforts to push his own division to the left, but he had scarcely begun when Longstreet's rushed forward, and with wild shouts of victory the entire 25,000 poured through the hole.

Davis' division was smothered, and scattered like chaff, its men slaughtered and trampled in the rush. Longstreet knifed directly through the heart of the Union army, unobstructed, then turned and in less than half an hour had reduced the entire right wing of the Union line to a helpless bloody mass, fleeing in rout for Chattanooga. With his one foul stroke, inspired by personal venom, General Wood all but destroyed the Union army.

McCook, Crittenden, even Rosecrans himself, were caught in the mad stampede. In utter despair Rosecrans turned to Garfield and asked him what he should do, and his staff chief's advice ruined the commander's last hope. Completely dashed, Garfield told Rosecrans to go to Chattanooga and try to save the remnants of the shattered right wing, while he himself would try to reach the left and order a swift retreat. His last vestige of courage gone, Rosecrans accepted the advice. When he reached his headquarters in Chattanooga he threw himself into a chair, his head in his hands, completely broken. McCook and Crittenden were with him, gloomy and speechless, when their silent despair was suddenly interrupted by a courier, who galloped up, rushed to Rosecrans and thrust a dispatch into his hands, crying, "It's from General Garfield." With nervous fingers, the commander opened the message and, with a dazed expression of disbelief, read,

"Thomas standing like a rock. Has seven divisions intact."

Rosecrans suddenly leaped to his feet, his face wild with joy. "Thomas is holding," he shouted. "We're not beaten yet." Calming abruptly, he turned to Crittenden and Mc-Cook and exclaimed, "This is no place for you, gentlemen. Go to your corps!"

It was no place for Rosecrans, either. If he had been alert, he could have collected ten thousand of the retreating men, thrown them on the flank and rear of Longstreet, and won one of the great victories of the war from the depths of defeat. But he was not equal to his opportunity. He stayed in his quarters and waited for more news. He did not return to the battle field.

When Longstreet had crashed through the Federal center and broken the right, he did not pursue the shattered regiments, the factor which gave Rosecrans his great chance. He allowed them to retreat unmolested and turned to crush Thomas, who still withstood every attack, suffering dreadful losses but refusing to be moved. Truly the "Rock of Chickamauga"—the rock of the Union Army always.

Now, in addition to the ceaseless attacks by Polk's heavily superior force, he was called upon to meet the vicious drive of Longstreet's victorious corps. But still he held. His flanks were bowed back until his face to the enemy on the slopes of Snodgrass Hill was almost a semi-circle. From three directions a force three times as great as his own stormed violently against him, but again he refused to yield. He moved through the thick of the fight, eyes alert for every threatened point of weakening, shifting his dwindling forces coolly to best meet each new assault, wholly unafraid, refusing to seek safety, inspiring every man in his exhausted ranks by his own matchless courage.

He was fighting the battle alone now and without quick reinforcements his position must become hopeless. His divisions had been mowed down to thin lines of men who beat back the enemy savagely above the bodies of their fallen comrades. Then, what Rosecrans failed to do—what Negley failed to do—was ventured by two generals who had the courage of their intelligence.

Three miles from the battle line, Generals Gordon Granger and James B. Steedman had been guarding the road to Rossville with the army reserve corps. The orders were unequivocal. They were to remain there and keep the enemy out of Rossville. But when word came of Thomas's predicament and the debacle of the right wing they did not hesitate. Daring to disobey orders in time of battle, one of the gravest offenses of which a soldier can be guilty, they left one brigade to guard the road and swung all the rest of the corps down the road at the double quick. As they drew near Snodgrass Hill, Granger galloped ahead and riding up to Thomas, his swarthy, heavily bearded face glowing, cried, "Where do you want us, general?"

New life surged along the beleaguered lines. With this new force added to his troops, Thomas rose to the heights. He hurled back attack after attack, then suddenly ordered his men from their position, commanded them to charge down the slope in pursuit of the reeling Confederates. Longstreet and Polk were stunned. The sudden drive of the blue line took them so completely by surprise they were wholly unprepared. From the very depths of the pit, Thomas dragged victory from crushing defeat. He drove the Confederates down the hill, charged on, and he was driving them from the field, sweeping back the vastly superior enemy, when Garfield rode back on the field and thrust a dispatch into his hands. Flushed with the prospect of triumph, Thomas opened the message and looked up like a man condemned. The dispatch was from Rosecrans, ordering an immediate retreat to Rossville. He turned and called his men back.

On the field lay nearly 35,000 dead and dying men, the bloodiest single day of the war, grim harvest of the errors of men who betrayed their trusts through stupidity, through venom, jealousy, incompetence or worse. Bragg admitted losing 40 percent of his whole army.

The only conceivable explanation of Wood's conduct is that he lost his head completely in the white rage Rosecrans had inspired in him. The thin-lipped Wood was a vitriolic, profane man, with a violent temper, but he was an excellent soldier and a good leader. With the exception of his action at Chickamauga his record during the Civil War was exceptional, and he was corps commander under Thomas, who spoke very highly of him, before the war was ended. Even at Chickamauga, he partly redeemed himself. Whether he was conscience-stricken, which is doubtful, or whether he had that peculiar indifference to the lives of common soldiers which so often imbues generals and felt that once Rosecrans was disgraced his debt was paid, he later in the day offered his division to Thomas. It was one of the seven which bore the brunt of the most fearful attacks of the day.

W. S. ROSECRANS

19.

Two Thousand Men a Day

STRANGELY, Washington had heard of Thomas at last. Rosecrans' star had set. He was relieved of command and his post was given to the man who should have had it at least a year before. It was a sorry legacy Thomas received. Contrary to Rosecrans' despairing conceptions, the Army of the Cumberland was reorganized at Chattanooga, well reorganized, within a few days after Chickamauga. But, due to Rosecrans' blunders, it now found itself practically besieged there. By his Chickamauga victory, Bragg was able to all but sever the Union force's lines of supply. For weeks Thomas's chief task was to keep his force from starving. Only then did Washington awaken to the gravity of the situation. Hooker, now in a subordinate position, where he belonged, was sent with two corps from the Army of the Potomac. Sherman hurried from Mississippi with two more corps. General Grant, too, started for Chattanooga.

"Hold on until I come," he telegraphed to Thomas.

"We'll hold on until we starve," Thomas wired back.

The last almost became necessary. Horses died by the hundreds until at last there were not enough left to handle one battery of artillery. The famine became so great that the men in the ranks were reduced to one raw ear of corn per day per man. It was no uncommon sight to see soldiers picking undigested grains of corn from the offal of animals, washing them carefully, parching them, and eating them.

Then Hooker arrived with food; and Sherman with more food. The Army of the Tennessee was brought from Corinth and united with that of Thomas. They were never separated for the balance of the war. And Grant came. So, the tide turned. But the greatest horror still was ahead.

Winter came and went, and it was 1864. Grant was called to take supreme command of all the United States armies. He was made a Lieutenant General on March 2, and ten days later he became general-in-chief. The reign of Halleck was over. For the first time grand strategy was introduced with all the forces of the Union working simultaneously to shatter the Confederacy under a single coördinated plan. For the first time, too, it was understood that the mere taking of ground meant nothing, that the hope of victory lay only in the destruction of the opposing armies. Sherman was given the direction of the western campaign, with Thomas as his second in command, to drive for Atlanta, cut the Confederacy in two and crush the army of Joseph E. Johnston. In the east, Grant was to take personal charge of Meade's Army of the Potomac and strike for Richmond, with his real purpose the annihilation of Lee's army.

Grant went to the Peninsula with a peculiar psychology. He was inclined to discount his opponent and attribute the consistent failure of the Union army against Lee to the incapacity of its many leaders, particularly their ineptitude on attack. He was right about their incompetence, but he was wholly wrong in his conception of Lee.

By spring of 1864 the Army of the Potomac had been increased to 140,000 men. Of these, Grant took 120,000, the flower of Northern manhood, and moved to the Rapidan, 65 miles from Richmond, to come to grips with Lee. He had 318 field guns and his equipment surpassed anything ever seen before. His baggage and supply train alone was over 60 miles long, and would have extended the entire distance to the Confederate capital from his concentration point.

Opposed to him, Lee once more had his army recruited to its normal strength of 62,000.

Grant was no battle strategist. He appeared to believe that subtle maneuvering and skillful tactics denoted weakness on the part of the general who employed them. "Keep hammering" was his only slogan, his only strategy, a policy which involves a total disregard for the men in the ranks as men, and is predicated upon an unlimited supply of them. Grant followed it. It gave him the name of "butcher" and so he was, the worst. But this much must be said for him. The war had many butchers, and without exception they were made so through ambition, vanity, ruthless self-seeking, jealousy, personal venom and incredible stupidity. Whatever was wrong with Grant, and his faults were many, in his 1864 campaign against Lee, he had no personal considerations whatever. He was actuated only by a dogged, sincere effort to end the war. His mind was that of a bulldog and nothing else. He conscientiously believed he was right in the course he pursued as the only one which offered a possibility of success. The result could not but be appalling.

From the day he struck his first blow, a wave of horror swept the country which rose and swelled day by day as the frightful, futile drive went on without relief. All the grisly slaughter which had gone before was as nothing compared to that which came now.

On May 5 he crossed the Rapidan and moved into the Wilderness where Lee was waiting for him. It was a dismal, ominous region of heavy woods, ravines and mantraps, its growths so tangled and dense that it was impossible for the fighting men to see each other more than a few yards, friend or foe. Lee knew every inch of it, knew how to make the most of its every natural feature. Grant knew it not at all.

He hurled his strength against the leaf-and-timber-hidden lines of Lee's men, the desperate 62,000 who swore he should not pass. All day of May 5, with not an inch gained. All day of May 6, and not only had the Union force been stopped, it had been thrust back in defeat. And Grant had lost 18,387 men—in two days. Lee's army had lost heavily, too, but far from as heavily as Grant, and the Confederate force was intact. The first frontal "hammering" had failed.

Grant shouldered his way to the left, determined to outflank Lee, but the Virginian outguessed him. On May 9, Grant had reached Spottsylvania Courthouse to turn Lee's right, but Lee arrived there first and it was to be frontal attack once more.

Lee had his army arranged in a huge salient, much like an irregular, inverted "V," its east side running north and south, its north line east and west, converging in a sharp angle, two miles north of the courthouse. On May 9 Grant hammered at its sides and was sent reeling back. On May 10 he sent his whole army crashing against it again, hour on hour, with the endless storm of lead cutting men down. At fearful cost, two regiments, led by Colonel Emory Upton and Colonel Samuel S. Carroll, drove through the Confederate lines, gained a foothold and seized 1,200 prisoners, but the gray forces swayed against them in might and they were hurled back. It was the first indentation which had been made on Lee's works, and in appreciation Grant promoted both Upton and Carroll to Brigadier Generals on the spot. Night came and morning again, and the armies were too wearied to continue in more than desultory firing for the day.

While they paused for breath Grant surveyed the situation grimly and sent his famous dispatch, "I propose to fight it out on this line if it takes all summer."

In the afternoon of May 11, a terrific storm burst, and drenched field and men for hours. All firing ceased. With the night, the rain stopped and the weather suddenly turned disagreeably cold. The chilled men gathered in small groups around half-drowned fires, some wrapping their tents around their shoulders, others burying themselves under the canvas folds on the soaked ground, all of them miserable, all trying to snatch brief sleep before the murderous struggles to come.

Some had no chance to sleep. During the night Major General Winfield S. Hancock, commander of the Second Union Corps, swung his men into position around the angle of Lee's salient, occupied by the brigade of General Edward

Johnson. Dawn came with the dense trees dripping, the air chill and a heavy mist lowering over the battle field. Through it, with the first streaks of daylight, Hancock's men advanced, stealthily, quietly, then with a wild yell and mad rush as the angled log breastworks rose suddenly before them.

Up the sides and over the top they lunged, a desperate dash, sweeping everything before them. Johnson's brigade was stunned, taken completely by surprise, and 3,000 men were prisoners within five minutes. The Union forces were inside Lee's lines at last. They pushed forward, spreading out as the angle widened, driving on toward the breastworks which cut across the salient and barred their way. But the alarm had been raised. Already the hail of fire was sweeping over Hancock's men. Then the way was blocked as a swarm of men in gray poured forward, and General John B. Gordon leaped before them, sword raised. But the order to charge was not given. A wild cheer had burst from the gray ranks, rolling down to the angle, and then its cause appeared, a stalwart, gray-haired figure on horseback, General Lee himself come to lead his men. But they would not have it. The life of the commander was too precious to be risked here. The cheers gave way to a new cry, "Lee to the rear! General Lee to the rear!" The figure on horseback stopped, his eyes glistening as he waved his arm to his men, and turned back, the cheers thundering out again as they saw him on his way to safety. Then they turned, and as General Gordon's sword flashed up again, the gray mass surged forward, faces tense, bayonets lowered, muskets roaring.

Before their rush, the Union hosts were swept back and

back into the angle, back against the entrenchments they had seized. The men in blue turned and fought with tiger-ish fury, refusing to give up what they had won. More men in blue surged over the breastworks, more men in gray swarmed into the angle—the "Bloody Angle." No strategy here, no maneuvers. Hundreds, thousands of battle-maddened men locked in death grips. Men fell and their comrades stumbled over their bodies to reach out and kill, and more men fell, spitted on bayonets, bodies shattered by lead, heads crushed by rifle stocks, hand to hand and body to body, a screaming maelstrom of frenzied madness.

More hundreds and thousands poured into the angle, eyes savage with the lust to kill. Muskets blazed into eyes inches from the barrel. Heads were blown off. The dead were piled in the ditches, four, five deep, blue and gray locked in each other's arms. Again and yet again the trenches were filled with dead, cleared out and filled again to make room for living men who rushed in to become the new dead. The battle flags waved dizzily above the holocaust, the Stars and Stripes swung savagely against the Stars and Bars. A color bearer in gray leaped forward, stopped as a shell burst and tore his arm from its socket. He stared at the spurting blood, saw his fallen standard, lunged at it with his other arm, raised it again with a wild, hoarse cry before he plunged into the mass of other dead he fell to join. A stunned, shattered company of men in gray cried, "We'll surrender. Cease firing! We'll surrender!" The rifles of the blue were lowered for a moment. Twenty of the graycoats rose above the entrenchments, arms raised to yield, but they never advanced a step. With roars of fury, their own comrades raked them with lead and the twenty fell in a huddled, bloody mass, every man dead.

Hour after hour, the blasts of hell swirled over the "Bloody Angle." Standard bearers lowered their flags to stab with the staffs into the faces of their enemies, clinched and fought with bestial frenzy. Two soldiers, their ammunition spent, choked each other to death on top of the entrenchments and rolled down among the torn and mangled bodies that filled the ditch. Men fought with gun swabs, hand-spikes, clubbed muskets, stones, fists, anything. Hour after hour—morning passed, noon, but no pause here for food, afternoon. And the hail of bullets never ceased. An oak tree, two feet in diameter, standing before the breastworks, was sheered off by rifle bullets alone, and fell among the men with a thundering crash. Night came and still the carnage went on. More soldiers came up and the horrors of the "Angle" went on while the death piles grew and the moans of the dying blended with the roar of gunfire and the savage cries of men that had no end. Through the black of the night, hour after hour, midnight, and still the blood-crazed men fought on, until at last at three o'clock in the morning, after nineteen hours of raging hell, the men who still lived sank exhausted in their tracks and neither mass had yielded an inch.

"On this line if it takes all summer!"

For five days more the red whirlwind raged about Spottsylvania, with no pause in the slaughter. Grant hurled his men against the desperate gray lines assault after assault, in the face of a torrent of bullet and shell which ripped his columns to bits. He found it impossible to believe the vastly inferior Confederate force would not yield under his weight.

In his certainty that he could crush it here, he refused to arrange a truce for burying the dead until May 17.

The burial parties found a horrible task before them. The dead—and the wounded who still breathed—were piled six layers deep in the trenches, and over them all swarmed a flock of vultures, who tore with reddened beaks at the bodies of dead and living alike. Spottsylvania had cost the blue another 18,399 men.

Then Grant moved again in another attempt to turn the gray left, but Lee divined his purpose. At the North Anna River, the gray commander once more arrived first. For five days, from May 23 to 27, Grant felt out the Confederate lines, attempting only one violent smash, as futile as all that had preceded it, and 3,986 more Union soldiers were gone. The nation stood appalled at the mounting toll, but the worst was yet to come.

Balked at the river, Grant shifted to the left anew and it was June 1. The blue legions stood before Cold Harbor—and before Lee, who had beaten them again. At six o'clock in the evening Grant threw two corps into a test attack. It lasted one hour and 2,200 men fell with Lee's position unbreached. The Union army rested on June 2, a hot, sweltering day, broken at last by a refreshing rain at five o'clock in the afternoon. Late at night Grant cast the die and ordered a direct frontal attack along the whole Confederate front to begin at 4:30 the following morning.

The soldiers knew what it meant. The last half hour before the assault witnessed a scene of grisly implication. Up and down the Union lines the men wrote their names and home addresses on little slips of paper which they pinned to their backs. "We who are about to die . . ."

Dawn came and the grim-faced men stood in line, awaiting a command which came all too soon. All night Lee had
prepared for this assault, had made his position perfect, his
breastworks impregnable. He was ready, fearfully ready.
Then came the attack and the blue hosts charged straight
into the pits of hell, a blasting inferno which flamed in
their helpless faces with a searing, endless eruption of
death-dealing lead and steel.

Nine thousand men in blue went down in eight minutes.

The frightful attack stopped in its own gory tracks. Just
one man reached the Confederate works. Colonel James P.
McMahon of the 164th New York seized the flag of his
regiment as his dying color-bearer fell, leaped on the para-
pet, planted his colors there and fell dead near the ditch,
bleeding from a dozen wounds.

The order came to renew the assault. At a few scattered
points brief charges were made by isolated units only to
fall back almost immediately. No human being could advance in that murderous fire. It was all over in less than
an hour. A third order came to attack. It was flatly refused.

The scene which followed was monstrous. Through three
days and nights the shrieks and groans of the wounded
arose from the field in an endless symphony of agony. No
truce was asked by Grant. Major General William F.
Smith says, "Common rumor gave as a reason that there
was a fear of refusal, as there were no dead or wounded of
the enemy to be cared for." But Major General Martin T.
McMahon offers, "An impression prevails in the popular
mind that a commander who sends a flag of truce asking
permission to bury his dead and bring in his wounded has

lost the field of battle. Hence the reluctance on our part to ask a flag of truce."

So there was no truce. Maddened by the cries which arose from the field, many Union soldiers heroically crept out under a hail of lead to bring in their wounded comrades, but there were hundreds who could not be reached and, says General Smith, "The groans of these grew fainter and fainter until they ceased."

Even Grant yielded in the end, and on June 7 the truce was arranged. When the burial parties went out to clear the shambles, they moved through an endless vista of blood in dark and slippery pools—dead horses; dead men, some mangled and trampled into unrecognizable masses of flesh; legs; arms; torn bits of bodies—in an upheaval of crimsoned mud. Every man on the field was dead but two.

Thirty days had passed since Grant began his "hammering" and he now had lost 60,000 men—two thousand men a day!

For twelve days after Cold Harbor the opposing forces rested on their arms. Then Grant, with reinforcements on hand and plenty of new men with whom to hammer, swung south and west—still to the left—and tried to capture Petersburg where Beauregarde was in command. On June 16 he hurled three army corps against Beauregarde's defenses and managed to capture four redoubts. At daylight of the next day he again crashed against Beauregarde and forced the Confederates out of their first line of defense, but they obstinately refused to yield farther, although Grant poured fresh troops into the assault until their blood flowed like water. As the third day dawned the terrific attack was renewed, but Lee had brought reinforcements to Beauregarde. The blue waves broke in shattered despair against the impregnable ranks of gray, and rolled back, leaving their dead piled high once more. At dusk Grant gave up. He had lost 10,587 more men and had failed again.

He changed his tactics, planned a coup, prepared to breach the Confederate works with a mine. Unfortunately, the man to whom this task was assigned was the incompetent Burnside. Instead of picking his best troops for the assault, he permitted his divisional chiefs to draw straws for the privilege. The "lucky" division was made up of some of the poorest material in the Union ranks. It was not well led and was given no special instructions. Every phase of the preparations was bungled.

The mine was exploded on the morning of July 30. Three hundred Confederates were hurled to their deaths and a pit was left 300 feet long and 65 feet wide. The attacking force went forward, but treated the matter as if it were a sight-seeing tour. The men crowded about the edge of the pit in a solid mass, gazing curiously at the results of the explosion instead of driving through. When they finally started they were met by a brigade of North Carolinians who had had plenty of time to come up.

The Union column became entangled in the jagged hole, floundered about confusedly under heavy fire, and began to crawl along without regard for its real objective. Burnside threw regiment after regiment into the breach, but the Confederates ringed it on three sides with blazing rifles and the Federals were cut to pieces like trapped rats. In his folly Burnside sent a regiment of negro troops into the attack. The sight of their black faces drove the Confederates to frenzy. The explosion pit became a blood-filled slaughter pen and when the futile assault finally ceased, it held 4,008 Union dead and wounded, while the Stars and Bars still flew above Petersburg.

This was enough for Grant. The "summer" was only half gone but he ceased to "follow this line." He had failed completely. He had lost nearly 75,000 men and he still was twenty miles from Richmond, while Lee's army, the primary objective, was intact and as efficient as ever. One benefit was derived. Grant learned at last to respect his foe.

After Grant's final failure at Petersburg, Lee was so confident of his ability to hold the bulldog in check that he sent General Jubal Early with about 20,000 men to make a demonstration against Washington. When this failed to draw Grant's force away from the Peninsula Early retired into the Shenandoah Valley, where, it became evident, Lee intended to leave him as a constant threat against the Union capital.

Grant decided to eliminate this menace and for that purpose organized the Army of the Shenandoah, assigning to it 40,000 infantry and 15,000 cavalry, a force almost three times as large as Early's. In command, he placed Philip Henry Sheridan—and another storied "hero" was given the chance to make his bid for glory.

Sheridan emerged from the war with the halo of the romantic chevalier of the North, to become an almost legendary figure of greatness, the dashing knight in shining armor who always won. The last was true. Sheridan is an outstanding proof that "nothing succeeds like success." From the time he first entered the limelight, he never lost a battle—eventually. In the light of this the manner of his winning has not been given much consideration and the public is reluctant to give up its heroes.

When Sheridan began his advance on August 7, 1864, the bearded Early began a series of maneuvers worthy of a "Stonewall" Jackson. For more than five weeks he played tag with his dashing foe, who chased him madly all over the valley until Early suddenly turned. At this Sheridan retreated precipitately. Then, learning that Early had been forced to send some of his troops back to Lee and was reduced to 15,000, Sheridan decided to attack. Instead of trying to envelop a force he outnumbered almost four to one, Sheridan used Grant's already outmoded hammering tactics. On September 19 at Winchester he made a direct frontal attack, and by sheer weight of numbers managed to drive Early from the field, but not until he had sacrificed 5,000 men. Early had 1,800 killed and wounded.

Three days later Sheridan attacked again, at Fisher's Hill, with a golden opportunity to surround Early's force, but the Confederate leader extricated himself again and escaped almost intact. Lee now restored some men to the valley commander and Early once more had a force of about 20,000. Despite the segregation of various detachments, Sheridan still had more than 40,000, but after one feeble and unsuccessful cavalry effort to destroy the Manassas Gap Railroad he began a general retirement, spending his time devastating the valley granaries until he reached Cedar Creek. Then, not certain what next to do, he left his force there and went to Washington to find out.

While he was on his way back Early suddenly attacked the flank of the army at Cedar Creek with his meager force and threw the Union troops into a disorderly stampede. Sheridan suddenly arrived after his renowned "Ride," and by a desperate rally reformed his lines and made a counter-attack which Early's inferior force could not withstand. But the Confederate commander left the field with enough captured supplies to take care of his needs for some time. In this near defeat, Sheridan lost another 5,600, while Early's casualties were 2,900.

After that nothing happened except a few insignificant skirmishes, with Early obstinately refusing to be cowed by the overwhelmingly superior force aligned against him. The great valley campaign ended in the middle of November when Early was called back to join Lee, and Grant summoned Sheridan to return to his own forces at Petersburg.

In all this glorified episode which brought Sheridan his reputed heroic stature, he never once routed his opponent, met him in battle only three times, completely failed to crush him, and in the final contest barely escaped disastrous defeat himself. In the campaign he had uselessly tossed away 17,000 men, almost one third of his entire command.

In the west a different story had been written. On May 7, two days after Grant first struck in the Wilderness, General Sherman started for Atlanta with 100,000 men, opposed by 65,000 Confederates. On September 2 Grant was before Petersburg, still twenty miles from Richmond. On that same day Sherman marched into Atlanta, completely victorious and ready to start the "March to the Sea" which sliced the Confederacy in two and cut off Lee's last hope of escape from Virginia.

In a desperate effort to force Sherman to retreat General John B. Hood, the most reckless waster of lives in the Confederate armies, circled Sherman's army and struck at his line of communications in Tennessee. The Union commander refused to be drawn back, but he provided for the stopping of Hood. He did not send an army, but he sent the equivalent of an army. He detached General George Thomas from his command and assigned him to the task. So, with poetic justice, in this last great campaign of the war the South's most "fatal general" was pitted against the most brilliant conserver of men the North could boast.

It was Thomas's first opportunity to conduct an entire campaign on his own. The results aroused more tragically regretful "might-have-beens" than any passage in the war. He started without an army against an enemy who had 54,000 men. He picked up detachments where he could find them along the way, added regiments of new recruits whom he stopped on their way to join Sherman. With this heterogeneous and disorganized array he fenced brilliantly with Hood, holding him at bay and inflicting heavy losses at every contact, while he slowly drew back upon his chosen concentration point at Nashville.

He did not risk a real stand until he reached Franklin on November 30, when his army had grown to about 27,000. Leaving Major General John M. Schofield in command to hold back Hood as long as possible, he himself hurried the extra twenty miles to Nashville, to prepare for the defense there.

Hood attacked Schofield on November 30, and the fury of the assault made Franklin, in its brief duration, one of

WILLIAM T. SHERMAN

the bloodiest battles of the war. After some initial success Hood was completely repulsed with a loss of 6,252 of his best men, including nine generals, five of whom were killed outright, three wounded and one captured. Schofield lost 2,326. The Union general retreated immediately afterward, and on December 2 was safely in Nashville, which Hood promptly besieged.

Thomas's ill-assorted force grew swiftly from day to day, but he refused to move against Hood until he was thoroughly ready, in the face of an endless stream of telegrams which came from Grant, day and night, irritably demanding that he attack. On December 15, while General John A. Logan was speeding westward to relieve him of command, Thomas struck.

At five o'clock in the morning he sent 43,260 men into battle against Hood's 37,937 well-entrenched veterans. The battle lasted all day of the 15th and for one hour on the 16th. Thomas did not defeat Hood's force. He pulverized it! In the entire war no army was so completely crushed and overthrown as was Hood's at Nashville. Fifty minutes after the second day's attack began, what was left of Hood's array was in shattered confusion, fleeing for very existence, every man for himself, all organization lost. In the two days' battle Hood lost nearly 10,000 killed and wounded, 5,000 prisoners, 53 guns and two thirds of all his equipment. The remnants of his army were reduced to a disorganized and useless mob. It ceased to exist as a factor in the war.

Thomas lost 3,087 men. At this insignificant price he had destroyed the last hope of Southern victory. The

dwindling forces of the Confederacy hung on, grimly, desperately. But Appomatox came at last and the guns ceased
firing because there had been a Thomas and a Sherman to
redeem the murderous blunders of the commanders who
had preceded them.

20.

Massacres—White and Red

DURING the latter days of the Civil War, butchery of quite a different sort was under way in a sector far removed from the Southern battlefields. The Indians of the central plains region, from the Missouri River to the Rocky Mountains, witnessed the outbreak of hostilities between the palefaces with savage satisfaction. Considering the hour propitious, they seized the opportunity for an attempt to restore some of their own lost supremacy.

From the early days of the war, they became increasingly troublesome, so much so that the soldiers of the far western states who enlisted for service in the fratricidal war between North and South, found themselves fully occupied with the Indians instead. In 1863 a semblance of quiet was restored with the redskins, but it proved only a dubious truce.

On June 1, 1864, the entire array of plains tribes—Sioux, Kiowas, Comanches, Apaches, Arapahoes and Cheyennes—burst forth simultaneously. From Canada to Texas they swept the prairie country, burning and massacring in all directions, wiping out lonely ranches and stage stations and destroying innumerable small settlements. The Indian is never a sustained campaigner, however, and in the face of rapidly developing resistance the early momentum of the outbreak passed.

Late in the summer Chiefs Left Hand of the Arapahoes and Black Kettle of the Cheyennes voluntarily came to Governor John Evans of the Colorado Territory and offered to halt the hostilities of their own tribes if they were assured protection from white attack. This plea was readily granted and the governor suggested that they camp along Sand Creek near Fort Lyon. The Indians accepted and gradually gathered at the camp in growing numbers. By November some 800 members of the two tribes were there, living peacefully, molesting no one, spending their time hunting and fishing.

Elsewhere, however, redskin depredations continued in scattered fashion with no sequestered settler immune from danger. To suppress these outrages, Governor Evans authorized the organization of the Third Colorado Volunteer Cavalry and its command was given to Colonel John M. Chivington. The colonel was presiding elder of the Methodist Church in Colorado, a preacher and a religious fanatic, imbued with an insatiable desire to wipe out all heathen, among whom he classed the Plains Indians. He was a mountain of a man, six feet seven inches tall, familiarly known among his admirers as "the Giant of the Lord."

His distorted zeal led him to decide upon a monstrous act, in the weird belief that its very horror would bring all the redskins to their knees to sue for peace. Late in

November, without orders while Governor Evans was absent in Washington, he hastily gathered his regiment, picked up a battery of field artillery en route, and rushed to Sand Creek with a thousand men. On the way he arrested everyone he met to prevent his objective from becoming known.

At dawn of November 27 he suddenly swooped down on the peaceful Indian camp and opened fire without warning. The opening gun launched the massacre which is the worst blot on all the shoddy record of white treatment of the Indians. With an inhuman savagery surpassing the worst atrocities of which Indians ever have been guilty, Chivington's white force slaughtered the hapless redskins in a bloody shambles without a parallel. Black Kettle raised the United States flag, whose protection had been guaranteed him, but Chivington paid no attention to this. Left Hand, unarmed and unresisting, faced the butchers with arms folded and was shot down in cold blood as he stood.

Mercy was shown to no one. Squaws, bucks, boys, girls, even papooses in their cradles, were cut down by the scores while their murderers cheered. It is a matter of record that three troopers, standing side by side, took alternate potshots at a toddling three-year-old who was sobbingly trying to escape, until one of the white men brought him down amid the laughing applause of his comrades.

Black Kettle finally managed to escape with some 200 Indians, and after he was gone the whites overran the camp. They scalped every dead and wounded man, woman and child they found—and there were more than 600 of these! Not content with this, they mutilated the bodies of their victims. Fingers were chopped off for the rings they held, arms for their bracelets, heads for the silver bands which encircled the necks. From this mangling, the men of the presiding elder went on to worse atrocities, too loathsome to describe. Then, with colors flying and the air filled with their shouts of victory, the gallant troopers proudly returned to Denver, where they paraded through the streets in triumph, waving their grisly trophies.

Horrified revulsion swept the entire country. Violent demands were made for the utmost penalty to be imposed upon those guilty of the shameful slaughter, and eventually Chivington was brought before a court-martial—in Colorado. After the most perfunctory trial he was acquitted with acclaim. The territorial legislature of Colorado passed a resolution commending him for his act!

The results, otherwise, were slightly different than Chivington had hoped for. Driven to a vengeful frenzy, the Indians arose with unprecedented fury and this time their vigor did not abate. Within six months, with Black Kettle as their outstanding leader, they were in scalp-knife control of the entire plains country. White traffic all but ceased. Not a single settler remained alive outside the more crowded settlements. At every military post the garrison was driven behind its stockade and held in a state of siege. For four years the war raged on before the Federal Government finally gained the upper hand.

It was ended primarily by the return to battle limelight of the dashing cavalier, Philip Sheridan, and another man who had been one of his cavalry leaders in the Civil War, also a *beau sabreur*, destined for an undying fame which he never won—General George Armstrong Custer.

After the Civil War Sheridan had been sent to Louisiana as the military dictator of that state during the tragic reconstruction days and immediately proceeded to tarnish his halo. Apparently under the impression that he still was at war with them, he treated the Louisianans with a vindictive ruthlessness which finally made it necessary to remove him. He then was sent to command the Department of the Missouri with the duty of suppressing the Indians. There he had a happy reunion with Custer.

The Custer myth is one of the most glamorous on America's pages. He is pictured—almost canonized—as the romantic, impetuous warrior who died with lustrous nobility, giving his life for his country in a heroic battle with the Sioux Indians. The facts are somewhat different.

Custer was impetuous—which almost sums up the total of his qualities and abilities. Throughout his brief life he was nothing more than a ruthless seeker for glory, and he sacrificed every consideration of decent human relationship, soldierly conduct and friendship in his relentless pursuit of personal grandeur. In his early days he was almost unbelievably lucky. His slashing, ill-considered cavalry actions during the Civil War turned out so fortunately that he was breveted a Major General in 1864, at the age of twenty-five, winning the title of "boy general." To no small degree it was his foolhardy recklessness which cost Sheridan's cavalry more than 3,000 men during the abortive Shenandoah Valley campaign.

In 1868, as Sheridan's right-hand bower in the Missouri valley, he led the unpardonable massacre of Black Kettle's warriors at Washita. He was lucky again. He handled his troops in the most muddled manner possible, but he was credited with a great victory. Inexcusable as was the slaughter of the Indians, it paled beside Custer's abandonment of twenty of his own men during the "fight." These, led by Major Joel Elliot were trapped by the redskins. Though he had a strong force only two miles away, Custer deliberately refused to attempt their rescue and all of them were killed and mutilated.

Washita paved the way for Indian peace which was arranged by treaty shortly afterward. For the next eight years Custer went on his shoddy way, accomplishing nothing worthy of note but always dashing hither and yon with saber swinging as scattered Indian bands became unruly, never passing a chance to boast that his regiment, the Seventh Cavalry, could wipe out all the Indians on the plains without other help.

In 1876 he made a serious mistake in his desperate pursuit of the limelight. The corruption scandal had burst about the head of President Grant's Secretary of War, William Belknap, and impeachment proceedings were under way. Custer thrust himself into this situation with a series of wholly unsupported charges against Belknap involving military matters in the west. He was summoned to Washington, placed on the witness stand, and made such a sorry spectacle of himself that, in his squirming, he soared continually higher in the wild aspersions he tossed about freely until he touched Grant himself. Custer already had won the contemptuous disdain of General Sherman, then commander-in-chief, by his conduct in Washington. Now he incurred the bitter enmity of Grant and found himself in official disgrace.

Mortified, he dashed back to Dakota, hoping to lead the

proposed expedition against the Sioux who were in open warfare against the whites but found officialdom had slammed the door of this opportunity in his face. Finally, through the friendly and wholly voluntary intervention of General L. H. Terry, who was to command the expedition, he was permitted to go along. He promptly planned to reward Terry's kindness in the true Custer manner, openly intimating his intention to draw away from the expedition with his beloved Seventh Cavalry once it reached the open country, wage his own campaign and gather all the glory himself. To insure himself the maximum of publicity, he took with him Mark Kellogg, correspondent of the New York *Herald*, although he had been directed specifically to have no newspaper men with him.

On June 24, 1876, Custer acted in accordance with his expressed intentions. Taking 203 cavalrymen—and Kellogg—with him, he started on a lone and unordered foray. Discarding the most elemental prudence and violating every principle of plains warfare, he led his men directly into certain destruction of which he had been fully warned. The next day the consequences of his ambitious folly overtook him. Several thousand Sioux warriors trapped his meager command on the Little Big Horn on June 25, 1876, and every man, including Custer and Kellogg, was killed.

"Custer's Last Fight" was not a fight. It was a rout. He did not gather his men about him and make a heroic stand. He fled for his life. His men were brave enough, but the story that Custer gathered his two hundred to fall in one great fighting circle, defying the Sioux to the last, is pure fiction. The bodies of Custer's men were found scattered far and wide over a distance of three miles, revealing their desperate and wholly justified rush to escape. Custer himself was found on the crest of a hill with only thirty men about him. It was these who made the "last stand" when they finally were trapped beyond hope. They did not deserve to die—not there. They simply were sacrificed to the insatiable glory-lust of their commander. Ironically enough, with his spectacular death, he gained the undeserved adulation for which he had struggled ignobly and futilely all his life.

21.

Just a Backyard War

FOR six years after the Sioux War ended, shortly after Custer had led his men to the slaughter, Sheridan continued his far from flawless service in keeping the Indians quiet. The actions in which his troops took part were small affairs but they eventually overcame the redskins, and after 1882 the country enjoyed almost complete peace for sixteen years. Then, on February 24, 1898, the battleship *Maine* was sunk in the harbor of Havana and the country suddenly found itself in a fight with Spain.

As a war, the Spanish-American affair did not amount to much. Its few months' duration served only to prove that Spain had rotted to a decrepit shell and that the United States, via its War Department, still retained its unaltered faculty for chosing incompetent generals.

On April 23, 1898, President William McKinley called for 125,000 volunteers for immediate field service in the National Guard. In two weeks the rolls were complete. On May 25 he asked for 75,000 more and acquired them as rapidly. But once they had signed enlistment papers Secretary of War Russell A. Alger had not the faintest conception of what to do with them. He had no place to put them. He had no transportation ready. He had no uniforms, no arms and no ammunition. All he had was men.

For generals, he could find no officers with field experience except aging veterans of the Civil War, so he appointed these. Within a week or two, eight of these honorable but ancient gentlemen had new stars on their shoulders—General Nelson A. Miles, commander-in-chief, William R. Shafter, Joseph B. Wheeler (former Confederate cavalry general), James H. Wilson (former Union cavalry general), Hamilton S. Hamilton, Charles A. Wikoff, Elwell S. Otis and John H. Brooke. To these men was assigned the major burden of carrying on the campaigns in the fever-ridden areas of Cuba and Puerto Rico where most of the fighting was certain to take place.

The prospective new army bogged down at once. Few of the state units were fully equipped and many were not equipped at all. Instead of mobilizing the first 40,000 in ten days as planned, Alger discovered it was impossible even to muster them in that time. The rusty and badly organized War Department machinery of transportation, supplies, hospital service and the rest was wholly inadequate for the strain suddenly put upon it. "The poor old system of military administration, with its coils of red tape and its vast clerical force devoted to details began to groan and creak, to break down here and to stop there and to produce a vast crop of delays, blunders and, what was worse, needless suffering, disease and death to the brave men in the field."*

It broke down so completely that the first of June found only 15,000 troops at Tampa, Fla., sufficiently ready to move, including the regular army and three regiments of volunteers—the 71st New York, the 2nd Massachusetts and the 1st U. S. Volunteer Cavalry (the "Rough Riders," commanded by Colonel Leonard Wood and Lieutenant Colonel Theodore Roosevelt). In the meanwhile the Atlantic Fleet, under Admiral Sampson, bottled up Admiral Cervera's Spanish fleet in Santiago harbor and it became obvious that the first land campaign was to be an attempt to capture Santiago in conjunction with the fleet. Alger decided to send his 15,000 available soldiers immediately, gave the command of the expedition to General Shafter, and on the night of June 7 ordered the troops to leave next day.

Matters went into hopeless confusion at once. Due to bungled railroad operations, hours instead of minutes were required for the troops to reach the port from Tampa. Arrived there, it was discovered that no proper transport arrangements had been made. Some ships were left empty while others had two or even three regiments assigned to quarters intended for one, but after a lengthy scramble the soldiers finally embarked after a fashion, but not to start for Santiago.

Several United States warships passing far off shore were reported to be Spanish vessels waiting to sink the transports and the army was kept sweltering aboard the crowded troop ships at wharves surrounded by water festering with sewage. Hundreds of men became sick and had to be

* Lodge, Henry Cabot: *Our War With Spain.*

sent back to Tampa. A great many died. And the transports remained where they were for six days. When they
finally left, on June 14, the boats were in such wretched
condition that it took them six more days to reach the landing point at Daiquiri, fifteen miles east of Santiago. Now it
was discovered that the transport fleet had no launches or
lighters to convey the troops to shore. They had been
omitted, forgotten or lost. Eventually, the Navy had to
provide the ship-to-shore boats.

Whatever the degree of General Shafter's responsibility
for the method in which the expeditionary force had been
shipped, he carried on nimbly in the same spirit. That he
was east of Santiago, he knew. That there was a distinct
probability of the presence of Spanish soldiers between
Daiquiri and Santiago, he also knew. So, two days after
landing, without any advance scouting, he sent forward
his dismounted cavalry to drive the Spaniards out of wher-
ever they might be, location uncertain.

The troops marched by two roads, so completely shut in
by dense undergrowth, it was almost impossible to throw
out flankers or deploy the lines, and wholly impossible to
see what lay in the underbrush on either side. The underbrush gave its own answer. Sporadic volleys of rifle fire
swept the advancing cavalrymen from securely hidden foes
against whom they were helpless. Fortunately, the Spanish
marksmanship was so bad that only a few Americans were
killed and their comrades exacted a quick revenge.

The two columns, emerging from the chaparral, joined
forces, and with a total of 964 men advanced against Las
Guasinamas Ridge, from which so many rifles were blazing that it was evident a considerable force of Spanish held

the crest. As a matter of fact, there were more than 3,000 of the enemy there, but they had no stomach for the American rush. At a trifling cost—16 killed and 52 wounded—the ridge was taken, the Spanish fled from the field in disorder and the Americans had won their first land triumph.

The results were fatal. General Shafter promptly became convinced the American troops needed only to press forward to drive the Spaniards out of their path and take Santiago in 48 hours. This might have happened had he pursued the routed enemy at once, but, having reached his conclusion as to the invincibility of his army, he sat down quietly and for a full week did nothing except watch the Spanish throw up extensive defenses. This was easy. From El Pozo Hill the Americans could see the enemy at work with the naked eye. However, Shafter graciously refrained from interfering with the Spaniards' vigorous efforts to strengthen their defense system, although a battery planted on El Pozo would have been able to use point-blank fire, so near and so visible were the enemy entrenchments.

Shafter had brought only eight field guns ashore, two batteries of 12-pounders. Not until his week of waiting was over and the Spanish were entirely ready for him, did he place one of the batteries on El Pozo. Then, in a haphazard manner, the army moved forward. Shafter appears to have ordered no scouting whatever. The only American reconnoitering was done on his own responsibility by General Adna R. Chaffee, who scouted the ground all the way to the heights of El Caney, the strongest post the Spanish held. The other powerful defense barrier of the enemy was on San Juan Hill, not far from El Caney.

Shafter decided these two forts should be taken now that they were as strong as the Spanish could make them. His general plan was hazy but engaging. Half the army was to move up and attack El Caney, supported by the other battery of 12-pounders. The rest of the army was to be prepared to attack San Juan as soon as he gave the word. Shafter made a rough estimate that it probably would take his troops about half an hour to capture El Caney. Then they were to swing to the left and take San Juan Hill in flank, while the balance of the army made a frontal attack on that position.

On the afternoon of June 30 the order went out for the forward movement to begin. Shafter had allowed two hours for his troops to reach their position for a late sunset drive. They started at four o'clock in the afternoon. They reached their attacking position shortly after dawn the next day, having marched all night.

Seven thousand men assembled below El Caney's height. To wait for the signal to attack San Juan, the Cuban insurrectos with the Americans, the Rough Riders and the 10th Cavalry were massed about the battery on El Pozo Hill. The rest of the San Juan party was distributed between El Pozo and the San Juan River, also waiting for orders.

Matters now began briskly. Shafter's four pea-shooters below El Caney began firing at 6:30 in the morning, with no effect aside from slicing bits of stone from the walls of the fort above. Also, the smoke from the black powder used in the guns accurately revealed the American position, offering a splendid target to the hidden Spanish above. The attack proper began half an hour later and something went wrong with the half-hour schedule. While the pathetic artillery fire continued, the advancing infantry suffered heavily, creeping forward a foot at a time, seeking such protection as they could while they moved on through the blazing heat of the tropical midsummer.

At 1:30 they were barely holding their own and the situation was so unfavorable that Shafter suddenly ordered the force to abandon the attack and try its luck at San Juan. As the crowning commentary on Shafter's leadership, the order simply was ignored. Not a soldier made a move to leave the field. Instead, the infantry became infuriated at the absurd manner in which the drive was being conducted, leaped into the open, and without orders charged the fort. After two and one half hours more of savage work, El Caney was captured at four o'clock. The American casualties numbered 444, more than half the total Spanish garrison.

Meanwhile other notable events were in the making. At 7 o'clock in the morning the battery on El Pozo Hill opened a bombardment in the general direction of the Spanish lines and displayed to the Spanish the finest visible target of massed troops yet offered them. The return fire became heavier by the minute, mowing down many of the helpless troopers who stood waiting for orders which did not come. Finally, they, too, issued a declaration of independence and without waiting for word from Shafter, who seemed to have forgotten them, started down the road to Santiago. Soon nearly 8,000 men were gathered in comparative safety around the San Juan River ford and the road leading to it. But now another of Shafter's inspirations began to operate.

A captive observation balloon was sent into the air—

above the ford! Just why there should have been an observation balloon at all is a mystery, unless Shafter wished to prove to the Spaniards that he had one. The enemy lines could be seen without a glass from El Pozo Hill and their disposition was known to every man in the American army. As it was, the balloon offered another perfect target while revealing the concentration point of the troops. Within five minutes the guns of San Juan were aimed unanimously at the ford. The balloon was destroyed but the damage of its presence had been done, giving the Spanish the exact range on the massed Americans. Under the galling fire, men fell on all sides and the shells were falling over such a wide area that there was no escape in any direction.

What happened next was wholly spontaneous. No orders of any sort were given, but with nothing to gain by retreat the whole force, by common impulse, suddenly moved forward to attack. And that is how the historic Battle of San Juan Hill began. Roosevelt, now in command of the Rough Riders since Wood's promotion to Brigadier General a day or two before, finally gave form to the drive. Politely requesting the 9th Infantry to let him pass, he led his regiment out of the woods and started up the hill. The 9th immediately fell in behind, then the others joined in the rush and the charge began, infantry alone, wholly unsupported by artillery. It was a recklessly mad adventure, yet it was the lesser of two evils. The Americans were taking the surest course to save their own lives. There was no movement by units. As the charge gained momentum, half a dozen regiments were intermingled, but this did not interfere with the rush. The Spanish morale was not equal to the grim assault. When the Americans stormed over the top of the hill the enemy turned and ran. Thus was won the most spectacular land victory of the war, a victory achieved wholly by accident. An unsupported infantry attack, the losses could not but be heavy, even against such poor shots as the Spanish. Of the 7,919 Americans who took part in the assault, 1,614 were killed or wounded.

After these two victories Shafter went into a deep fit of discouragement and sent a wild dispatch to the War Department, screaming for reinforcements. Even while he was writing it, Admiral Sampson was relieving him of all necessities for worrying. On July 2 Admiral Cervera attempted to steam out of Santiago harbor with his fleet. Two hours later every Spanish ship had been destroyed. With the fleet gone, the Spanish occupation of Santiago was hopeless. On July 17 the city surrendered.

This was fortunate for the American army. Matters had gone from bad to worse. The troops were badly fed— Roosevelt's regiment had to subsist on rations abandoned by the Spaniards—transportation was slow, supplies were scarce, tropical fever struck the troops and the hospital service proved utterly inadequate.

At the time Santiago surrendered, General Miles already was ready to launch the next campaign on Puerto Rico and it was presumed the American force at Santiago would be available for service with him. It was a vain presumption. Only 3,300 men could go to Puerto Rico. All the rest —more than 11,000—were sick, and many of them died. In fact, during the Spanish-American War, hospital facilities were so badly prepared that five times as many men died of disease as of battle wounds.

The surrender of Santiago ended the only appreciable land campaign of the war. Shafter was lionized. He had won. Nothing else mattered. The Puerto Rico campaign conducted by General Miles was little more than a picnic jaunt. Miles handled his men with efficiency and he faced little strenuous opposition anywhere, so the casualties were negligible. The whole war was ended so quickly it was difficult to realize it had even begun. Between May 1 and the end of August, two Spanish fleets had been completely destroyed and three small Spanish armies had been routed, one each in Cuba, Puerto Rico and the Philippines. By that time Spain was ready to concede anything and the war ended, with the name of one more American commanding general added to the list of incompetents.

22.

The World Goes Mad

EACH major war in which the United States has been involved has carried its own unique significance in the nation's development and progress. And, in a sense, each war has paved the way directly to the next.

The continuity is curious. The Revolutionary War created a loosely knit republic. In the conditions under which the country began its struggle for life, another war, particularly another war with England, was inevitable and 1812 was the result. It finished the work of the Revolution and served notice that the United States was deserving of recognition throughout the world. Of equal importance, it launched the great national expansion movement within the limits of the continent which opened the direct road to the war with Mexico. Despite the doubtful quality of the motives which instigated the Mexican War, it demonstrated the growing might of the country to all the world. At the same time, however, it made acute the long-smouldering differences between the North and South which resulted in the Civil War. From that bitter conflict emerged a solidarity which led to such steadily increasing national power that the country quickly became the undisputed, dominant nation of the western world, and as such began to look with a fatherly eye at small, suffering neighbors within its own immediate radius. It was this protective sentiment which led to the Spanish-American War. While there was more than a touch of imperialism motivating the national government in that conflict, the public at large supported it entirely in the spirit of helping down-trodden Spanish possessions in distress. As a result of the war, diminutive as it was, the United States was definitely established as a world power of the first rank, the first step toward its eventual involvement in the greatest contest of international power the world has seen.

From the beginning of the twentieth century the importance of the United States in the family of nations increased so rapidly that within a decade it was acknowledged as one of the three most powerful countries on the face of the earth. It maintained peace with all the world, and with no axes to grind felt hopeful of steering clear of international complications. But its economic, industrial and financial operations had extended their tentacles throughout the world to a degree which made certain that any sort of international conflict of major proportions could not but affect it to a serious extent, impossible at any time during the latter half of the nineteenth century.

In Europe the carefully nurtured balance of power among nations who viewed one another with jealous and avaricious eyes maintained an uneasy armed peace for more than forty years after the Franco-Prussian War, a period of development along curiously contrasting lines. They were forty years marked by greater progress in science and invention for the advancement of life, living and civilization than the forty centuries which preceded them. Through the same forty years, science and invention produced methods unsurpassed for inflicting quick and violent extinction.

By 1914 people throughout the world were speaking in hushed tones of the frightful possibilities of the newly evolved war equipment. Everyone knew that the panoplied warfare of five thousand years had passed before a mechanized era which had learned how to deal wholesale death in monstrous form even though the possibilities had not been tested. The very horror of the prospect was believed to be the surest guarantee of the preservation of peace. It was said that only a nation gone stark mad would entertain the remotest thought of actual war. But on August 1, 1914, the whole world went mad.

The United States managed to keep out of the maelstrom for two and a half years. Perhaps its eventual entry was inevitable from the start since conditions were so ripe for the manipulation of affairs to force its entry. But it did have two and a half years of grace, during which its people witnessed the useless butchery of men on a scale to make all the "fatal generals" of human history stand as pygmies beside those who now were pulling the strings. They were years destined to have an enormous effect on America's own conduct when it stepped in at last.

The outbreak of the war was accepted throughout the world with a dazed sort of non-comprehension. Nothing could have been more complete than the universal lack of understanding of what the war would mean in terms

of human bloodshed. The dreaded hideousness of a machine war with human beings as the grist surpassed every
previous conception, and with it vanished all the fabled
glory of war.

There was no room for a romantic Paul Revere's Ride
in a conflict in which radio, telegraph or telephone could
span the world while Revere was saddling his horse. There
could be no thrilling scout of the enemy's position when
the enemy's position was an unbroken line extending for
three hundred miles and the scouting was done from the
skies with cameras which saw what the eye could not.
There could be no gallant charge to spike the enemy's
guns when the enemy's guns could lie back fifteen or forty
miles to hurl their messengers of death with an accuracy
in which sight played no part. There could be no forlorn
hope defense of a fortress against an enemy's assault when
half a dozen shells from distant, unseen guns could blast
the fortress to bits without an assailant in sight.

Battle deaths in horrible new forms had been introduced,
too. The new engines of war did not merely wound or
kill. They blew the soldiers to bits in wholesale lots. They
burnt them alive with liquid fire. They sent them choking
to death in clouds of poison gas. They ripped them to
shreds with lead-spraying machine guns. And there were no
truces to bury the dead. Those that could not be snatched
from the field by comrades under fire lay where they fell,
soon to be joined by others, so that useless bits of ground
which were fought over savagely became miry cesspools
of blood and muck and rotting flesh of what had once been
men, while more long-dead bodies were spewed up with
every crashing shell-burst.

In this war the men in the ranks ceased to be men. They were mere pawns. A life, a thousand lives, a hundred thousand, meant nothing when the scales were balanced by nothing short of millions. The casualty figures reached totals so stupefying that the human mind could not even think in the terms demanded. In the American Civil War, the North and South all told mobilized less than 3,500,000 men in four years, and the actual battle deaths numbered less than 200,000. In the World War the number of soldiers mobilized reached the incomprehensible total of 60,000,000, and the battle deaths alone numbered 7,694,336—more than twice as many as the grand total of soldiers who bore arms in the Civil War.

Some inkling of what was to be came with the First Battle of the Marne, September 6-10, 1914, one month after the war began. In that first great battle, the greatest the world ever had seen, 2,000,000 men fought for five days and the casualties totalled more than 300,000. U. S. Grant's thirty-day "butchery" of 60,000 men in the Richmond campaign of 1864 was just an average single day's toll along the Marne. And this was just the beginning. The World War was one Cold Harbor after another, day in and day out, expanded on a scale which staggered the imagination.

In its 1916 attacks on Verdun, Germany tossed away 500,000 men and gained nothing. A few months later, in the gigantic Battles of the Somme, from July to December, 1916, the British lost 450,000, the French 250,000 and the Germans 600,000—1,300,000 casualties on one sector in five and a half months and the results did not hasten the war's end by a day.

These figures are so enormous as to be without meaning.

It is almost impossible to picture 1,300,000 dead and dying men as the toll of a single, prolonged battle. From Paris to Verdun is 120 miles. Standing shoulder to shoulder, 300,000 men could line up in that distance, which means that the men who fell at the Somme alone would have presented an array four ranks deep all the way from Paris to Verdun.

"It is the machine war," was the reason given, while the world stood dazed at the ghastly massacre of youth. But it was only a little while before those who watched from afar suddenly realized that the machines were being operated by human hands and human minds, that, unfortunately, the machines had not eliminated the human element, and, once more as always, the needless slaughter of boys was being directed by butchery-minded men whose criminal incompetence was sending the marching ranks to their doom.

It was this that the people of the United States saw for two and a half years and prayed that if we were drawn into the pit our men might not this time, as they so often had been in the past, be led by such men—"fatal generals," all.

Of the British who commanded in the field, Sir Philip Gibbs has said:

"Among them there was not one whose personality had that mysterious but essential quality of great generalship. 'The Staff' made men attack impossible positions, sent down conflicting orders, issued a litter of documents containing impracticable instructions. The British generalship made many mistakes, some of them no doubt unavoidable because it is human to err, and some of them due to sheer, simple, impregnable stupidity.

"In the Battles of the Somme they attacked isolated objectives on narrow fronts so that the enemy swept our men with fire by artillery concentrated from all points, instead of having to disperse his fire during a general attack on a wide front. In the days of trench warfare, when the enemy artillery was much stronger than ours and when his infantry strength was enormously greater, our generals insisted upon the British troops maintaining an 'aggressive' attitude with the result that they were shot to pieces."*

The French, with their professional army of more than a million men, did little better. The first commander, Joffre, was an almost complete failure. His victory at the first Marne only partially redeemed the monumental blunders with which he began. He threw away thousands of lives in abortive and meaningless offensives during the early weeks of the war, while Germany overran northern France and took a foothold she did not release until the last week of the conflict. It was Joffre who launched upon the costly attritional policy which aimed to wear out Germany by sheer preponderance of numbers and served only to wear down France and decimate her ranks. In April, 1917, one of his successors, Nivelle, launched an offensive in the Champagne region worthy of a Burnside or a Grant. Ill-advised and poorly conceived, it was a total failure and lost more than 100,000 men the first day.

As they watched these things with growing uneasiness the people of the United States had but one thought, "If

* Gibbs, Sir Philip: *Now It Can Be Told,* page 45.

we are drawn into this, will our generals learn anything from this and profit by it for the salvation of our own men?" But there was no means of knowing.

Then, in 1916, the attention of the United States was distracted for a moment. Early in the year a Mexican bandit named Pancho Villa crossed the border and raided Columbus, N. M., raised a brief flurry of death and destruction and sped back into Mexico. The United States government demanded and received permission to pursue him with an armed force. The man to whom the task of leading the American expedition went was a veteran of the regular army, Brigadier General John J. Pershing. His name was unknown to the public at large and considerable wonder was expressed as to who he was and what he could do.

Pershing was faced with a hopeless task from the outset, so far as the capture of Villa was concerned, but he made of his invasion a most effective gesture at a time when the relations between Mexico and the United States were such that Mexico needed a bit of impressing. And gradually word began drifting through the country that the expedition had been a model of soldierliness, conducted with more than ordinary skill in the trying conditions faced by the invading Americans. It was said, too, that while displaying plenty of daring Pershing never had taken a useless risk. This was all. The expedition was not a highly important affair against the background of a world aflame across the Atlantic. The most important result was that the name of Pershing became more generally and more favorably known.

Then attention reverted back to Europe where the staggering waste of life was going on as unintelligently and as uninterruptedly as before. But the titanic blunders of the Allied generals were now surpassed by Germany's greatest and most incomprehensible error. At the end of 1916 Germany almost had won the war. Then she went mad and guaranteed her defeat by challenging the United States with the institution of an unrestricted submarine campaign against neutral shipping.

On February 3, 1917, the United States severed diplomatic relations with Germany. On April 6 war was declared. The time of grace was over. America was in.

23.

The Third Great Captain

CONSIDERABLE surprise was expressed throughout the country when President Woodrow Wilson suddenly announced that the commander-in-chief of the United States army and its field leader in France would be General Pershing. In some quarters, particularly in high military circles, the surprise took the form of deep resentment. After all, Pershing was merely a Brigadier, whereas the country had quite a supply of Major Generals, all of whom were his military seniors. Most people had expected Major General Leonard Wood to receive the command. Pershing's only claim to public attention had been his Mexican expedition which had had little material result, whereas Wood still carried something of a halo as the first chief of the Rough Riders during the Spanish-American War.

The dark suggestions were many that politics played a notable part in the appointment, and to some extent this undoubtedly was true. Not on Pershing's part. Few commanders in history have been so completely free of the tinge of personal interest in politics. But, in all honesty, the situation was somewhat like that which faced President Polk at the outset of the Mexican War in the fact that the commander-in-chief of the army, Winfield Scott, had his eye on the presidency.

In 1917 a Democratic President also faced the fact that the leading candidate for military honors also was a Republican with presidential aspirations. To some extent, this may have been the reason for passing Wood by, but it does not necessarily explain the choice of Pershing. The country had plenty of other generals who were Pershing's military senior. After Wood was eliminated, there was only one obvious reason why Wilson chose Pershing. He believed him the best man available for the job.

As it turned out, the selection of Pershing was a miracle of good luck for the country and the Allied cause in the war. It was an action which will go down in history as one of Wilson's wisest. But, even greater in many respects, was Wilson's bestowal of absolute authority upon the commander for his operations in France, with the guarantee that no one would be permitted to interfere with that authority. No other general in the history of the United States has been awarded such autocratic power. It was not misplaced.

The direct result was a record for the United States which was unique, not only in the World War but in its own history. For the first time an American general was permitted to conduct a war without the slightest political interference. For the first time since George Washington the United States had the right general at the head of its forces from the start, instead of going through the grievous and costly "trial and error" system. This does not mean that the United States troops in France did not suffer from "fatal generalship." Two of the most highly lauded of American victories bear this blemish—the capture of Cantigny and the immortal conquest of Belleau Wood—so that even in the World War, with all the lessons of two and a half years, American lives were sacrificed needlessly. But, because we had Pershing, those two engagements are almost the only stains.

Pershing was one of the greatest yet one of the least appreciated military commanders of American history. The country has had three truly great captains at the head of its armies since the republic began. The first was Washington, the second, Thomas and the third, Pershing.

The story of America's part on the battle-front is the story of Pershing. To no small degree, the story of the Allies' swift success in the last one hundred days of the war is the story of Pershing, entirely aside from his battle contribution.

For three and a half years the Allies floundered through their war activities, always on the narrow brink of defeat, because their mutual jealousy prevented the sane coördination of their efforts, and they refused to learn their lesson although they had before them the example of a numerically inferior foe, holding them at bay and all but crushing them because his direction of all fronts was unified.

Pershing saw unity of Allied command as the vital necessity to success from the outset. In June, 1917, when he was sailing for France, he said, aboard ship, that "some one man—it did not matter whether he was a Frenchman or a Briton—must have the power of coördinating effort and plans and of making decisions in the midst of action on the Western front."

From the time he landed he continued to express this view. In the early days of the American Expeditionary Force the limitations of the army made it of little influence in Allied military councils. But Pershing kept on prodding for unity of command. As his army grew, he became more insistent. The Allied chiefs grew a little weary of hearing him on the subject, but this did not discourage him. It required a dismaying crisis to produce action but in March, 1918, when Ludendorff's first great offensive rocked the Allies back on their heels, something approximating unified command was established under Foch as the generalissimo, and in six and a half months Germany was suing for peace.

Wholly new to large commands, Pershing displayed an extraordinarily comprehensive grasp of the needs of the situation he faced. In spite of all the difficulties encountered at times, the American army in France was a miracle of organization from the front line to the farthest rear supply base. He thought in terms of millions of soldiers. As a result, the United States was able to send 2,000,000 soldiers to France and 1,400,000 of them reached the battle front when they were most needed, completely equipped and ready for the fight. He was tireless, his energy boundless, his every act aimed at getting as many soldiers into the battle lines as possible, sending them there prepared for what they would be called upon to face, and seeing that they were properly taken care of.

All the while, he was forced to wage an endless, bitter, behind-the-scenes fight from the day he landed until the last shot was fired. Even before the first American soldier reached French soil, Marshal Foch, Sir Douglas Haig, Premier Clemenceau and Prime Minister Lloyd George attempted to have the flood of American troops turned over to the English and French commands as replacements, to be used in their ranks without identity as an army of their own.

The persistence of this campaign was amazing. All the combined international pressure possible to gather was brought to bear upon President Wilson to command him to accede to this request, but Wilson kept his promise and referred them to Pershing. Then everything possible was done to discredit Pershing. Rumors were permitted to emanate that the field commanders and governmental officials of France and England were dissatisfied with Pershing. Which was definitely true, but not for the reason implied.

Pershing flatly refused every request to have his men transformed into mere gun fodder to fill the depleted ranks of nations who had wasted their own men so prodigally. He insisted upon an independent American army, not because he cared for the personal glory of leading it, but because he knew the value of the Americans would be nullified if they simply became replacements. Their morale which played so great a part in their field successes would have been shattered. Moreover, an impossible situation would have resulted which could easily have been ruinous, since little personal love was lost between the Americans and their co-fighters in the other Allied forces.

It is a pity that the record should have been marred by

Cantigny and Belleau Wood. There was no military necessity for the attack on Cantigny. It was simply a publicity
stunt, staged to prove that Americans can fight intelligently
—something they had been demonstrating for 150 years.
The capture of the town could serve no strategic purpose
at the time. The attack was made on a sector only a mile
and a quarter in length and involved an advance of only a
few hundred yards. From a military standpoint, it was a
perfect piece of work. For publicity purposes, the timing
also was supposed to be perfect, as it was scheduled for
May 28, 1918, when it was assumed the front would be quiet
and the American exploit could capture plenty of headlines. Unfortunately, the German commander, Ludendorff,
stepped in a day ahead of time and stole the headlines by
launching his third great offensive on May 27, gobbling up
villages by the dozen and completely eclipsing the one-
village drive of the Americans. Nevertheless, the Cantigny
attack was made, at a cost of 1,057 killed and wounded, for
a publicity feat which was a dud.

Belleau Wood is a magic name and always will symbolize
the ultimate in enduring heroism of American troops. It
should. There can be no words exalted enough for the men
who fought through that grim machine-gun stronghold for
twenty heart-breaking days and defeated the flower of the
German army.

Less can be said for the men who ordered the attack.
In a war whose supreme lesson had been that assault without the most thorough artillery preparation means holocaust
for the infantry, the Marines were hurled into certain
destruction on June 6, when the attack began, almost with-

out artillery preparation of any kind. Not until they had been fighting through the wood for eighteen days was adequate artillery assistance given—and then they finished the job in two days. But the 5th and 6th Marines of the Second Division and the regiment of the Third which had accomplished it lost 9,777 killed and wounded—133 per cent. of their original strength. This can not be charged to Pershing and Major General Omar Bundy, head of the Second Division and Brigadier General James G. Harbord, chief of the Marine Brigade distinguished themselves through the remainder of the war.

As to generalship, Pershing had two great opportunities to prove his ability. The first was his attack on the St. Mihiel salient. This sharp angle in the Allied line, east of the Meuse River, had withstood every effort to reduce it for four years, though France had expended tens of thousands of lives in the attempt. Pershing wiped it out completely in two days on September 12 and 13. He used 250,000 men for the attack, sustained less than 7,000 total casualties—including the French troops involved—captured 14,439 prisoners and 443 field guns.

His supreme test came in the Meuse-Argonne offensive, the greatest battle in American history. Launched on September 26, it continued without interruption for 47 days to the end of the war. Here the Americans were called upon for the crucial drive of Foch's entire victory offensive. Its objective was the Sedan-Mezieres Railroad, the chief "feeder" line for the entire German army from the Alps to Belgium. With this line of communications cut, the Germans would be compelled to evacuate all of northern

France. To prevent this disaster, Germany had more congested lines of defense on this sector than anywhere on the front, and during the battle, fighting as she was for her life, she threw against the American soldiers every available man she could lay hands on.

The battle was one of continuous attack in the face of desperate defense, the most costly kind of warfare. During the 47 days, 1,400,000 Americans served in the front line. The battle had to be fought over the most difficult terrain on the Allied front, a desolate region of tangled woods, deep ravines, rolling hills, the entire region a mire from continuous rain and only one or two roads leading through the whole sector. The continued attack was made against the last word in death-dealing weapons, machine guns so thickly and shrewdly placed that they raked every square inch of the battle area, hand grenades, rifles, tremendous concentrations of field guns which hurled high explosive and gas into the advancing lines night and day.

Exactly six weeks after the fight began American shells were crashing in Sedan. The railroad was cut. Five days later the Germans were on their knees and the Armistice was signed. During the 47 days the total American casualties were 117,939, less than ten percent of the soldiers who took part, an almost incredibly low figure. But under Pershing all the American casualties were incredibly low, despite the fact that the A. E. F. was attacking without interruption from May 28, when Cantigny was taken, until the Armistice. From October 17, 1917, when the first American shot was fired on a World War front to November 11, 1918, the total battle casualties of the Americans were 48,909 killed and 237,135 wounded, a minimum without parallel in the war.

The reason was that Pershing's first consideration always was the welfare of his men, their protection and their safety to the ultimate degree possible consistent with the necessity for defeating the enemy with the least delay. Under his authority the fatal type of general never was allowed to command combat troops. Pershing managed to stop most of them before they had a chance to leave the United States. Plenty of them appeared there, as the ever-changing array of the starred personnel at the cantonments proved. But they did not reach the battle front. Those who arrived in France found themselves curiously assigned to insignificant duty in back areas when they were not hustled back to the United States at once. Pershing had no need to apologize for any of the generals he permitted on the firing line.

Plenty of American soldiers died during the war whose lives should not have been lost, but few of these were on the battle field. Some of them may be charged to cantonment generals who did not know how to take care of the troops under their command, but the chief fault lies, as always, at the door of politics to whose expediency the lives of helpless men never mean anything.

Due to politics America had some sadly located training camps where health conditions were atrocious—as at Deming, N. M., for instance, where the soldiers at Camp Cody were subject to tremendous daily changes in temperature and where choking sand-storms swirled over the tents to stifle and blind the men sent there to learn how to become soldiers. Many youthful lungs gave way before those violences of nature and their owners died of pneumonia and tuberculosis. There were others but little better.

There were many who died in France because of the rotten raincoats sent by the government—raincoats which never kept out the rain on a battle front where rain fell incessantly. And there were shoddy overcoats which did not keep out the cold, as well as other causes for complaint. But, perhaps, these things must always be in a war though it is hard to excuse them.

The army did have a great commander and, therefore, the World War is the brightest war chapter in the nation's history.

24.

To Whom Honor Is Due

FOR nearly twenty years, the United States has been at peace since the World War, but this is no guarantee of perpetual peace, else there would be no reason for so unpleasant a narration as this book contains. As this is written, the whole world is in a state of uneasy upheaval with the "wars and rumors of wars" more insistent than they have been at any time since the July days of 1914. There may be another war of vast proportions, if not now, before many years have passed. The United States may escape this one, but it cannot always escape.

There will be more wars and Americans will fight, as they always have been willing to fight, for their country. It would seem but little to ask that no more of their lives be thrown away as in the past, that the commanders who hold over them the power of life and death shall be wise men who not only know how to fight and win but how to do so without needless blood waste.

For them to be fighters alone is not enough. Some of our

"most fatal generals" have been vigorous fighters—Sullivan, Taylor, Scott, Grant, Burnside, Hooker, Rosecrans, McClellan, Meade, Sheridan, Custer. Most of them have been winners, too. But this does not wipe out the desolation of empty homes into which they have brought the agony of death undeserved and unneeded. Nor does it restore the virile young manhood they destroyed. Unfortunately, it is not just the average man who dies on the battle field. War demands the fittest, the select, the flower of a nation's youth, and will be satisfied with none less.

Needless deaths in war build the world's greatest and most continued tragedy and the United States has been one of the most pronounced victims. With the exception of the World War, it has been the unvarying American formula to sink close to defeat under inept commanders before the right leaders were found. Due to the field-testing of its generals which has appeared to be an inherent part of its military code, the country often has had to be blessed with abnormal luck to survive until the capable leaders appeared.

Even with Washington at the helm, the ineptitude of some of his subordinate commanders, over whom he had little control, made the blessings of great luck a vital necessity in winning the Revolutionary War. But for luck, particularly the luck of having Sir William Howe as the British commander until the middle of 1778, Washington might never have overcome the evil works of Sullivan, Charles Lee and Gates.

In the War of 1812 the nation was extremely lucky in the fact that most of Britain's military might was held in

Europe to fight Napoleon until Andrew Jackson arose with the power to stop the Peninsular veterans.

The luck of finding Mexico vastly weaker than had been expected was all that saved Taylor's army in 1846, and Scott, too, had to have the same sort of luck to make his successful drive on the capital city.

The same sort of luck, intensified, saved the United States from the brutal consequences of Shafter's incompetence. But Spain proved weaker than Mexico had been, so only a few lives were tossed away and Shafter's luck held.

This would seem a sweeping indictment of ability in American military commanders, and so it is—for the majority of them as individuals. It is part of the story which the public has a right to know if it is ever to find a remedy for the inexcusable massacre of its sons in war.

It is not an indictment of the inherent military ability of Americans. Always, great generals have finally come to the fore to undo the costly work of their incompetent predecessors and produce eventual victory. The painful factor has been the difficulty which always has confronted these men before they were granted the opportunity to demonstrate their worth.

The United States has had more bad generals than good ones, more than it has been possible to touch upon. All of them cannot even be listed. Unfortunately, it is much easier to proclaim the brief list of those who were conspicuously capable and to whom all honor is due. It is these who have given the country its heritage of bravery, military brilliance in the hour of need and uninterrupted success, gifts which have enabled the nation to move on its progressive way with ever-increasing momentum. Yet all of them had to struggle to gain the heights, usually over personal antagonisms, political preference and unnumbered prejudices.

George Washington always had a behind-the-scenes fight on his hands with Congress, and, times without number, he was retained at the head of the Continental armies by no more than an eyelash. When Philip Schuyler was hounded out of the service and Benedict Arnold was incapacitated by his wounds, Washington had to fight again to gain recognition for his new right arm, Nathaniel Greene, so he might make the most of Greene's abilities.

Andrew Jackson, William Henry Harrison and Jacob Brown, who saved the day on land for the United States in the War of 1812, had to batter their way through the fog of poltroonery which tried to hold them back.

In the Mexican War, Scott, by far the better of the two commanders of the United States troops and the man who eventually won the war, was withheld from the battle field for a long period for political reasons.

George H. Thomas did not receive his chance until the Civil War was nearly at an end—although it was his efforts which did much to bring the end so near—and, even then, he was harried to distraction by Grant and, twice within two weeks, was threatened with the loss of his command. Sherman had to undergo humiliation and degradation before he was given a chance to prove himself.

Robert E. Lee, universally beloved as he was in the Confederacy, was not immune to the jealous hectoring of General James Longstreet, who missed no opportunity to criticize the commanding general. Joseph E. Johnston was hampered constantly by the disfavor of President Jefferson Davis.

Fortunate as he was in the support of President Wilson, Pershing was the prey of constant bickering and back-biting in Washington which attempted to undo him.

The record of Pershing in the World War offers a magnificent criterion, but unfortunately it does not offer a guarantee, and there never will be a guarantee against "fatal generals" until the country devises some means of insuring wise choices to prevent its soldiers from being led to the slaughter. Such means do not appear to be visible as yet.

The list of those who have shone on America's battle fields is a painfully scanty one for one hundred and sixty years of national life—Washington, Schuyler, Arnold, Andrew Jackson, Harrison, Brown, Thomas, Sherman, Lee, "Stonewall" Jackson, Joseph E. Johnston, Pershing. And of these, the three great stand out—Washington, Thomas, Pershing—men who fought wisely, men who won brilliantly, men who never spent blood uselessly.

Bibliography

THE information upon which this book is based has been the accumulation of many years of interested delving below the surface of American history. In fact, it was the material itself which suggested the book. To a large extent, original sources and contemporary documents were employed. The published works of many historical societies have been drawn upon freely, particularly those of Massachusetts, New Hampshire, New York, Pennsylvania, Maryland, Michigan, Indiana, Ohio, Virginia, Kentucky, Tennessee and Louisiana. To cite a complete list of the sources would be impossible. The available literature on the Civil and World Wars alone would require several lifetimes of continuous reading. The objective has been to sift out those most pertinent to the subject at hand. Of these the most important and most informative are those listed below. The date and place of publication are shown.

GENERAL

Bancroft, George: *History of the United States,* 6 vol., Boston, 1837-74.

Channing, Edward: *History of the United States,* 6 vol., Macmillan & Co., New York, 1906-25.

McMaster, John Bach: *Brief History of the United States,* American Book Company, New York, 1907.

Wilson, Woodrow: *History of the American People,* 5 vol., New York, 1909.

Winsor, Justin: *Narrative and Critical History of the American People,* Boston, 1909-12.

REVOLUTIONARY WAR

Adams, John: *Works,* 10 vol. Little, Brown & Co., Boston, 1856. Edited by Charles Francis Adams.

Allen, Paul: *History of the American Revolution,* F. Betts, Baltimore, 1821.

André, John: *Journal.* Edited by Henry Cabot Lodge. 101 copies published for Bibliophile Society by Houghton & Co., Boston, 1903.

Arnold, Benedict: *Present State of the American Rebel Army, Navy and Finances.* Transmitted to British government in October, 1780. Edited by Paul Leicester Ford. Brooklyn Historical Printing Club, 1891.

Arnold, Charles Henry: *A New and Impartial Universal History of North and South America,* London, 1783.

Arnold, Isaac Newton: *Life of Benedict Arnold.* (The author was not a relative of his subject.) New York, 1880.

Atlee, Colonel Samuel John: *Journal of the Battle of Long Island*, New York, 1847.

Bancroft, George: *American Revolution*, Little, Brown & Co., 1858.

Becker, Carl Lotus: *Struggle for Independence*, Yale University Press, New Haven, 1918.

Belcher, Henry: *First American Civil War*, 2 vol., London, 1911.

Carrington, E. F.: *Battles of the American Revolutionary War*, Boston, 1902.

Carroll, Charles: *Journal of Charles Carroll of Carrollton During His Visit To Canada in 1776 as One of the Commissioners of Congress*, Maryland Historical Society, Baltimore, 1876.

Coffin, Charles: *Life of Major General John Thomas*, Boston, 1897.

Congress: *Journals of the Continental Congress*, Washington, Government Printing Office, 1889.

Congress: *Secret Journals of the Acts and Proceedings of Congress*, Boston, 1821.

Cullum, George Washington: *Struggle for the Hudson*, Boston, 1884.

Deane, Silas: *Papers of Silas Deane*, Seventy-Six Society, Philadelphia, 1855.

Emmet, Thomas Addis: *Some Popular Myths of American History*, Magazine of History, New York, February, 1905.

Fisher, Sidney George: *True History of the American Revolution*, J. P. Lippincott & Co., Philadelphia, 1902.

Fiske, John: *American Revolution*, 2 vol., Houghton, Mifflin & Co., Boston, 1886.

Franklin, Benjamin: *Political Pieces,* London, 1779.

Frost, John: *Stories of the American Revolution,* Gregg & Elliott, Philadelphia, 1847.

Gaskell, Caleb (fifer of the Newburyport, Mass., Company at Quebec, 1775-76): *Diary,* Magazine of History, Extra No. 86.

Gordon, William: *History of the Rise, Progress and Establishment of the Independence of the United States of America,* London, 1788.

Greene, Major General Francis Vinton: *The Revolutionary War,* Charles Scribner's & Son, New York, 1911.

Griswold, Rufus Wilmot: *Washington and the Generals of the American Revolution,* Philadelphia, 1847.

Hatch, Louis Clinton: *Administration of the American Revolutionary Army,* Longmans, Green & Co., New York, 1904.

Headley, Joel T.: *Washington and His Generals,* Baker & Scribner, New York, 1847.

Hubley, Bernard: *History of the American Revolution.* (Including Events and Resolutions of Congress, letters and orders of General Washington.) Northumberland, Pa., 1805.

Huddleston, F. J.: *Gentleman Johnny Burgoyne,* London, 1927.

Hughes, Rupert: *Life of George Washington,* 3 vol., W. Morrow, New York, 1926-30.

Irving, Washington: *Life of George Washington,* 5 vol., G. Putnam, New York, 1855-59.

Johnson, Arthur: *Myths and Facts of the American Revolution,* W. Briggs, Toronto, 1908.

La Fayette, Marie Joseph Paul Roch Yves Gilbert de Motier, Marquis de: *Autobiography*, J. Deighton, London, 1793.

Lamb, Roger: *Original and Authentic Journal of Occurrences During the Late American War*, Dublin, 1809.

Landers, Lieutenant Colonel H. L.: *Battle of Camden*, Government Printing Office, Washington, 1929.

Lecky, William E. H.: *American Revolution*, D. Appleton & Co., 1898.

Lee, Henry: *Memoirs of the War*, Bradford & Inskeep, Philadelphia, 1812.

Lee, Richard Henry: *Letters*. Edited by James Curtis Ballagh. Macmillan & Co., New York, 1911.

Letters and Journals Relating to the War of the American Revolution, Albany, 1867.

Lossing, Benson J.: *Life and Times of Philip Schuyler*, New York, 1860.

Lossing, Benson J.: *Pictorial Field Book of the Revolution*, New York, 1852.

Moore, Frank: *Diary of the American Revolution*. (From Newspapers and Original Documents.) Privately Printed, New York, 1865.

Morris, Margaret: *Private Journal*, Privately Printed, Philadelphia, 1836.

Moylan, Col. Stephen: *Correspondence*, Philadelphia, 1913.

Nickerson, Hoffman: *Turning Point of the Revolution*, New York, 1928.

Official Journal of Crown Point, 1776-77.

Old South Leaflets, Boston, 1889.

Orderly Books of the Continental Forces, Washington, 1877.

Pemberton, Thomas: *An Historical Journal of the American War,* Boston, 1810.

Percy, Hugh, Earl of, 2nd Duke of Northumberland: *Letters From Boston and New York,* Boston, 1910.

Riedesel, Countess Friedericka Charlotte: *Letters and Journals,* New York, 1868.

Rising, Oscar E.: *A New Hampshire Lawyer in the Revolution,* Geneva, N. Y., 1915.

Sparks, Edwin Erle: *Men Who Made the Nation,* New York, 1922.

Sparks, Jared: *Correspondence of the American Revolution,* Boston, 1853.

Sparks, Jared: *Life of Major General John Sullivan,* Library of American Biography, Boston, 1834.

Sparks, Jared: *Writings of George Washington,* New York, 1847.

Stevens, John Austin: *Gates at Camden,* New York, 1903.

St. Clair Papers, National Archives.

Sullivan, Major General John: *Letters and Papers.* Edited by Otis G. Hammond, Concord, New Hampshire, 1930.

Thacher, James, M. D.: *Military Journal During the Revolutionary War,* Hartford, 1854.

Trevelyan, Sir George Otto, Bart.: *American Revolution,* London, 1899.

Washington, George: *Official Letters to the Honourable American Congress, 1775-78,* 1795.

Watson, John F., and others: *American Historical and Literary Curiosities,* New York, 1847.

Wister, Sally: *Journal, Privately Printed,* New York City, 1789.

FROM THE REVOLUTION TO 1812

Chinard, Professor Gilbert: *Thomas Jefferson, the Apostle of Americanism*, New York, 1929.

Clark, William: *Journal of General Wayne's Campaign*, Mississippi Valley Historical Review, vol. I.

Gayarre, Charles: *History of Louisiana*, 4 vol., 1854.

James, Marquis: *Andrew Jackson, the Border Captain*, 1933.

Marshall, Humphrey: *History of Kentucky*, 2 vol., 1812 and 1824.

McCaleb, Dr. Walter F.: *The Aaron Burr Conspiracy*, 1903.

Roosevelt, Theodore: *The Winning of the West*, 4 vol., New York, 1896.

St. Clair, Arthur: *Papers*, National Archives.

Secret Correspondence Between James Wilkinson and the Spanish Authorities in America, MSS. record in New York Public Library.

Shreve, Royal Ornan: *The Finished Scoundrel*, New York, 1933.

Wandell, S. M., and Meade Minnegerode: *Aaron Burr*, New York, 1925.

Watson, Thomas E.: *Life and Times of Thomas Jefferson*, New York, 1903.

Wells, Elbert: *James Wilkinson, the Study of a Traitor*, Chicago University MSS.

Wilkinson, James: *Memoirs of My Own Times*, 3 vol. (Probably the most mendacious autobiography ever written.) Published by the author, Washington, 1811.

WAR OF 1812

Armstrong, John, Secretary of War, 1813-14: *Notices of the War of 1812*, New York, 1836-40.

Beall, William K.: *Journal, July-August, 1812*, Historical Review, New York, 1912.

Bouchette, Raoul: *Canada*, Toronto, 1842.

Brackenridge, Henry M.: *History of the Late War*, Baltimore, 1818.

Christie, J. R.: *History of the War Upon the Canadas*, 1824.

Davis, Paris M.: *Authentic History of the Late War*, New York, 1836.

Dudley, Thomas P.: *Battle and Massacre at Frenchtown, Michigan*, Western Reserve Historical Society Tracts, 1878.

Halbert, H.: *The Creek War of 1813-14*, Chicago, 1895.

Hart, Albert Bushnell: *War of 1812*, New York, 1916.

Headley, Joel T.: *Second War with England*, New York, 1853.

Lossing, Benson J.: *Pictorial Field Book of the War of 1812*, New York, 1868.

Madison, James: *Papers*. Edited by H. D. Gilpin, 1841.

McCarty, William: *History of the American War of 1812*, Philadelphia, 1816.

O'Connor, Thomas: *Important and Correct History of the War Between the United States and England*, New York, 1816.

Papers Relating to the War of 1812, Western Reserve Historical Society, Cleveland, Tracts No. 3, 7, 12, 15, 17, 18, 19, 28.

Parton, James: *Life of Andrew Jackson,* 3 vol., New York, 1870.

Record of the Court-martial of James Wilkinson in 1815.

MEXICAN WAR

Brady, Cyrus Townsend: *Conquest of the Southwest,* New York, 1905.

Davis, Jefferson: *Letters and Papers,* Mississippi Department of Archives & History, 1923.

Frost, John: *Pictorial History of Mexico and the Mexican War,* Philadelphia, 1848.

Furber, George C.: *The Twelve Months Volunteer,* Journal of a Private in the Mexican War, Cincinnati, 1848.

Henry, W. S.: *Campaign Sketches of the War with Mexico,* New York, 1847.

Jenkins, John Stilwell: *History of the War Between The United States and Mexico,* Auburn, N. Y., 1849.

Mansfield, Edward Deering: *The Mexican War,* New York, 1851.

Ripley, R. S.: *War With Mexico,* New York, 1849.

Smith, Justin H.: *War with Mexico,* 2 vol., New York, 1919.

Scott, Winfield: *Memoirs.*

Scott, Winfield: *Correspondence with the Secretaries of War,* New York *Evening Post,* June 10, 1846.

Stephenson, Nathaniel W.: *Texas and the Mexican War,* Yale University Press, 1921.

CIVIL WAR

Hundreds of volumes were consulted for the Civil War data. More than 24,000 books have been written about this conflict, the great majority of them prejudiced, argumentative, disputatious and violently contradictory. The problem lay in sifting out the truth from those pertinent to the subject at hand but the very partisanship of the writers, when one was compared with the others, usually revealed the high road to fact. As is usually the case in this type of research, the basic material eventually simmered down to comparatively few books, aside from the countless digests which have been written.

Badeau, Adam: *Military History of Ulysses S. Grant,* New York, 1885.

Confederate States of America: *Report of Special Committee on Recent Disasters at Forts Henry and Donelson,* Richmond, 1862.

Cory, Eugene A.: *A Private's Recollections of Fredericksburg,* Soldiers & Sailors Historical Society of Rhode Island, 1884.

Davis, Jefferson: *Rise and Fall of the Confederacy,* New York, 1881.

Dodge, Lieutenant Colonel Theodore Ayrault: *Bird's Eye View of the Civil War,* Boston, 1883.

Duncan, Louis C.: *The Bloodiest Day in American History,* Chicago, 1913.

Early, Major General Jubal Anderson: *Autobiography,* Philadelphia, 1912.

Fiske, John: *Mississippi Valley in the Civil War*, Boston, 1909.

Freeman, Douglas Southall: *R. E. Lee*, 4 vol., New York, 1934-35.

Gordon, Major General John B.: *Reminiscences of the Civil War*, New York, 1905.

Gracie, Colonel Archibald: *The Truth About Chickamauga*, Boston, 1911.

Grant, General Ulysses S.: *Personal Memoirs*, 2 vol., New York, 1894.

Johnson, Robert Underwood & Clarence Clough Beal: *Battles And Leaders of the Civil War*, 4 vol. (These volumes include quite the most comprehensive statements concerning the various campaigns to be found, most of them from the pens of the commanding generals involved. While frequently contradictory, they reveal a wealth of information often surpassing the Official Records themselves.) New York, 1884-87.

Johnston, General Joseph Eggleston: *Narrative of Military Operations*, New York, 1874.

Lee, Guy Carleton: *True History of the Civil War*, Philadelphia, 1903.

Lee, Captain Robert E.: *Recollections and Letters of General Robert E. Lee*, New York, 1913.

Lincoln, Abraham: *Works*, New York, 1920.

Longstreet, Lieutenant General James: *From Manassas to Appomattox*, New York, 1887.

Lossing, Benson J.: *Pictorial Field Book of the Civil War*, 3 vol., New York, 1876.

Lyman, Colonel Theodore: *General Meade's Headquarters, 1863-65*, Boston, 1921.

McCann, Thomas H.: *Campaigns of the Civil War*, Hoboken, N. J., 1915.

McClellan, George Brinton: *McClellan's Own Story*, New York, 1887.

Meade, Major General George Gordon: *Life and Letters*, New York, 1913.

Official Records of the War of the Rebellion. (Includes Official Reports, Correspondence, Orders, etc., of both Union and Confederate Forces. Published in accordance with an Act of Congress, at the Government Printing Office, Washington, 1885. In general, the most acceptable source of information, particularly the orders and correspondence, written under stress, when the generals were not taking time to think how favorable the report might be made.)

Patterson, Major General Robert: *Narrative of the Campaign in the Shenandoah Valley in 1861*, Philadelphia, 1865.

Phisterer, Frederick: *Statistical Record of the Armies of the United States*, New York, 1885.

Pittsburg Landing, Shiloh and the Investment of Corinth from Original Sources, Beadle & Co., New York, 1862.

Sheridan, Major General Philip Henry: *Personal Memoirs*, New York, 1902.

Sherman, Major General William Tecumseh: *Personal Memoirs*, New York, 1890.

Wallace, Major General Lew: *Autobiography*, New York, 1906.

THE WARS WITH THE PLAINS INDIANS

Bates, Charles F.: *Fifty Years After the Little Big Horn Battle*, New York, 1926.

Benteen, Captain Frederick William: *The Custer Fight,* Privately Published, Hollywood, 1933.

Byrne, P. E.: *The Custer Myth,* North Dakota Historical Quarterly, Bismarck, 1932.

Custer, Elizabeth Bacon: *Boots and Saddles,* New York, 1885.

Custer, Major General George Armstrong: *My Life On The Plains,* New York, 1875.

Dodge, Lieutenant Colonel T. A.: *Our Wild Indians,* New York, 1889.

Keim, De B.: *On the Border with Sheridan,* New York, 1875.

McKim, G. H.: *The Story of the Indian.*

Milner, Joe E.: *California Joe,* Caldwell, Idaho, 1935.

Van de Water, Frederick F.: *Glory Hunter,* New York, 1934.

SPANISH-AMERICAN WAR

Alger, Russell A. (Secretary of War in 1898): *The Spanish-American War,* New York, 1901.

Davis, Richard Harding: *The Cuban and Porto Rican Campaigns,* New York, 1898.

Lee, Fitzhugh: *Cuba's Struggle Against Spain,* New York, 1899.

Lodge, Henry Cabot: *The War With Spain,* Boston, 1899.

Morris, Charles: *The War With Spain,* Philadelphia, 1899.

Norris, Frank: *The Surrender of Santiago,* San Francisco, 1917.

Roosevelt, Theodore: *The Rough Riders,* New York, 1899.

United States, Adjutant General's Office: *Correspondence*

Relating to the War With Spain, Government Printing Office, Washington, 1902.

WORLD WAR

The literature of the World War is so vast that it has seemed best to cite only the minimum number of volumes which offered the most valuable digest of the material needed.

Beamish, Richard J. & Francis A. March, Ph. D.: *America's Part in the World War*, Philadelphia, 1919.

Clemenceau, Georges: *The Grandeur And Misery of Victory*, New York, 1924.

Gibbs, Sir Philip: *Now It can be Told*, New York, 1920.

Halsey, Francis Whiting: *History of the World War*, New York, 1919.

McPherson, William: *Strategy of the Great War*, New York, 1919.

Page, Captain Arthur: *Our 110 Days Fighting*, New York, 1919.

Palmer, Colonel Frederick: *America in France*, New York, 1918.

Pattullo, George: *The Inside Story of the A. E. F.*, Published serially in the *Saturday Evening Post*, April-May, 1922.

Pershing, General John J.: *My Personal Experiences in the World War*, New York, 1931.

Simonds, Frank H.: *History of the World War*, New York, 1919.